The
ECONOMICS
of
PEACE

KENNETH E. BOULDING

Iowa State College

❧

New York   **PRENTICE-HALL, INC.**   *1946*

First Printing ....January 1945
Second Printing ....June 1945
Third Printing ....May 1946
Fourth Printing.........June 1946
Fifth Printing ....August 1946
Sixth Printing ......September 1946

To Elise

Preface

The main key to the economics of the postwar world is a simple truism—that the rate of accumulation is equal to the rate of production less the rate of consumption. This is the "Bathtub Theorem." Production may be likened to the flow of water from the faucet, consumption to the flow down the drain. The difference between these two flows is the rate at which the water in the bathtub—the total stockpile of all goods—is accumulating.

War drains the economic bathtub in a great waste of consumption. The first problem of reconstruction is to rebuild the stockpile. It can be rebuilt only by widening the gap between production and consumption, or, in the case of a single country, by importing more than is exported. It is difficult for a ravaged country to increase either its production or its net imports. Unless it can obtain outside help, therefore, it must suffer a drastic restriction of consumption. Frequently the only way consumption can be restricted is by inflation. Here, therefore, is the key to the most fundamental problems of reconstruction.

As the reconstruction period ends, however, a new shadow falls across the economic scene. Accumulation cannot proceed forever. The time must come, as the stockpile continues to grow, when the world has enough buildings, machines, equipment, raw materials, and other goods in its inventory. With two crops of wheat in our warehouses there is not much point in adding a third. A time will come, therefore, when the rate of accumulation must decline—that is, when the gap between production- and consumption-flows must shrink. This decline can take place in only two ways—by an expansion of consumption, or by a contraction of production. Depressions—and especially great depressions—are a symptom of the attempt to solve the problem of overstuffed stockpiles by the most stupid method possible—by a restriction of production. This restriction is brought about by deflation—for deflation reduces production by making it unprofitable.

If a free economy cannot avoid deflation and mass unemployment, it is doomed. I believe, however, that a policy for full employment can be devised. It consists of two elements: an "adjustable tax plan" designed to support consumption and prevent deflation, coupled with proposals to prevent the penalization of investment and encourage capitalists to hold goods. Such a policy could not prevent local depressions nor unemployment caused by maladjustments of industry. It could, however, prevent disasters such as the Great Depression of the 'thirties. It would mend the most fundamental flaw in the noncentralized economy and give economic and political freedom a new lease on life.

Instability and unemployment, while they seem to be the big problems of mature capitalism, are not the prime cause of the hideous poverty under which the mass of mankind groans. It is the sheer unproductiveness of human labor, rather than unemployment, that condemns two thirds or more of the world's people to a life of semi-starvation. In the long view, therefore, economic progress is still the world's greatest economic problem, and the world's best hope.

For all its darkness, this is a millenial age. For the first time in human history, a world without poverty and without war is technically possible. It may be, of course, that in the smallness of our minds we shall dash from each other's mouths the cup of plenty that our skills have fashioned. Yet it is not impossible for our ideas to keep pace with our techniques. It may well be, when the history of the last two or three decades is written, that a silent revolution in economic thought may bulk larger than the frenzy of dictators or the fortunes of war. If a free world is to survive, these new ideas must spread beyond the circle of professional economists, and there is dire need for intellectual middlemen who can assist in their distribution. It is to that task that I have endeavored to dedicate myself in this book.

My obligation to the ideas of Lord Keynes is almost too

obvious to mention. I am indebted to my colleagues at Iowa State College for many helpful suggestions and criticisms. I am particularly indebted to my friend Albert G. Hart, to whom I owe many of my best ideas.

K. E. B.

Ames, Iowa,
December, 1944

Contents

PART I

THE ECONOMICS OF RECONSTRUCTION

PART II

THE ECONOMICS OF REFORM

Part I

THE ECONOMICS OF RECONSTRUCTION

CHAPTER 1

Physical Reconstruction

The nature of war's destructiveness

At the end of the war the economic life of the world will be in a sad condition. The most obvious and dramatic weakness will lie in those areas where the physical destructiveness of war has been most apparent. There will be battlefields churned in a nightmare of dirt and destruction; bombed areas like gaping wounds in the cities of Europe and Asia; the dead and the maimed. The most obvious task of reconstruction is that of the builders, the farmers, and the surgeons, in the physical restoration of shattered buildings, soils, and men. This task, although it is the most obvious, is not the greatest. It is an odd paradox of modern warfare that the destructiveness lies not so much in the efficiency as in the expense of its destruction. It is doubtful whether, with all the immense technical changes in the art of war, in spite of airplanes, bombs, and high explosives, war has become much more efficient as a means of destruction than it was in ancient times. No modern city has, as yet, suffered quite the fate of Carthage or of Jerusalem, and in spite of the advance of science, the most efficient and perhaps the cheapest instrument of destruction is still the lighted torch. The actual physical destruction of World War II, as of World War I, can be repaired in a few years. This is true, strangely enough, even

1

of land. Observers who saw the battlefields of Flanders in 1919 debated whether the hideous scene would ever be fit for agriculture again and seriously proposed turning the whole area back to forest. Yet, as early as 1921 the battlefields had recovered in the production of cereals to a greater extent than the rest of Europe, and by 1924 had even recovered their livestock industry.

The destruction of human resources

More serious than the destruction of land and building is the destruction of human resources. There will be two great gaps in the population of those countries most affected by the war. One, affecting mainly the male sex, is the gap in the war generation itself—those who fought and will never return. Many of these men would have been the leaders of the postwar world, and the gap is likely to be felt in quality as well as in quantity. The other gap, affecting both male and female populations, is the legion of the unborn. This may be even larger than the number of those who died. The illustration below shows the age distribution of the German population in 1925: *A* shows the gap of the

AGE DISTRIBUTION OF THE POPULATION OF GERMANY
(Census of 1925)

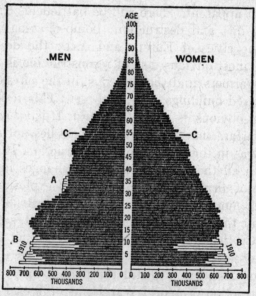

Adapted from *Statistisches Jahrbuch für das Deutsche Reich, 1928, Graphische Darstellungen*, p. II.

war dead; *B* shows the gap of the unborn. These gaps persist for decades. Thus the gap of the unborn in the War of 1870 is apparent at *C* in the age distribution of 1925, when there were fewer people of 55 than there should have been.

The invisible cost of war

But the most serious destruction of war lies not in visible ruins or in visible gaps in the generations. It lies in the fact that the whole economic, political, and psychological apparatus of the warring nations has been turned to war. Huge war industries have been developed. The ordinary channels of trade have been blocked, and the flow of the materials of commerce goes through unaccustomed and perhaps temporary channels. Millions of men have lived for years in the armed forces where the habits of responsibility have been destroyed, and many have become unfit for the tasks of civilian life. Millions of other men have gravitated to war industries where there is now no demand for their services. Machines, even machine tools, may be specialized for war and are not easily adapted to the production of the goods of peace. This is the "real" cost of war—the diversion of so large a proportion of economic resources to produce that most expensive and often most disappointing of all commodities —victory.

The real cost of war

In thinking about the cost of war, the astronomical billions of dollars mean very little, except as they tell us what proportion of the national income is diverted to the war industry. The significant cost is the "real" cost—that is, the goods and the services that are *not produced* because the resources—men, land, and machines—that might have produced them are instead producing arms and ammunition. The resources used in war may be partly obtained, it is true, by absorbing unemployed men and equipment. Insofar as this is true, the war effort has no real cost. But, in a big war, the war industry eats up resources that might have been engaged in producing other things, and the loss of these things constitutes the major portion of the real cost of the war. The number of houses, for instance, *not built* because of the war effort is probably greater than the number of houses destroyed by bombs.

Capital consumption

The "real" cost falls on two groups. Part of the sacrifice is endured at the time of the war through the reduced consumption of the people. Part of it, however, falls on the postwar generation because of the consumption of capital during the war. Resources are obtained for the war effort by using up the existing equipment of society without replacing it. Houses are not repaired, railroads, machines, and factories deteriorate, soils are depleted, education is neglected; at the end of a long war the whole equipment of civilized life, both physical and mental, is on a lower level than it was at the beginning. The task of restoring this equipment involves real sacrifices from the postwar generation. This is true no matter how the war is financed: it is not the national debt that constitutes the burden on future generations, but rather the absence of real equipment which they might otherwise have possessed.

Reconstruction is capital rebuilding

Essentially, the economic problem of reconstruction is that of rebuilding the capital of society. It is not only the physical capital that needs to be built up—new houses, new factories, new machines. War damages psychological capital as well as physical capital, and lowers the economic value of human minds and wills. Despair is more destructive than dynamite, and the greatest obstacle to reconstruction may be the apathy of a war-worn people. This is so particularly in the defeated nations, where the tremendous sacrifices of war have apparently been made in vain. War also tends to destroy the subtle, moral bonds that are the unseen underpinning of all economic life. This is as true in the victorious countries as it is in the vanquished. The trust and confidence of man for man on which the whole economic structure is raised suffers as a result of war. The governmental regulation and the inflation which usually accompany war provide a medium in which large gains can be made by the unscrupulous. A class of *nouveau riches* may arise whose conduct is not subject to the restraints of an older aristocracy. The honest man finds himself beaten to the wall in a maze of governmental regulations and prohibitions; he finds unscrupulous competitors, who know the "black market" not only in commodities but in men, getting rich at his expense. Little wonder, then, that the temptations to dishonesty grow, that power is abused, and that the moral fabric weakens. No monetary value is usually placed upon an honest man; but in a very real sense, when honesty decays, the true capital values of society decline.

The meaning of "capital"

This concept of capital-rebuilding is so important that it may be desirable to digress for a moment. In the broadest sense of the word, *capital* means the sum total of the valuable things possessed by the individuals of a society, excluding "claims," that is, mere titles to property. The word is used to mean both the *inventory* of these valuable things—the houses, factories, machines, livestock, stocks of raw materials, and goods in all stages of completion—and also to mean the sum of the *values* of these things. It should generally be clear from the context which of these two meanings is intended.[1]

Production adds to capital, consumption destroys it

Every time something valuable is created, there is an act of production. That is to say, all production adds, however momentarily, to the stock of capital. The farmer who grows wheat, the miner who mines coal, the builder who builds houses, the tailor who makes clothes, are all, in those acts, increasing the stock of capital, for they are adding to the existing stock of values. Even a singer may be conceived as creating a very short-lived capital good in the form of sound waves. Conversely, all consumption subtracts from the stock of capital. Consumption means destroying values in the way in which they were intended to be destroyed. Thus, when we eat a loaf of bread, wear out a suit of clothes, burn coal, or use

---

[1] Claims and titles, such as shares of stock, bonds, notes, securities of all kinds, bank deposits, and so forth, are not counted in the total of capital, although they represent *assets* to individuals. However, any claim or title which is an asset to one individual is a liability to another. Thus, a bond is an asset to its owner, but a liability to the company that issued it. A bank deposit is an asset to its owner, but a liability to the bank. Hence, if we were to add up the balance sheets of all individuals and organizations in society, we should find that the claims would cancel out, and we should be left with the inventory of capital goods on the one side, and an equal total of personal net worths on the other. For a fuller discussion see Boulding, Kenneth E., *Economic Analysis,* Chapter 14. New York: Harper, 1941.

furniture, we are by these acts diminishing the total stock of capital. There is nothing wrong about this; indeed, the whole aim of production is consumption. There is no particular virtue in having a stock of capital. It merely so happens that we cannot do many of the things which are necessary to living without consuming capital, and hence production is necessary in order to replace the capital destroyed. If we all had wishing wands, there would be very little need for capital; yet our satisfactions and our general welfare might be enormously increased, provided that we were wise enough to wish for the right things. Production is necessary because we cannot eat without destroying our stocks of foods, clothe ourselves without wearing out our garments, or build houses that will not crumble.

Rate of increase of capital = production minus consumption

The rate of increase of the stock of capital is equal to the difference between production and consumption. This difference is sometimes called "saving," but since this word is ambiguous, it should be avoided as far as possible. If, for instance, production in a community is worth 1,000,000 dollars a year, and consumption amounts to 900,000 dollars' worth a year, there will be a net increase of 100,000 dollars in the value of the stock of capital. Thus a community can increase its rate of accumulation of capital only by increasing production, by decreasing consumption, or by some combination of the two.

Production depends on capital, both material and spiritual

A complicating factor is introduced, however, because the rate of production itself is dependent on the amount and the character of the stock of capital goods previously accumulated. Without a stock of food sufficient to last from one harvest to the next, a community cannot occupy itself with agriculture, but must scratch a living from the woods. No modern method of production can be carried on without machinery and equipment of all kinds. In the accumulation of capital goods each kind of commodity tends to be accumulated to a point where further accumulation does not bring returns sufficient to compensate for the sacrifice involved. Thus, a community will increase its stock of wheat up to the point where there is no danger of running short between harvests, or in bad years, but will not normally increase its stock beyond that point unless through governmental intervention. The same will be true of all other items, whether raw materials, goods in process, finished goods, or machinery, tools, and equipment.

The rate of production itself depends primarily on two things: the state of knowledge and character of the people, and on the material goods which they possess. In one sense these are both aspects of capital, for the state of knowledge and character is itself a result of the educational processes of society, which bear a striking resemblance to the process of investment. Just as we value a house or a machine, so we might value the minds and bodies of persons according to their productive capacity, and in a broad sense the process of education consists in increasing the capital value of minds and bodies.

The more capital, the faster it grows

In the economic, as in the spiritual sphere, to him that hath shall be given. A rich society, possessing much capital, finds the process of accumulating more capital relatively easy, for its great capital enables it to have great production, and with great production it is easy to have a large excess of production over consumption. A poor society, on the other hand, with little capital, finds accumulation difficult, for even at low levels of consumption nearly all its meager production is consumed and there is little margin for accumulation. Very poor societies may never even be able to start accumulating capital, for production may never exceed that minimum below which the level of consumption cannot fall. In this miserable state production and consumption are equal yet both are at a level so low that consumption cannot be lowered further. Savage societies are nearly all in this condition, and even the relatively advanced societies of India and China are not far from it. Such a society cannot better its condition except by some intrusion from without, such as missionaries, teachers, businessmen, investors, or plague.[2]

---

[2] The Black Death in the 14th century, by effecting a sudden reduction in population in Europe, left the survivors with increased equipment per head and apparently started a snowball of economic progress.

The chain of production

The process of production is a long, chain-like structure with many links, connected in many ways. In the course of this process, certain goods, known as intermediate products, are transformed into other goods closer to the form in which they are finally consumed. Grass becomes wool, wool becomes yarn, yarn becomes cloth, cloth becomes clothes, and clothes become warmth. Some of these chains are even circular: manure becomes fodder, fodder becomes manure. Most of the chains have branches, either meeting where a number of things combine to make one commodity, or diverging, where one commodity is used to make a number of different things. Thus coal, iron ore, and limestone combine economically to become steel; the steel assumes the form of automobiles, bridges, buildings, cooking utensils, or a host of other things—and eventually becomes scrap, which in turn becomes a raw material of steel again.

The vicious circle and the benevolent spiral

The circularity of the production process is of the greatest importance in interpreting the growth of capital and of production itself. This is seen particularly if we recognize a link that often goes unnoticed—the link between human consumption and human energy and creativeness. Up to a point, consumption goods are transformed into human energy, which in turn is a factor of production. This "circle" may be "vicious" or may be entirely beneficial, depending on whether it is a closed circle or a rising spiral. In very poor societies, poverty is both a result and a cause of the low energy level of the people. Since the people are poor, they do not produce enough food and warmth to keep their bodies and minds active. Because their bodies and minds are not active, they do not have the energy to produce enough food and warmth. Societies caught in this vicious circle —as are all savage societies and even many sections of civilized society—find it impossible to break the circle except through some outside intervention or fortuitous favorable circumstances, such as an accidental discovery of new lands or new techniques.

Once the circle is broken, however, nothing can prevent the

improvement of the life of the people, for the circle has become a spiral: increased production leads to improved nutrition; improved nutrition leads to increased energy; increased energy leads to increased production, and so onward and upward until a new and higher equilibrium is reached. One of the great long-run problems of the world is that of how to turn the vicious circle, in which half or three-quarters of the world's population is trapped, into a benevolent spiral of increasing production. On a smaller scale, this problem is involved in postwar reconstruction, and in this case also the speed of reconstruction depends greatly on the extent to which outside help is available in restoring the capital structure, by permitting the distressed area to import without exporting.

The importance of "outside" help

What is true of a poor society is also true of a section made poor by the destructive effects of war. Such a devastated area may recover very slowly unless it receives help from outside in the form of gifts or investments. Had the battlefields of World War I been cut off from the rest of the world, they would still be devastated areas. Their rapid recovery arose from the fact that they were able to import great quantities of food, materials, livestock, equipment, and labor without paying for these things by exports. In the years following 1918 a large volume of goods poured into the devastated areas; the inhabitants were fed and clothed from outside and were able to devote their time to rebuilding houses and farms, filling up trenches and shell holes, ploughing the devastated fields, restoring the shattered factories and towns, and so on. Imagine the situation had there been no flow of commodities from the outside. The inhabitants would have had to devote almost their whole energies to growing food, often with very inadequate implements. Crops would have been poor and livestock scanty for many years. Not until a little reserve of food had been accumulated could they have devoted much time to rebuilding buildings, or to making equipment and machines. It would have taken many years to restore the cattle, sheep, and horses, for these are slow-breeding animals; meanwhile, the people would have been desperately short of meat and milk, for where animals have to be used for breeding purposes, they cannot, of course, be used for food.

It can hardly be too strongly emphasized, therefore, that where devastation is confined to certain areas, the speed of reconstruction depends mainly on the ability of these areas to receive net imports from the world outside. This is still true, even for areas where physical devastation has not been extensive, but where the economic strain of conducting a war has led to a general wastage of all capital. Although the capital losses of these areas of general decay are less spectacular than those of devastated areas, they are usually large in volume, if only because the areas of actual devastation are small compared with the areas of general decay. As we shall see later, the whole *financial* problem of reconstruction centers around the attempt of the decayed or devastated areas to obtain net imports of commodities.

The hierarchy of need

Another point of apparently purely theoretical interest, but actually of the utmost importance in understanding the economics of reconstruction, is that in the process of the accumulation or restoration of capital, there is a kind of hierarchy of needs. It is not merely the *quantity* of capital that is significant, but the kind of goods in which the values are embodied. There would be no point in building up vast stocks of wheat in a devastated area where there were no machines, ploughs, tractors, or horses. Similarly, there would be no point in sending harvesting equipment to a district that had no seed, nor even in sending seed to a place that had not enough bread to keep the people alive till harvest time. Thus it is that in a badly devastated or decayed area, relief must always precede reconstruction. Where economic life has almost come to a standstill, the first essential imports are food, clothing, fuel, and simple raw materials, so that the people may have strength to get back to work and materials with which to work. For the same reason, the first step in permanent reconstruction is either the restoration of agricultural production or else the restoration of export industries, the products of which will buy food elsewhere.

The "bottlenecks" produced by war

Not merely the *quantity* of imports but the *character* of imports is a vital factor in the restoration of production. The obvious general rule may be given that those commodities which have become the most seriously deficient should be imported first. As a result of a war, not only does the quantity of physical capital diminish, but the whole *relative* quantities of different kinds of goods change, and the balance of the capital structure is upset. In the normal operations of the economic system, we will find that the quantities of various capital goods bear a certain fairly stable proportion one to another: the number of harnesses is usually roughly proportionate to the number of horses, the number of trucks and coaches is proportionate to the number of railroad engines, the numbers of livestock to the supplies of feed, the stocks of yarn to the number of looms, and so on. War distorts this whole structure of relative proportions, and the decline in production which is observed as a result of war is perhaps even more due to the distortion of the relative structure of capital than to any absolute decline. One reason is clear: in any process involving the co-operation of many elements, the pace of the slowest sets the pace of the whole. A convoy can go no faster than the slowest ship, and a process of production can go no faster than the pace set by the tightest bottleneck. There is no use for looms if we have no yarn, no use for trucks if there are no engines, no use for harnesses if there are no horses. The factors of production are most efficient where combined in certain proportions; where these proportions are changed, the efficiency of the whole productive process falls off.

The problem of maintenance—in agriculture and industry

One important example of the effects of distortion in the "relative structure" occurs where the instruments of production have to be maintained. Perhaps the best example may be found in the production of livestock products, and especially in the production of milk. The feeding stuffs given to an animal perform two functions; one is to maintain the body of the animal, and the other is to produce its characteristic product, whether it be meat, milk, or eggs. That part which is necessary for maintenance is called the "maintenance ration," and that part necessary for production is called the "production ration." When the amount of food given to an animal is cut down, therefore, a greater proportion of the food is used for maintenance, as the absolute amount needed for maintenance is fairly constant, and consequently a smaller proportion goes to producing the animal's product. Accordingly if the diet of cows is restricted, their first reaction is to lessen, or even to abandon, their production of milk. Similarly, the hungry steer will not fatten nor will the hungry hen lay eggs. If there is a serious decline in the quantity of feeding stuffs available, but the livestock population is *not* reduced in proportion, the decline in the production of livestock products may be out of all proportion to the decline in feeding stuffs; the available feeding stuffs have to be used merely to keep the animals alive and are therefore not transformed into meat, milk, or eggs. The tragic decline in milk production in Germany during and after World War I was due not to any decline in the number of cows—in fact, in some parts of the country, the number of cows actually increased—but was due to a decline in the quantity of feeding stuffs. Nearly all the short supply of feeding stuffs went to keeping the animals alive.

This phenomenon is not so likely to occur in industry, where the problem of maintenance of machines is not so serious as the maintenance of livestock. But even here the problem arises in a small degree. The decline in industrial output in Germany was associated with a great scarcity of lubricating oil and a consequent rapid deterioration of machinery. Even more serious was the shortage of coal, and hence of power, which may have been the most serious bottleneck as far as industrial recovery was concerned.

Improper distribution of goods in process and of foodstuffs

Another example of a defective "relative structure" is the distribution of the existing capital goods among various classes of owners. If a war is followed, as it usually is, by a period of inflation, raw materials and commodities generally become the subjects of an unusual degree of speculation. When prices of all things are rising rapidly, profits can be made simply by holding stocks of commodities in warehouses. At such a time, therefore, the distribution of raw materials and goods in process between speculators and manufacturers is likely to move in favor of the speculators, and to the disadvantage of the manufacturers. Hence, even the small stocks of raw materials in the country may not be properly employed, as a proportion of them may be withheld from the productive process by speculators.

The distribution of food, as well as its absolute scarcity, is likewise an important factor. It has been estimated that in 1919, in Germany, there was enough food to supply everyone with the scanty, but adequate diet of 3000 calories per day. Because of the breakdown of the exchange between town and country, however, the farmers ate an average of about 4000 calories apiece whereas the city populations were near starvation on a diet yielding only 2000 calories per head. The problem of getting existing supplies into the right hands, therefore, may be quite as important as the problem of augmenting the total supply.

Food shortage may be due to decline in industrial production

In this connection, it should be noticed that a food shortage may be as much a result of a decline in industrial production as in agricultural production. The supply of food to the cities depends in the last analysis on the ability of the cities to pay for this food by supplying city-made goods to the country. The only exception to this rule occurs when the landlords of the country live in the city; then the country pays its rent mainly in the form of foodstuffs sent to the city. We can think of this case as one in which the city exchanges the services of land, owned by some of its inhabitants, for foodstuffs and other products of the country. When there is a revolution, as frequently happens after a war, and the landlords are dispossessed, a great strain is thrown on the ability of the cities to provide themselves with food. During the war the industries of the cities are turned over to war purposes. Consequently, by the end of the war, the cities are not producing anything which can be given to the farmers in exchange for food. This breakdown of exchange is the principal cause of the "city famine" so characteristic of a postwar period. It was the most important factor in the Russian Revolution of 1917: the refusal of the peasants to pay their rents, coupled with the fact that almost the whole industrial equipment of the country had been turned over to war purposes, meant that the cities had practically nothing to give to the country in exchange for food except increasingly depreciating money. It was the cessation of the flow of food to the cities rather than any sharp decline in agricultural production itself that brought about the revolution. In 1919, in Germany also, as we have seen, the famine was due not only to the decline in agricultural production, but also to the fact that the cities and towns could not get food which did exist in the country, largely because they had so little to offer the country in exchange. This is, in a way, part of the general problem of capital rebuilding—how to get imports without immediately paying for them by exports. As will be shown in the next chapter, the financial consequences of the breakdown in exchange are profound, and the inflationary conditions which follow a war are in no small measure due to the breakdown in the city-country exchange.

The significance of "subsistence-goods" industries

All these phenomena are related to the "hierarchy of needs" mentioned previously. The point is so fundamental to the understanding of any broad economic problem that it may be worth while to digress somewhat to examine it further. The ability of a society to increase in wealth depends, as we have seen, on its existing degree of wealth. A rich society can increase its wealth much more rapidly than a poor one, and below a certain level of poverty, a society becomes incapable of improvement. The degree of wealth of a society depends mainly upon its techniques of production and particularly upon the efficiency of labor. The best measure of wealth is product per man-hour, and we can say without much hesitation that anything which increases the product per man-hour in any occupation has the effect of increasing wealth. The effects of an improvement in methods of production are not the same in all occupations, however. Some occupations, notably agriculture, produce what may be called "subsistence goods"—that is, goods whose main function is the preservation of the health, abilities, and energies of the actively productive members of society. Other occupations produce "luxuries," in the sense of goods that contribute relatively little to productive efficiency, but do, of course, contribute to the satisfactions and enjoyments of the people. No hard and fast line can be drawn between these two kinds of commodities—many foods, for instance, contribute more to enjoyment than they do to health and energy, while many "luxuries," such as movies, may contribute indirectly to health and energy by providing opportunities for psychological relaxation. In spite of the vagueness, however, the distinction is of supreme importance, for an improvement in the techniques of production of subsistence goods, except in very rich societies, is likely to have a greater effect on the degree of wealth than a similar improvement in the techniques of production of luxury goods.[3]

How wealth depends on techniques in subsistence industries

The ability of any closed society to support cities and to produce luxuries depends mainly on the techniques of production in the subsistence industries and especially in food production. The size of the industrial population depends on the surplus produce of agriculture and other food industries. If methods of production in agriculture are so poor that the average farmer and his family eat all the food that they produce on their farm, then clearly there can be no cities and no industries. If the farmer and his household produce twice as much as they eat themselves, then about half the population will be in agriculture and the other half in industry. If the farmer's household can produce food for ten other households, as in the most advanced countries, then only a tenth of the population needs to be on the soil and nine tenths are available to produce the luxuries and conveniences of life.

Why "agricultural" countries are weak

A society always gets into difficulties when it tries to maintain a superstructure of nonsubsistence occupations that is too

---

[3] For a fuller discussion of this problem, see Boulding, Kenneth E., "Equilibrium and Wealth." *The Canadian Journal of Economics and Political Science,* February, 1939.

large to be supported by its existing agricultural techniques. The Roman Empire, especially in its declining years, was a case in point; it tried to maintain a great military establishment and a host of parasitical cities when the agricultural techniques did not provide an adequate surplus of food, over and above the consumption of the agricultural population. But any country during a long and severe war is apt to find itself in the same position. War is a "luxury" industry, not a subsistence industry. The ability of a nation, or a group of nations, to wage war depends mainly on the degree of wealth and particularly on the state of agricultural techniques. A country of "subsistence farmers" or poor peasants, whose techniques and resources are so poor that they consume almost all their produce, can never support a large army or a large war industry. The profound military weakness of the so-called backward "agricultural" countries—that is, countries in which the output per man in agriculture is low, and therefore the agricultural population is high—is a standing testimony to this principle. During war, however, a nation tries to devote as great an absolute amount of resources to the war industry as possible and especially in militaristic nations the coercive power of the state is used to build up a superstructure of warlike activity far greater than the agricultural foundations can support. The result is invariably economic collapse and defeat. This goes far to explain one of the paradoxes of history— that the commercially minded and relatively peaceable peoples have on the whole been most successful in war.

Importance of reconstructing "subsistence-industries"

The economic difficulties of a postwar period often arise, therefore, from the fact that during the war there has been a diversion of economic resources away from the "subsistence" industries into the "luxury" industry of war. Consequently, at the end of a war, the nation has too small an output of subsistence goods to support the people in other occupations. This state of affairs may, of course, be only temporary; but, one of the main tasks of reconstruction is to increase the output of subsistence-goods industries and so release resources for the rebuilding of capital.

Importance of transport

It remains to mention another vital phase of the problem of physical reconstruction—the restoration of the transport industry. The transport system is the veins and arteries of the economic body; without it, exchange would be impossible, specialization would cease, and we would be reduced to poverty-stricken subsistence farm units. In that breakdown of exchange, which is perhaps the most critical problem of reconstruction, the decline in the facilities for transport plays an important part. During a war the transport system shares the general decay of capital. On the railroads, repairs are not made and the rolling stock and road-bed deteriorate. Roads are not repaired; vehicles are not repaired or replaced as they wear out; ships are sunk in great numbers. So, at the end of a war, there is an acute crisis in transportation, which presents one of the most serious *physical* obstacles to reconstruction. There may be people starving in Europe while great stocks of food pile up in countries overseas; there may be relative plenty in one place and famine in another. Industries languish for lack of raw materials, while the raw material producers cannot get shipments for their accumulated stocks. In any system of priorities in the reconstruction period, transport both by land and sea must stand very high, even perhaps before the "subsistence" industries, for, unless the produce of the subsistence industries can be transported to the workers in the other industries, no substantial reconstruction can take place. The transportation problem is frequently aggravated by political factors. The war may result in the creation of more independent countries through the breakup of old empires, as in the case of Austria-Hungary in 1919. Then these new states will generally interfere with transport across their boundaries, through restrictions on trade. There may also be difficulties and delays in adjusting the transport system itself to the new political conditions. The restoration of the Danube Basin in the years following 1918 was greatly hindered by the fact that the old Austro-Hungarian Empire, occupying a relatively compact and self-sufficient economic region, had been broken up into the succession states. Each of these states interfered with trade crossing its boundary, either by outright prohibition, or by quotas, or tariffs. There was also a long dispute regarding the distribution of the rolling stock of the old Empire which immobilized much of it just at the time when it was most critically needed.

The conclusions of this chapter may now be summarized:

1. The problem of physical reconstruction is essentially that of the *rapid* accumulation of capital.

2. The net rate of accumulation of capital in any region is equal to Production + Imports—Consumption—Exports. The problem therefore resolves itself into increasing production and net imports, and diminishing consumption and net exports.

3. Besides the quantitative problem, there is an important qualitative problem in restoring the "relative structure" of capital goods. In this connection, the restoration of agriculture and transport is of peculiar significance.

CHAPTER 2

The Financial Problem of Reconstruction

Valuations involve us in a financial system

In the first chapter we have considered the *physical* problem of reconstruction. The physical problem is not, however, the only one. In this world, physical goods are clothed with values, and their production and consumption entangles us in a complex web of financial relationships involving costs and receipts, incomes and expenditures, debts and credits. Although the most fundamental economic problems are physical, in the sense that they involve work and goods rather than wages and money, yet corresponding to all the physical processes of economic life there must be financial processes. If the financial processes break down, or function improperly, then the physical processes are profoundly affected. We see this most clearly in the sequence of booms and depressions that we call the "business cycle." Although there are some aspects of the physical process of production which are sufficient to cause small fluctuations in the productive process, the wild ups and downs of our present economic system are not primarily the result of physical, but of financial causes. It is our defective financial organization, rather than a defective physical organization, that makes the swings of the business cycle so large and so destructive. This weakness in our financial system itself produces great effects on physical production. In the depths of a depression, for instance, there is a great volume of unemployment, and the total output of society is much less than would be physically possible. Similarly at the height of a boom, the behavior of the financial system causes bad investments to be made in physical goods; a distortion of the physical structure of capital ensues which is in part responsible for the subsequent depression.

Physical problems underlie financial problems

The problem of physical reconstruction, therefore, is complicated considerably by the necessity for solving *financial* problems as well as purely physical problems. These financial problems are, however, largely conditioned by the underlying physical structure and cannot be understood unless we see the matter not merely as a problem in finances, but also as a problem in terms of goods and services. It may be well, therefore, to digress once again from the main theme in order to consider the general relationship which exists between the financial and the physical structures of the economic system.

Why have a financial system?

By the *physical* structure of economic life we mean the quantities of various commodities, materials, and capital goods of all kinds that exist at a moment of time, together with the rates of production and consumption of all these things, including not only material goods but also human bodies and minds, and certain spiritual or mental commodities such as "ability." By the financial structure we mean the values and prices of these goods, the money incomes and expenditures to which their production and consumption gives rise, and the structure of debt and ownership of the goods in existence. The unsophisticated individual may quite reasonably ask, "why do we have to have a financial structure at all—if what is really important is the physical structure, the doing of work and the production and consumption of commodities, why do we have to bother with all this complicated business of money, prices, wages, incomes, debts, and so on; why cannot we do our daily work, and take what we want from the shops just as we do now, without all the additional trouble of accounting, of paying and being paid for things?" The question is a good one, and in the answer lies the clue to much that is puzzling in economic life.

Example—prices fixed too low or too high

The answer to the question "what would happen if we abolished money and prices" is seen clearly when a government interferes with prices. There have been innumerable instances where a government has fixed a price "too low." Then the commodity in question has disappeared from the market. On the one hand, it does not pay producers to produce it at the low price; on the other hand, consumers are encouraged to consume it. Stocks are consumed and are not replaced, and the commodity disappears, or at least is produced only in a very much reduced quantity. Meat and butter in certain parts of the United States provide a recent example; the war of 1914-18 produced many more examples. Butter disappeared from the markets of Germany when the government fixed the price—farmers preferred to use it as a lubricant instead of the high-priced axle grease! The control of rents during and after the war caused an almost universal housing shortage, for it did not pay investors to build houses at the existing level of rents.

Similarly, when prices have been fixed at too high a level, production has been unduly encouraged and consumption discouraged, so that unwieldy stocks of the commodity have piled up. Many agricultural commodities provide examples of such a policy. A classic case is that of Brazilian coffee. As Brazil has a near-monopoly of the production of coffee, the Brazilian government formed an export monopoly, and so was able to raise the price of coffee. The high price of coffee encouraged producers in Brazil—and in other parts of the world—with the result that world production increased and consumption failed to increase proportionately. Stocks of coffee therefore began to accumulate in the warehouses of Brazil until there was a year's supply in stock at the time of the new harvest of 1928. Great quantities were as a result dumped in the sea or otherwise destroyed.

The "rationing function" of price

These examples give us the clue to the real function of prices —the real job that they have to perform. It is the job of "rationing"—that is, of apportioning available supplies, whether of productive agents or of the goods produced, among the various claimants, so that the amount that people wish to buy is just equal to the amount people wish to sell. If this process is interfered with, some substitute must be found, either in direct rationing of consumption or in control of production.

Financial system permits separation of ownership and control

There is also another important job that is performed by the financial system—that of permitting specialization to take place between the ownership and the administration of capital. This is the principal job that has to be done by the system of *debt*, and by the whole system of "financial instruments"—stocks, bonds, mortgages, securities of all kinds. Consider, for instance, a man who wishes to be a farmer, but who does not own any land, or very much property of any kind. There are several alternatives open to him. He may rent a farm, either for a money rent or for a share of the crop. Or, if he has a little money, he can buy a farm and pay part of the cost by borrowing on a mortgage. Suppose, for instance, that he buys a farm for $10,000, paying $1,000 of his own money and borrowing $9,000 on a mortgage,, with the farm as security. It is evident that he does not really "own" the farm in one sense—that is, in the sense of possessing its full value. He only owns $1,000 worth of it, and the mortgage holder owns $9,000 worth. Nevertheless, the farmer does own it in the sense of administering it, as long as his mortgage is not foreclosed. The relation of the mortgage holder to the farm is different from that of a landlord: a landlord is responsible for the administration of his land in a much more direct and intimate sense than the mortgage holder. Similarly with any other form of debt: the creditor in one sense owns the value of the assets of the debtor up to the amount of his debt; but the debtor administers these physical assets, and organizes them into some kind of a process of production. The main purpose of the financial system is to enable the ultimate owners of property—the capitalists—to combine that ownership with as little, or as much, responsibility for administration as they wish, and by so doing, enable those individuals who own little property but are skilled in its administration to administer far more property than they actually own. Thus the owner of a bond or a mortgage, as long as the debt is not defaulted, has no responsibility whatever for the administration of the property which "secures" and gives value to his security. The owner of ordinary shares of stock has a certain responsibility for the ultimate management of the concern through the election of a board of directors, who in turn appoint the administrative officials. Even this theoretical responsibility may be evaded in practice, and a concern may be run by its board of directors or by its managers without much consideration for the interests of the shareholders. At the other end of the scale, we have the paid manager, or the managing director, who may have little or no share in the ownership of the concern, but who is in practice responsible for its policy. Without a system of debts, bonds, shares, and other financial instruments, only those who possessed capital could administer it no matter how bad a job they might do, and those with managerial ability, but with no capital, would be deprived of an opportunity to exercise their talents.

The finance of reconstruction

These considerations may seem somewhat far removed from the problem of reconstruction. However, they are essential to its understanding. In the previous chapter, it was shown that the problem of reconstruction, in a physical sense, is the problem of the accumulation of physical capital at a more rapid rate than is normally achieved. This can be done in two ways: either by a severe restriction of *internal* consumption within the affected country or region, or by bringing a marked excess of imports of physical goods from *external* sources into the affected area during the reconstruction period. Both these methods involve a financial problem. The first involves the problem of obtaining a sufficient volume of internal saving. The second involves the problem of obtaining foreign loans, credits, gifts, or other sources of foreign purchasing power. Any combination of the two methods may be adopted, since they are not exclusive.

Finance by direct accumulation

Let us consider first the case of a country which cannot obtain any outside loans so that its reconstruction must be accomplished out of its own resources—through producing more than it consumes. In financial terms, this is reflected in the *value* of production being greater than the *value* of consumption. The result is an increase in the net worth of the society—that is, an increase in the value of its physical assets, assuming for the moment that there is no change in prices. The greater the value of production and the less the value of consumption, the greater will be the rate of accumulation and the more rapid will be the reconstruction. The problem, therefore, is how to keep production at the highest possible level, and yet restrict consumption to the lowest level consistent with efficient production.

Voluntary saving

If this restriction of consumption is performed voluntarily, through the saving of individual consumers, there is no financial difficulty. The restriction of consumption on the part of consumers means that they will spend less money than they earn. The difference between earnings and spendings represents in the first instance an increase in the holdings of money. There is no point in an individual merely accumulating money, that is, cash, beyond a certain point. This money, therefore, will be used to buy securities of some kind—that is, if the consumer does not want to spend it in any productive process himself, he can lend it to someone who will spend it in buying factors of production and creating goods. By this means, capital is accumulated.

Inflation and involuntary saving

Suppose now that the "investors"—the people who want to spend money in the creation of goods—have the power to create money. This may be done by the government directly by the printing of bills, or it may be done by borrowing from the banks, with two effects. In the first place, unless the factors of production were unemployed to start with, the new producers will attract labor and equipment away from old occupations and may actually reduce the amount of consumers' goods that are currently coming on the market. In the second place, the new money will provide increased cash incomes—probably to an extent greater than the initial expenditure of the new money, for the people who receive it also spend it, and their payees also spend it, and so on. The result of there being more money to spend, and fewer goods to buy, is inevitably a rise in prices. This rise in prices is a method of forcing consumers to restrict their consumption. This rise in prices will not take place if there is voluntary restriction of consumption and therefore voluntary saving. If, however, consumers are unwilling to restrict consumption to the extent necessitated by the investment program, a rise in prices is inevitable.

Why inflation follows war

This perhaps is the most fundamental explanation why severe inflation of prices has always followed great wars./Both a war and a reconstruction period necessitate restrictions in consumption—simply because in the war period a large proportion of productive capacity must be turned over to the war industry, and therefore is not available for the production of consumers' goods; in the reconstruction period a large proportion of productive capacity must likewise be turned over to the "capital-goods" industries and again cannot be used immediately in the production of consumers' goods/This restriction of consumption is the primary problem of "finance," whether of war finance or of reconstruction finance./It is generally easier to solve during the war, for then the public is in a mood to accept sacrifices, is willing to accept high taxation, rationing, and all manner of restrictions on consumption. After the war is over, however, the mood of the public changes and the real danger of inflation begins. Even in defeated countries the postwar mood is not one of sacrifice and asceticism—rather it is likely to be one of selfishness and extravagance. The war is over; the burden is lifted; people want to come out of the years of toil, darkness, and tears, and reap the reward of their sufferings. Workers press for higher wages and threaten revolution if their demands are not satisfied. The rich make full use of their opportunities for extravagant consumption which the war has denied them. The tax system tends to break down; the unwillingness to pay taxes grows to such a point that evasion becomes the rule rather than the exception. The government consequently finds it impossible to balance the budget; the war leaves a great aftermath of expenditure; reconstruction, insofar as it is financed by the government, demands even further expenditure. On the other hand, taxes are defaulted, and the public becomes unwilling to lend to the government, either because they mistrust its solvency or because they are generally unwilling to accept the sacrifices that lending would involve. The result is inflationary governmental finance, either through borrowing from the banks or through the direct printing of money. This adds to the inflationary elements already present in the society.

Inflation may restrict consumption

Inflation *may* solve the problem of the restriction of consumption, or it may not. After the last war inflation solved the problem for France and Italy, though at a considerable cost in injustice. It failed to solve the problem for Germany, although even there in the early stages it undoubtedly helped. Inflation operates to restrict consumption as long as prices rise faster than consumers' incomes. The consuming power of an individual depends on two things—his money income, and the prices of the things that he buys. His consuming power may be decreased *either* by a reduction in his money income, prices being the same, *or* by a rise in prices, his income being the same. If his income rises, then prices must rise in a greater proportion if his consuming power is to be reduced. In the early stages of inflation the restriction of consumption may be very considerable. In the first place, there is an important class of people in any country whose incomes are fixed in terms of money: pension holders, bondholders, annuity holders, and the like. These are the first and the greatest sufferers through inflation. These are the people who really "pay" the most for war and reconstruction, when financed by inflation, for these are the people who are forced to curtail their expenditures most drastically. Hundreds of thousands of people in Germany and other countries who, before World War I, had a comfortable income, were reduced to poverty by the postwar inflations. Salaried workers, teachers, officials, and others whose money income rises slowly, lagging behind the rise in prices, also find their purchasing power reduced and consequently may reduce their consumption. The working class in general may find wages lagging behind prices and so will have to reduce its consumption, although in the case of strongly organized workers this is less likely to be the case. Finally, the people whose consuming power is increased by inflation are the merchants, the businessmen, and the speculators —the whole general class of people whose income is derived from profits—from buying and selling. If, now, those whose con-

suming power is increased by inflation do not take advantage
of this increase, but continue to consume pretty much as before, the inflation will result in a net decline of consumption in
the society, and therefore in an increased rate of accumulation.
The inflation is also likely to stimulate production, at least in
its early stages, for profits in almost all forms of enterprise are
high. Unemployment is likely to be practically nonexistent, and
though the inflation may cause production to be directed into
wrong channels in some instances, nevertheless the total will be
close to a maximum.

Inflation and employment

The connection between inflation and employment is an
important one, not only for problems of immediate reconstruction but also for the long view. It may be wise, therefore, to consider it in more detail. Consider what happens when an employer
hires a man for a week. This act of employment is in reality
an *exchange*. At the beginning of the week, the employer has
in his possession, say, $40 in cash. At the end of the week he
must give the $40 cash to the worker as wages, but in return
the employer owns the *product* of the work done by the workman. For instance, the worker is a coal miner; as a result of the
week's work, suppose ten tons of coal are brought out of the
mine, where they have no value, to the pithead where they can
be sold. By employing the miner, the employer has in effect
exchanged $40 in cash for a certain value of coal—he has ex-
changed *liquid* property (cash) for nonliquid property (coal).
Unless the value of the coal in the above case were at least
equal to the miner's wage, the man would not be employed, for
an employer does not willingly give up·in exchange something
(money) which has a greater value than the product of the work
(goods). If the miner's wage were $40, when the coal that he
produced was worth only $35, it would not pay to employ him.
If the coal was worth $45, however, it would pay to employ him.[1]
Generally speaking, an employer will increase the number of

---

[1] In calculating what the coal is "worth" to the employer, account must, of
course, be taken of changes in his other assets which the extraction of the coal
has entailed.

men he employs as long as the value of the product of the work of the last man employed is greater than that man's wage.

Inflation increases the demand for labor

Now, the product of a man's labor is usually sold some time *after* the labor has been performed. The value of that product depends therefore on the price of the final article at the time when it is sold—perhaps a week, a month, or even years after the labor has been performed and payment made. If the general level of prices is rising, the present value of the product of labor depends on the expected price at some future date, and may therefore be expected to be large by comparison with the wage level, which depends more on the *current* level of prices. Hence the *expectation* of rising prices nearly always leads to a rise in employment. Similarly, the expectation of a fall in prices is likely to lead to a decline in employment, for it leads to a decline in the estimated value of the product of labor.[2]

Inflation may pass into "hyperinflation"

We see, therefore, that inflation may be a method of capital accumulation. This is only true however, up to a point. Beyond a certain stage the whole system of accountancy begins to break down; there is a flight "out of money"; contracts are not made in the depreciating money, but in terms of commodities or foreign currencies. As soon as money comes into people's hands, they rush to spend it, and the rise in prices may not be rapid enough to check this wild rush of expenditure. At this point any effect of inflation in restricting consumption is lost, for the fear of rising prices of itself actually stimulates consumption. When this effect is strong enough, it overrides the deterrent effect due to the shift in consuming power. We can use a medical analogy and say that inflation is a drug, whose effect declines with increasing doses. Consequently, as inflation proceeds, it becomes less and less effective in performing the task of restricting consumption. Larger and larger doses have to be given, and the pace tends to accelerate until it ends in the wild and uncontrolled scramble of hyperinflation, where its effectiveness is nil, or even negative.

---

[2] In the general case, it is the anticipated changes in the demand for the firm's product that is the cause of changes in demand for labor.

The success of inflation depends on how far it is unexpected

It is clear that while inflation may be a way out of an otherwise impossible situation, it is a way fraught with grave dangers and is certainly not to be recommended. Its success as a capital-forming device depends largely on the degree to which it is unexpected. It is because taxation is all too clearly an act of government, and saving all too clearly an act of the individual, that inflation may be able to restrict consumption when all other means fail, for most individuals regard a rise in prices as in some way an act of nature for which nobody has any particular responsibility. Accordingly—quite irrationally—the reaction to a rise in prices may be different from the reaction to increased taxation. This difference arises partly from the astonishing faith which mankind seems to possess in the stability of the purchasing power of money—a faith totally without foundation in history, but apparently strong in human nature. It is a question of great importance for the future of Europe whether this faith has been destroyed by the experiences of World War I. If it has, if people fear inflation and act accordingly, inflation is much less likely to be successful in achieving its true end than it was in the last reconstruction period, for the stimulative effects of inflation on consumption depend on the degree of anticipation. If everyone fears and expects inflation, it will pass almost immediately into the stage at which it stimulates instead of restricts consumption—that is, into hyperinflation, even if the actual level of prices has not risen very far.

The function of imports

In the above discussion we have assumed a self-contained economy, trying to reconstruct itself solely out of its own resources. As we have seen, however, it is possible for a region to be reconstructed partly, or almost entirely, from outside—by importing more than it exports. The simple, "orthodox" way to do this is of course by loans or gifts. The financial mechanism here operates through the balance of payments and, in the case of an independent country, through the foreign exchanges. Consider first the case of a country, such as France in 1919, which has to reconstruct a devastated area, comprising only a small part of the country, largely out of the resources of the relatively undisturbed provinces. In physical terms, the devastated area must import food and raw materials of all kinds from the rest of the country; it has very little, however, to export, as its industries and its agriculture are in part ruined. There is here a problem in the balance of payments, even though it does not result in a "foreign exchange" problem, for the question arises immediately, how can the devastated area pay for this excess of imports. Normally, the sale of its exports would put money into the hands of the people, with which they would buy imports. Now, however, the amount of money that can be acquired in this way is very limited, while the need for imports is great. Some other way must be found, therefore, to put money into the hands of the inhabitants of the devastated area. This may be done partly by loans, or partly by insurance payments or by gifts—for example, compensation paid by the government for war losses.

Finance by loans

When the reconstruction is financed by loans, the ultimate ownership of the reconstructed capital lies in the hands of the lenders—that is, in the hands of people outside the devastated area. This may be quite "sound" financially, as long as the value of the capital equipment constructed by the loans is equal to, or greater than, the amount of the loans. It does mean, however, that the main burden of the war is still borne by the people of the devastated area, for, until the loan is paid off, they do not "really" own their newly-built capital; though they may eventually succeed in paying off the loans and so regain the equity in their property, this can only be done by restricting their consumption of "imports" below their production of "exports." The total effect of the loan, assuming that it is eventually paid off, is that the lenders restrict consumption, or investment elsewhere, for a short period, in order to permit the borrowers to import without exporting. In the long run, however, the lenders do not suffer, but are actually paid in interest for their restriction of consumption at the time of the loan. The net result of the loan, therefore, is to increase the total consuming power of the lenders over the whole period of the loan. The borrowers, on the other hand, over the whole period of the loan must restrict their consumption to an even greater extent than the amount of rebuilt capital. That is to say, a loan enables the inhabitants of the devastated area to spread the restriction of their consumption over a longer period than would be the case if they had to reconstruct their capital wholly out of their own immediate current resources; the total amount of restriction necessary is not lessened, but rather is increased by the loan, as interest must be paid. The whole "real cost" of reconstruction is then ultimately borne by the people of the devastated area.[3]

Finance by gifts

This is not the case, of course, where reconstruction is paid for by the national government, through compensation, as was largely the case in France after World War I. Then the whole nation must restrict its consumption (including foreign investment) without any future benefits accruing. This is undoubtedly the fairer method, as the costs of a war and reconstruction should be spread over a whole society that is responsible, rather than confined to the individuals whose property is destroyed.

International finance

Turning now to the problem of the reconstruction of a whole nation, it may generally be assumed that this will only in small part be achieved by gifts from outside. There may be, indeed, charitable individuals and organizations whose sense of brotherhood is world-wide and who therefore will freely assist in the reconstruction of a foreign or even of an enemy country. Many people in the United States, for instance, gave money to help to feed the children of Germany in the period after World War I. These gifts, however, are likely to be small in comparison with the desperate need for imports, and there will, therefore, be

---

[3] This does not mean, of course, that there is anything irrational about borrowing: even though interest is paid, it may be preferable to restrict consumption by a larger amount spread over a long period than by a smaller amount squeezed into a small space of time. In one sense also interest is paid out of the increased productivity which the loan creates.

attempts to obtain loans from outside. As in the case of a region within a country, these loans may be quite "sound"—that is, they may result in the creation of exporting power sufficient not only to pay interest but also eventually to repay the loans. On an international scale, however, loans are not unlikely to be financially unsound. Both lenders and borrowers may be inexperienced, and the purchasing power acquired by the borrower may be frittered away in unprofitable enterprises and may not result in a permanent increase in capital values. Or, the conditions of international trade may create a "transfer problem" so as to prevent the repayment, or even the payment of interest across national boundaries. In such a case, the loan may be defaulted, and the greater part of it may then be regarded, from the long-run point of view, as a "gift" obtained under false pretenses, or rather, false expectations.

Finance of imports by inflation and exchange depreciation

Inflation enters the picture here also as an attempted solution of the problem of obtaining imports without paying for them. In the early stages of reconstruction after a war, when international trade is just reviving, and when the foreign exchange markets are beginning to function again, a country that is experiencing an internal inflation and is in dire need of imports will find its foreign exchange rate depreciating. The price of its currency will fall in terms of foreign currencies, and the price of foreign currencies will rise. This is part of the general inflationary movement; the price of foreign currencies rises just as the price of everything else rises—because there is more of the national money being offered, and possibly less of the purchased articles, that is, the foreign currencies. In the case of foreign currencies, the rise in price is a direct result of the attempt to import more than is exported, for imports are purchased from foreigners, who come into possession of the domestic money which they wish to sell, while exports result in nationals coming into possession of foreign money. The abundant imports and scanty exports mean that there is a great deal of domestic money on the market, trying to exchange itself for a small quantity of foreign money. The result is a fall in the price of domestic money.[4]

Effect of falling exchange rate

This in itself, however, will have the effect of discouraging imports, for it means that if the prices of imported goods in the foreign money do not change, the prices in the domestic money rise. Thus, an automobile that was priced at $1000 in American money, would be priced at 5000 marks when marks were 5 to the dollar, that is, when dollars were 0.2 to the mark, but would be priced at 10,000 marks when marks were 10 to the dollar and dollars were 0.1 to the mark. Similarly, there will be a favorable effect on the volume of exports, for if the domestic price of exports remained the same, the foreign price would fall and this would encourage sales. Of itself, these movements would bring the value of imports and of exports to an equilibrium, and the depreciation of the foreign exchange rate would cease. If, however, the internal inflation continues, the domestic price of imported goods will continue to rise, there will be a further excess of the domestic currency in the foreign exchange market, and the currency will depreciate still further.

Exchange depreciation may make foreigners finance
reconstruction unwittingly

Just as domestic inflation in the early stages may be a desperate, last-resort device to try to force the people to restrict their consumption, so also inflation in its early stages may enable a country to import goods without paying for them by exports and so force foreigners to contribute to building up the country's capital. This may happen as long as the foreigners do not anticipate a rate of inflation as rapid as that which takes place. Suppose that an American merchant sold wheat to Germany at a price of 10 marks a bushel when the exchange rate was 5 marks to the dollar. Not counting costs of transport,

---

[4] Suppose, for instance, that Germany imported from America 20,000,000 marks' worth of goods, and exported to America $1,000,000 worth. The exchange rate would stand at about 20 marks = $1, assuming that there were no other countries and no loans. If imports increase to 30,000,000 marks' worth the mark would fall to 30 marks = $1. (See Boulding, Kenneth E., *Economic Analysis*, Chapter 6. New York: Harper, 1941.)

the price in dollars that he expected to get would be $2 a bushel. If, however, by the time he buys his dollars in the foreign exchange market, the value of the mark has sunk to 10 marks to the dollar, he will only realize a price of $1 a bushel, at which, perhaps, it does not pay him to sell the wheat. If he had anticipated the movement of the exchanges correctly, of course he would never have sold the wheat, but his faulty expectations led him to sell wheat to Germany at a price of $1 a bushel instead of $2.

In a like manner, foreign speculators may contribute to a nation's capital import in time of inflation if they purchase the currency for speculative purposes, expecting it to recover its value; when in fact it depreciates still further. During the great German inflation from 1919-1923 a great deal of money was lost by incautious speculators in other countries who, observing that the value of the mark was very low, bought marks in the expectation of a rise. But the value of the mark fell almost to zero, and these speculators lost almost the whole value of their holdings. What was lost by these non-German speculators, however, was a real gain to Germany; it provided her with foreign currency at the time when the marks were bought which enabled her to increase her imports, and the marks were never used, or used only with greatly diminished purchasing power, to buy German exports. An analogous situation arises internally, when people believe that the inflation has gone as far as it can, and therefore refrain from consumption in order to hoard money—money which actually loses its value, so that the abstention from consumption gives these people no future claim on goods and services.

This effect also depends on faulty expectations

It should be emphasized, however, that the effect of inflation in forcing foreigners to finance, unwittingly and unwillingly, a part of the capital rebuilding, depends as does the effect of domestic inflation, on the fact of faulty anticipations. If foreigners anticipate the course of inflation correctly, they will refuse to import except at prices high enough to compensate for the expected fall in the exchange rate, and they will not purchase the depreciating currency for speculative purposes. Once all faith has been lost in the restoration, or even in the stability, of a currency's value, the stage of hyperinflation sets in on the foreign exchange market as on the domestic markets, and inflation makes no further contribution, and indeed will be an active hindrance, towards solving the problem of *physical* reconstruction.

Reparations and reconstruction

A word may be added at this point concerning the effect of reparation payments on the progress of reconstruction. After a war the victorious party frequently imposes an "indemnity" or "reparation" payment on the defeated nation in an attempt to make the vanquished pay the victor at least part of the cost of the war. If the war has not severely impaired the productive powers of the nations concerned, and if the indemnity is a small one, it may contribute to the recovery of the victor at some cost to the vanquished. The indemnity exacted from France by Germany in 1871 was a case in point. If, however, the war has been a severe one, so that both victor and vanquished are exhausted and their productive powers are impaired, the attempt to exact an indemnity may be quite unsuccessful. In "real" or physical terms, the payment of an indemnity means that the defeated people must restrict their consumption in order to provide an excess of exports, while the victorious people can enjoy an excess of imports and hence can rebuild their capital without restricting consumption as much as they otherwise would have had to do. We have seen already, however, that the problem of obtaining a restriction of consumption sufficient even for restoring domestic capital is a serious and sometimes an almost insoluble problem after a great war. If, in addition, a large indemnity has to be paid, the problem may become completely insoluble, and total financial breakdown may result, as in Germany in 1923. This whole problem is considered in more detail in the next chapter.

Deflation and reconstruction

The prevention, or at least the control, of inflation is not the only financial problem which may have to be faced during a reconstruction period. A government which follows too straight a path of financial rectitude, balances its budget and prevents the inflation of its currency may find itself in a deflationary situation, with falling prices, a rising value of its money on the foreign exchange markets, unemployment, and trade depression. Deflation is a much greater enemy of capital formation than inflation, for a fall in prices may encourage consumption and at the same time discourage production. Inflation may eventually fail to restrict consumption, but in its initial stages it is likely to discourage consumption and to encourage production. Deflation, on the other hand, has a doubly adverse effect on the restoration of physical capital—directly encouraging consumption, if prices fall faster than incomes, and discouraging production through destroying profits. It is almost impossible to make profits when prices are falling, for the very essence of profit-making is to buy something at one time and sell it later in some form or other at a higher price. If prices generally have fallen between the purchase and the sale, the likelihood of making profits is slim. Hence the demand for labor falls, and as wages do not usually fall immediately or do not fall sufficiently, there is unemployment.

Deflation also may have highly adverse effects on the foreign trade position of a country, especially if it is not anticipated, or if the foreign exchange rate, through speculation, gets out of line with domestic prices and incomes. In 1921-22 Czechoslovakia suffered a remarkable *appreciation* of her currency. This led to a severe depression in her export industries, which could not reduce costs quickly enough to meet the situation. Czech exports had to be sold for about the same prices in dollars or pounds as before, but these dollars and pounds could now be converted into fewer Czech crowns than previously.

CHAPTER 3

A Case Study: Europe, 1918-1928

Europe in 1918: Agriculture and industry

When the bells rang for the Armistice on November 11, 1918, Europe was in a condition of acute economic distress. In Russia the Communist government was in control, inflation was proceeding at a spectacular pace, production was at a low ebb, and civil war was raging. All over Europe, with the exception of the neutral countries, the production of food had declined to nearly 50 per cent of the prewar level. Communications were in a poor state; railroads and roads had deteriorated; rolling stock was badly in need of repairs. Stores of many essential commodities, especially those normally imported in quantity, such as fats, oils, and phosphates, were extremely low. A large proportion of the population was either in the military forces, being held as prisoners of war, or had been killed. In several areas where trench warfare had been waged, the devastation was almost complete. The Western Front in Flanders was a desolate chaos of mud, ruins, craters, trenches, and tree stumps. Along the Piave Valley in northern Italy was a line of similar, though less complete, destruction. In Poland, in Rumania, in Greece, the same story of devastation was repeated. But these devastated areas were small in comparison with the whole of Europe. Over most of Europe the buildings and fields were intact. Nevertheless an unseen decay, more important though less spectacular than the devastation of the battlefields had struck deep into the European economy. The farms were there; but the farmers were away in the army. The women and old people, in spite of many a gallant struggle, could not raise the crops that were raised before the war. The area under the plough through most of Europe, excluding Russia, had fallen by about 25 per cent. The yield per acre also had fallen by about 25 per cent. Fertilizers had not been available—at least, not in proper balance. Of the three main elements of artificial fertilizer, potash had been a German monopoly; nitrates had been largely imported from Chile, and hence were available to Britain, France, and Italy, but not to the Central Powers. Phosphates were in part produced from the by-products of the steel mills (basic slag), and in greater part were imported from North Africa and America. The whole plant diet of European Agriculture, insofar as it rested on artificial fertilizers, was thrown out of balance—the Central Powers had plenty of potash, but little in the way of nitrates[1] or phosphates. The Allies had nitrates and phosphates, but very little potash. Animal manures also had declined significantly in quantity and quality. In Germany the number of pigs had more than halved, and the number of cattle and sheep, had been reduced by more than ten per cent. More significant even than this: the imports of animal feeding stuffs (for example, Argentine maize and Russian barley) had been cut off during the war, and the quantity and quality of manure suffered in consequence. The lack of feeding stuffs, more than the lack of animals, caused a marked decline in the production of meat, eggs, and milk.

In industry, total output had fallen well below the 1913 level, and the output of civilian goods had fallen even further. Again, the significant fact is not the ruined factories and coal mines of northern France, important as these were. Over most of Europe, however, the factories and mines were still intact, if a little run down. But there were no young men in them and few raw materials. Morever, a large proportion of the industrial equipment had been turned over for war purposes and was producing the munitions of war, not the commodities of peace.

Rapid, though not uniform, recovery

The history of the years 1918-1928 is one of remarkable recovery from the desperate situation that followed the war. This recovery was neither regular in time nor uniform in space. Roughly speaking, the victorious countries recovered most rapidly. France recovered more rapidly than Germany, Italy

---

[1] The product of the new synthetic production (the Haber process) was used mainly for military purposes in explosives.

more rapidly than Austria. By 1928, however, the economic face of Europe looked almost as if the war had never been. Only in the gaps in the age distributions were the results of the war apparent. The battlefields were green and productive again. The ruined towns and villages had been rebuilt. Production had returned approximately to the 1913 level. International trade and transport had been largely restored.

Two periods of recovery: 1918-24 and 1924-28

The recovery period falls into two fairly well-defined periods. In the first period, from 1918 to about 1924 or 1925, recovery was marked in Western Europe, but Germany and Eastern Europe went through a wild period of inflation, political crises, civil wars, trade disturbances, and violent agricultural reform which prevented any large scale recovery in production. Even under these adverse circumstances a certain amount of recovery went on, but the recovery of Central and Eastern Europe dates mainly from 1924-1925. About that time currencies began to be stabilized, inflations were brought under control, trade barriers (especially in the Danube Valley), were lowered, the political outlook became more stable, and the whole European situation took a marked turn for the better.

The food situation

In the years immediately after the Armistice, the dominating economic problem was food, particularly in Central and Eastern Europe, and in Italy. The food situation was fairly satisfactory in Britain and France, for they had in part been fed by imports from overseas during the war, and these imports continued, financed in part by continued borrowings. France also has a smaller density of population than Central Europe, and is normally a food-surplus country. The areas affected most by food shortage—a shortage that amounted in places to famine—were the industrial cities of Germany, the great city of Vienna, the thickly populated areas of Eastern Europe, and, of course, Russia. The reasons for the famine were threefold. In the first place, there had been a great decline in agricultural production, due to the conscription of farmers and farm labor, the ruthless requisitioning of livestock and farm equipment, and the lack of imported feeds and fertilizers. In the second place, the whole system of trade and transportation had been disrupted, not only trade on an international scale, but also internal trade between city and country. This was due to political conditions, the creation of new frontiers, and the revolutionary character of many of the new governments. Thus the old, almost self-sufficient empire of Austria-Hungary was broken up into seven or more pieces. The great system of internal trade that had existed within the boundaries of the old empire was likewise disrupted, as each of the "Succession states"—Austria, Hungary, Czechoslavakia, Poland, Rumania, Jugoslavia, and Italy—tried to solve its own difficulties at the expense of its neighbors by setting up customs barriers and even prohibiting outright imports and exports across the frontiers of the new jigsaw puzzle. The most tragic case was that of Vienna, a city of over two million people—once the capital of a proud empire and now the bloated head of a little peasant republic of seven million. Before the war, Vienna had obtained its food from the whole empire, partly in exchange for manufactured products and commercial services, but also in payment of taxes to the government, and in payment of rents to absentee landlords, who owned great estates in various parts of the Empire but who lived in Vienna. After the war, of course, the taxes and rents ceased to come in, as the various parts of the Empire declared their independence and as the landlords were expropriated. The export of Vienna's manufactures and trading services also was seriously affected by the new frontiers.

The breakdown of exchange

This breakdown in the food supply of the cities was part of a widespread breakdown of exchange between city and country. Nowhere did this go so far as it did in Russia, but everywhere in Europe it was important. Even the trade barriers set up, especially by the agricultural states, were part of this phenomenon. In part the phenomenon was due to the perennial hostility felt by the country for the city, but more was it due to the fact that the city had nothing to give the country in exchange for what it bought, except depreciating money. Hence we find a marked tendency for agricultural areas to discourage exports.

Perhaps the extreme case was reached in Austria, where not only did the newly-formed countries place restrictions on exports, but even the tiny provinces of German Austria imposed restrictions on the sending of foodstuffs to Vienna.

Price policy

A third factor, at least in the years immediately following the war, was the price policy of many of the new governments. The government of Austria, for instance, seeking to ensure cheap milk for the workers of Vienna, fixed the price of milk at a level so low that it paid nobody to send milk to Vienna, and if it had not been for the "black market" the children of Vienna would have had no milk at all. The German government similarly attempted to fix the price of wheat and rye, with similar results, until it was forced to remove the restrictions in 1921. The fixing of house rents led to an acute housing shortage, only partially relieved by the building of governmentally or municipally financed homes. Perhaps the principal reason for these unfortunate policies lay in the fact that the power of the new governments rested mainly on the votes of a newly liberated but politically inexperienced working class, and hence the governments were often obliged to do things in the interest of apparent "cheapness" that in fact resulted in scarcity.

Continuance of fighting after 1918

Also, it must not be forgotten, in explaining the slow recovery of Central and Eastern Europe, that the war did not end for many of these countries in 1918. Poland was fighting the Red Armies right into 1920; Rumania invaded Hungary in 1919; Greece and Turkey were fighting until 1923. France, Britain, and America among them held part of Western Germany in military occupation for several years after the Armistice; France invaded the great German industrial area of the Ruhr in 1923, and was finally driven out only after a long and costly campaign of passive resistance that proved to be the last straw in the depreciation of the mark.

Inflation: movement of world prices

The problem that was perhaps dominant in men's minds in this period was that of monetary policy, and especially the

problem of inflation. The course of world prices in this period
was significant and provided a background against which the
monetary dramas of the various countries were played. Dollar
prices are perhaps the best index of world prices in this period;
these rose rapidly after the Armistice, reaching a peak in the
middle of 1920. A sharp deflation ensued, bringing with it a
severe, though short, depression, often called the "primary"
postwar depression. This was felt in almost all countries, even
in those in which internal inflation was going on. The depression lasted only for a year or two, however, and prices and employment in most countries recovered steadily from 1922 on,
leading finally into the boom years of 1925-1929.

The postwar boom, 1919-20

The reasons for this movement of world prices are not altogether clear, but the main facts stand out. The immediate
postwar inflation was due first to the general scarcity of commodities and the depletion of stocks which had taken place
during the war, and secondly to an increase in the velocity of
circulation of money, or, what is the same thing, a general increase in the money demand for commodities. This arose partly
from psychological reasons; the desires and demands which had
been pent-up during the war now were released, and money which
had been earned during the war but not spent now came out of its
hiding places, to be spent freely. Another reason for the "spending spree" was the sudden removal of many of the restrictions
and controls which had been established during the war. This
again was part of the general postwar intoxication; rationing
and price control had been accepted as part of the *war* program;
with the coming of peace, they were resented, and frequently
removed under pressure from the public—although the conditions which gave rise to them had by no means passed away
and the need for them was perhaps even more acute.

The postwar depression, 1920-22

By the middle of 1920, however, the "spending spree" was
over. Stocks of goods were beginning to accumulate again, and
the monetary demand for commodities underwent a sharp decline. The result was a dramatic fall in commodity prices, in

"gold" or dollar terms, on a world-wide scale, beginning in Japan, and spreading soon to every country. This represented in the main a readjustment from a level of prices that could have been maintained only by a permanent increase either in the quantity of money or in its velocity of circulation. The fall in prices caused acute distress, particularly in the areas specializing in the production of raw materials, for it was the prices of raw materials that fell the most. Ocean freight rates also fell drastically from the almost fabulous level to which the shortage of ships and the urgency of demand had forced them in 1919.

Effects of price fluctuations on farmers

This rise and fall in prices had world-wide consequences almost as profound, in their long-run effects, as the war. When prices were high in 1919 and 1920, for instance, farmers all over the world borrowed in order to buy land at inflated prices, expecting these prices to continue. When the price of agricultural produce, and the price of land, fell sharply in 1920, hundreds of thousands, possibly millions of farmers lost their farms; the value of their farms dropped sharply, but the money value of their debts and mortages remained the same. Thus, a farmer who bought a farm for $10,000 in 1919, borrowing $8,000 on a mortgage in order to pay for it, might have found in 1923 that the farm was worth only $5,000 and the mortgage, of course, was still $8,000.

The foreign exchange, 1918-24

In the foreign exchange market the period 1918-24 was one of extreme confusion. The war had destroyed the gold standard as an effective international mechanism linking together the currencies of various countries. Most countries had not yet developed techniques for controlling the foreign exchange rates without interfering drastically with international trade. Consequently, the exchange rates suffered wild fluctuations due to speculative movements coupled with spasmodic and frequently unintelligent governmental intervention. This unstable situation in the foreign exchange markets affected gold standard countries just as much as it affected those countries with no gold standard law, for what matters in international trade is the *relative* value of currencies. A depreciation of the mark in terms of the dollar is exactly the same thing as an appreciation of the dollar in terms of the mark; it has effects on American importers and exporters just as profound as the effects on German importers and exporters. Under these circumstances, international trade became extremely risky, for the merchant not only had to reckon with possible changes in the internal prices of his goods, but also with wild and often apparently unreasonable fluctuations in the exchange rates.

The financial conferences

Several conferences of financial experts were called during this period—for example, at Genoa in 1922 and at Brussels in 1925—to obtain the prescriptions of the financial doctors for the monetary troubles of sick Europe. The prescriptions were usually the same and followed the canons of good nineteenth century orthodoxy. The unsteady and slightly intoxicated governments of Europe were advised solemnly to balance their budgets, increase their taxation, reduce the governmental expenditures, remove trade barriers, remove restrictions on the foreign exchange market, and, as the culminating peak of virtue, return to the gold standard. Having delivered this good moral lecture, the financial experts polished their top hats and went home, and the naughty governments promised to be good, and also went home and did precisely the opposite of everything they had agreed upon at the conference. This indeed was a chronic condition of economic conferences all through the interwar period; the representatives of governments met and agreed that tariffs should be reduced, and immediately went home and raised them; or they agreed that the budget should be balanced, and immediately went home and developed even larger budget deficits than before.

The advice of experts neglected, for good reasons

It was not so much that there was anything wrong in the abstract with the advice of the financial experts, but rather that they concentrated too much on rule-of-thumb formulas and *secondary* ideals of financial policy, and did not go deeply enough into the fundamental economic problems that underlay the financial difficulties. As we saw in the previous chapter, the inflationary financial "policy"—if so haphazard and uncontrolled a phenomenon may be dignified by such a name—was a desperate attempt to solve underlying economic problems, notably the restriction of consumption, the encouragement of production, the transfer of resources from war to peace industries, and the development of an import surplus. Consequently, countries which followed the advice of the financial purists, such as Czechoslovakia, found themselves from an economic point of view temporarily worse off than their profligate neighbors. Economically sound financial policy is a delicate tightrope act, in which the operator is always in danger of falling into inflation on the one hand or deflation and unemployment on the other. If it is a matter of choice between the two, inflation may well be preferred as the lesser of two evils in a period when the desperate need is capital-formation; deflation is almost uniformly destructive to the formation of capital, whereas a *moderate* inflation may be highly favorable.

Varieties of inflationary experience, 1918-25

We may distinguish three groups of countries in regard to the degree of inflation experienced. In the first group the rise in prices was moderate and confined pretty much to what may be called the "world movement" described above. The price level did not rise above three times the prewar level, and fell in 1920-21 to about 40-50 per cent above the prewar level. The United States, most non-European countries, Britain, the European Neutrals (the Scandinavian countries, Switzerland, and Holland) fell under this category. In the second category may be placed countries that experienced a substantial and permanent, but still not spectacular, inflation in which the price level rose to a point six to ten times the prewar level. France, Italy, Rumania, and most of the Balkan countries fell into this group. It was perhaps this group that gained the most through inflation. The third group consists of those countries that experienced "hyperinflation," in which the price level rose to a point thousands, millions, or even a billion times above the prewar level. Russia and Germany provide the most dramatic examples; Poland, Austria, and Hungary also fell into this class. It is a matter for amazement that a society should go through such experiences as these and yet sur vive. Yet in one sense inflation represents a purging process that wipes the debt slate of the past and allows a country to start afresh. Through these inflations, countries wiped out their internal debts, governmental and private. While this meant ruin to many thousands, those who were ruined were, on the whole, the less productive members of society, and in their very ruin, by transferring real income to the worker and the entrepreneur, may have contributed to the future of the very society at whose hands they suffered.

War debts and reparations

The part played by the tangle of war debts and reparations in the general financial shambles may be mentioned at this point. As a result of the war and the peace treaty, the paper structure of obligations was as follows: Germany owed her European enemies, particularly France and Belgium, an immense but indeterminate sum in reparation for the damage caused by the war. France and the other European allies owed great sums to Great Britain; Great Britain owed an approximately equal amount to the United States; other European countries also owed smaller sums to the United States mainly because of relief loans. The British hoped to come out approximately even by offsetting continental credits against their own debt to the United States. France likewise hoped to offset her debts to Great Britain and the United States by reparations received from Germany. The net result of all these debts was that, in effect, German reparations were to have been paid to the United States, France and Great Britain being intermediaries. France and Great Britain naturally under these circumstances proposed the general canceling of debts, or alternatively, linking the payment of war debts closely with the settlement of the reparations question. The United States authorities took a highly legalistic view of the whole matter and insisted that the debt question was separate from the reparations question.

The conditions of settlement

In real terms, these paper obligations could only have been settled—or even partway settled—either by the transfer of the real equity in vast quantities of German property to Americans, or by a substantial increase in German net exports and American net imports. The second of these alternatives proved to be impossible. The United States was unwilling to increase her imports. The Allies did not want Germany to develop her exports—indeed, one of the minor causes of the war had been the growth of German exports in the world market and Great Britain's fear in particular that she would lose her privileged position. Applying a traditionally protectionist policy in the face of a totally new situation to which it was wholly inappropriate, the United States raised its tariff barrier. This in itself might not have been an insuperable barrier to the increase of American imports, for had the nineteenth-century gold standard been in full operation, even in the United States, in a situation demanding an excess of imports, the imposition of a tariff would merely have caused gold to flow to the United States until the resultant rise in the price level had made the tariff ineffective. This could not happen, however, or at least was unlikely to happen as long as the Federal Reserve System provided a "buffer" between the inflow of gold and the movement of domestic prices and incomes.

The Ruhr occupation and the Dawes Plan

In fact, Germany paid relatively little in reparations, measured in "real" terms. During the years of 1919-1923, some payments were made in kind; by the end of 1922, however, the obligations were hopelessly in default. As a consequence the French, with the co-operation of Belgians and Italians, occupied the Ruhr industrial area. The result of this occupation was an actual *reduction* of German exports to these countries—an excellent illustration of the fact that in a sensitive industrial economy military force is a highly ineffective weapon in obtaining economic gains. The "crisis years" came to an end with the Dawes Plan of 1924, the main feature being that the amount of reparations payment in each year should depend on an "index of prosperity." The plan also provided for a certain amount of external control of Germany's internal finances by an international Reparations Commission.

The collapse of reparations

The Dawes Plan apparently worked well in the years in which it was in operation (1924-1929). The payments were made regularly and it looked as if the reparations problem had been solved. So well indeed did the plan seem to be working that in 1929 it was replaced by what was supposed to be a permanent settlement, the "Young Plan" under which payments were fixed, no longer to be dependent on an "index of prosperity." Thus Germany recovered her financial autonomy. Nevertheless, in three years the whole structure of reparations and interallied debts had crashed in ruins. The "Great Depression" made all intergovernmental payments so difficult that in June, 1931, President Hoover of the United States declared a one-year moratorium, a moratorium which in effect, if not in law, exists to this day.

Reasons for the collapse

Why, then, did the system break down? Was there something inherently unstable and artificial about the situation from 1924 to 1929, or were there deeper causes at work that prevented the operation of a system of payment that was not inherently unsound? The smooth working of the reparations-war debts system from 1924 to 1929 was undoubtedly due to the fact that investors in the United States, and to a lesser extent in Britain, were making extensive loans of a private and commercial nature to German firms and municipalities during that period. In the balance of the international account what really was happening was the first alternative mentioned above —Americans were coming into possession of the equity in larger and larger amounts of German property. Americans made loans to Germans, Germany paid reparations to France, France paid war debts to Britain, and Britain paid war debts to America— there, in a nutshell, is the main structure of the international payments of the period. In effect, America was herself paying the war debts owed to her, and in the meantime was acquiring an extensive interest in German industry and municipalities. There was nothing inherently unsound in this. The ability of Germany to pay reparations at all in the long run depended on her ability to restore the productive capacity of her industry. Consequently it could have been a perfectly sound policy to *lend* to Germany in the immediate postwar years, so that the burden of reparations would not fall on her at the time when she so desperately needed an import surplus, in order that in future years she might have a large export surplus, and hence be in a position to pay a much greater sum in the long run. The same result would have been attained had the Allies from the very beginning proposed a reparations settlement of moderate size, with no payments in the first few years, or even perhaps payments *to* Germany in the early years. Such payments might be regarded as "pump priming" designed to increase the eventual flow. It can be said, in fact, that the Allies—and France in particular—were in the position of a dog that got nothing because in his greed he tried to get away with a bone too big to be carried.

The stoppage of loans to Germany

In spite of the fact that there was nothing necessarily unsound about the financial arrangements of the years 1924-1929, in reality many of the loans that were made to Germany were unsound, and were used for purposes (for example, the building of municipal swimming pools) not calculated to give Germany an increasing export surplus. The factors that finally wrecked the whole system of payments, however, must be sought outside the narrow field of the reparations question. The stock market boom of 1927-1929 had the effect of checking the export of capital from the United States; the crash of '29 and the subsequent depression stopped the flow of loans completely and abruptly. It was the abrupt cessation of the flow of loans to Germany that really broke down the system; but this stoppage was due to causes outside the field of international payments.

Uncertainty of reparations delayed recovery

One further element of the whole reparations problem should be mentioned. There is little doubt that the uncertainty of the *size* of reparations payments had a detrimental effect on the recovery of Germany. In the Treaty of Versailles, the amount of reparations was left undetermined. In theory, the victors wanted to make Germany pay the whole cost of the war to them—including such items as pensions. Even in England, where feeling against Germany was much less strong than in France, the popular cry was to "squeeze the orange till the pips squeak." In practice this was recognized to be absurd, and the final settlement was supposed to be according to Germany's "capacity to pay." Even the Dawes plan recognized this officially, in the provision for payment according to an "index of prosperity." This meant for the German people, however, that the more they recovered their prosperity, the more they would have to pay in reparations! Under these circumstances, there is little incentive for recovery. Just as a man will not exert himself to earn more income if *all* his additional income is to be taxed away, so a people will not exert themselves to increase their production if they know that the main result of such increased production will be a corresponding increase in their reparations obligations. There is little doubt that this factor contributed to the generally low morale of the German people in the immediate postwar years, and the provisional settlement of the reparations question under the Dawes plan equally led to a revival of the "will to work."

Unemployment and depression: Great Britain

We may conclude with some observations on the countries that suffered from deflation and depression during the postwar years. Of these, the most important was Great Britain. Like the rest of the world, Great Britain suffered the immediate postwar boom, depression, and recovery. The years 1925-1928, however, which in many countries were boom years, were in Great Britain years of moderate depression—not so severe as the great depression which followed, but nevertheless of an intensity severe enough to cause alarm. The number of unemployed hovered around one million; the export trades, especially coal, were most depressed. This depression, especially after 1925, when most other countries were enjoying prosperity, was closely associated with her monetary policy. In 1925, at a time when her internal price level was still markedly above the prewar level (the price index stood at about 140), the British Government decided to return to the gold standard at the old, prewar price of gold

(£3.17.10½ per standard ounce). This policy had the effect of fixing the exchange ratio of the pound to other currencies at a level at which the price of British exports in foreign countries was too high to stimulate an adequate volume of sales. Thus, the price of the pound in terms of dollars rose from around $4 to the old prewar par value of about $4.87. That is to say, an article which had previously sold in America for $4 would now have to sell for $4.87 in order to return the same amount of English money to the English manufacturer. If the British exporter charged a price abroad that might bring him a reasonable profit, his sales declined; on the other hand, if he took a cut in the price in order to preserve his market, the business was frequently unprofitable.

One possible solution—devaluation and why it was not applied

There was only one way out of this dilemma, assuming that the gold standard was to be retained at the old parity. The general level of *money* costs had to be reduced within Britain—that is, the level of money wages and money prices in Britain, expressed in pounds sterling, had to come down. Under the prewar gold standard, this would have been accomplished almost automatically, for the shrinkage of exports and the probable expansion of imports would have led to an adverse balance of payments and an outflow of gold to "pay for" the excess of imports. The decline in the gold stock would have caused a diminution in the amount of gold money in circulation and a diminution in bank reserves, with a consequent shrinkage in bank loans and bank deposits. The result would be a fall in demand for commodities and factors of production, which in a freely competitive market would force down the prices of commodities, the wages of labor, and the rents of land to the level necessary for the maintenence of international equilibrium.

In fact this did not happen. In the first place, the "new" gold standard differed from the old in that gold no longer circulated as coin but was concentrated in the reserve of the Bank of England. Consequently, the direct connection which had existed between the inflow or outflow of gold and the monetary system was not restored in the postwar gold standard. When gold flowed out, there was not the old necessity for a contraction of credit and monetary activity generally. In the second place, the development of the Trade Union movement and the generally militant attitude of workers made it difficult, both politically and economically, to lower money wages. Actually, the attempt to lower money wages after 1925 resulted in a great coal strike which led to the General Strike of 1926, in which virtually the whole organized labor movement came out on strike for about ten days, bringing the industry of the country almost to a standstill. Thus, while the general tenor of monetary policy in those years was mildly deflationary, political and economic forces prevented the necessary readjustment of Great Britain's internal price level. The result was a state of chronic depression which unquestionably hampered, quite unnecessarily, the readjustment of the British economy to the postwar world, particularly in those parts of the country which had previously depended on the export markets.

CHAPTER 4

The Lessons of Experience and Prospects for the Future

Will history repeat itself?

While these lines are being written, World War II is still in progress. Nevertheless, the day must come when the destruction ceases and the forces of reconstruction take hold once more. For this time we must be prepared; even in the midst of war we must think of the peace to come. But as our only guide to the future is our past experience, perhaps the most important question we can ask in this connection is "how far will history repeat herself;" how far will the circumstances of the last postwar period guide us in the period to come; how far can we be warned by the mistakes of the past generation, and so build on their experience?

1944 and 1918 compared

The similarities between the situation of 1918-1919 and the situation of 1944-1945 are striking. The protagonists in the war are approximately the same: Central Europe is ranged against the world. There are, however, important differences. The area under the control of the Central Powers—which now means practically Germany alone—was wider at its peak than it was in 1918; it included Holland, France, Norway, Italy, Greece, as well as all of Eastern and Central Europe. There are fewer neutrals—Sweden, Switzerland, Spain, and Portugal alone remain in Europe. There has been no entrenched Western Front. Russia is much stronger today than in the last war and may prove to be the decisive factor. Then, perhaps the most important difference—Japan is the center of another area of attempted expansion in the Far East. In spite of these differences, however, the broad picture of Europe is not dissimilar from that of 1918. The devastation is more widespread, as trench warfare has been replaced by aerial warfare and the "blitzkrieg." It is difficult at the present moment to assess the effects of aerial bombardment; it is possible that because of the widespread character of the damage more "key" establishments may be destroyed. The astonishing way in which the European and British cities have kept going through heavy bombing indicates that recovery may not be so difficult as might first be supposed. Nevertheless, it is probable that the destructive effect of a given weight of explosives will be greater when spread out over a wide area, as there is less chance of hitting something that has been already destroyed. Explosives that merely make an already ruined building somewhat more of a ruin, and therefore easier to clear away, make the task of reconstruction lighter than explosives which hit a building for the first time. In World War I the battle raged for so long over so small an area that the destruction in that small area was practically complete; nevertheless, in terms of the destruction per ton of explosives, it was probably small, as after the first year at least the battle area was in ruins anyway, and the further destruction of these ruins may even have made the task of reconstruction easier. It may reasonably be concluded, therefore, that the task of physical reconstruction after the present war will be substantially greater than after the first world war.

The short-run problem—relief

For the first few years after the end of hostilities the most pressing problem will be relief—the provision of the barest necessities of life. Housing will probably have to wait a while. In spite of the destruction of millions of homes by bombs, it will still be possible to house the people of Europe in some fashion or other, by reducing the number of rooms per family. Food, and to a lesser extent clothing, cannot wait. Unless the millions of Europe's cities can be fed, there can be no hope of reconstruction, for food is the fuel of the human machine, without which it cannot operate. The great question is therefore, "will the famine of 1919 be repeated." The answer is almost certainly "yes." Indeed, in parts of Europe—notably in Greece and Poland—famine stalks already. The year after the war may very well see a famine greater than that of 1919.

Reasons for fearing a famine: shrinkage in agricultural labor supply

Famines are due to two causes, as we have seen: first, a shrinkage in the production of food, and secondly, a breakdown in distribution. Although detailed figures are not available, it is probable that the same factors which brought about the catastrophic decline in the European production of food from 1914 to 1919 are operating today. There is first a great withdrawal of the agricultural labor supply into the armed forces and into the war industry. In view of the fact that in this war one soldier at the front requires even more men behind the lines to supply him than in the last war, it is quite likely that the withdrawal of labor from agriculture is more serious now than it was then. This labor cannot be adequately replaced either by women—who already work on European farms—or by the labor of prisoners.

The experience of the last war showed that prisoners are almost useless as a labor substitute since they hardly produce as much as they eat themselves. Agriculture is not a mechanical occupation. It requires skill and patience and the close attention of a proprietor or tenant. There is no substitute for the man who is away in the army or who is attracted to the war plants.

Shortage of power

Commensurate with the decline in man-power in agriculture there is a decline in other forms of power. The situation now differs from that of the last war in that motor power has to some extent displaced horsepower. Nevertheless, the demands of the military for motor fuel are even greater than their demand for horses. Germany has been desperately short of fuel even for her planes and tanks; there must have been very little to spare for tractors and trucks.

Shortage of fertilizers and feeding stuffs

Another vital factor in the decline of European food production in the last war was the lack of imported fertilizer and feeding stuffs. This condition also has repeated itself, with some modifications. The Allied blockade has not only cut off imports from overseas, but has also cut down Europe's internal trade in these essentials. Not only has there been a cessation in imports of maize and barley from South America, and of oilseeds from Africa and the East, but even the export of feeding-stuffs from Rumania to Germany has been greatly cut down. In normal times a good deal of Europe's internal trade is coastwise. Rumania's maize and barley, for instance, travel to Hamburg by way of the Black Sea, the Mediterranean, the Straits of Gibraltar, and the English Channel. The British blockade has rendered this part of Europe's internal trade impossible, and the already overburdened roads, railroads, and canals cannot carry the extra load. For the same reason, the acquisition of the Ukraine made little or no contribution to Germany's food supply. Even if the Ukraine had a large food surplus (which is not the case, because of the growth of its industrial population), it would be almost impossible to transport it to Germany because of the closing of the Mediterranean sea route.

The vital importance of phosphates

In regard to fertilizers, the essential shortage is in phosphates. Europe is self-sufficient in potash, as in the last war. She is also self-sufficient in nitrates, because of the development of the synthetic production of nitrogen compounds from the air. This is an important difference between the state of affairs in the first war and in the second: in 1914, Germany had only begun the production of synthetic nitrates and still relied upon imports from Chile for part of her supply. In 1939, Europe was actually a net exporter of nitrates, so great had been the development of the synthetic production. In regard to phosphates —the third great element of the fertilizer trinity—Europe is still dependent for about two thirds of her supply on sources outside the continent, notably North Africa and the United States. In the early years of the war, a limited amount of phosphate got through from North Africa, but later, even this meager supply was cut off.

The vital importance of this phosphate deficiency can hardly be overemphasized. It might be thought that nitrates and potash would be enough. Actually however, plants, like humans, must have a balanced diet, and a deficiency in one element is a deficiency in all. Without phosphates, the increased application of nitrates and potash may even diminish the yield of crops. Phosphates, then, may well be regarded as the kingpin of European reconstruction. The absence of phosphates will inevitably result in a drastic reduction in the yield of crops, and these yields cannot be restored until the import of phosphates is restored.

The decline in equipment and in herds

At the end of the war the physical equipment of agriculture in the war-torn countries will be seriously depleted. If the experience of the first world war is any criterion, the number of cattle will be down some 10 per cent, the number of sheep will be down rather more, and pigs and poultry will be reduced in places to one third of their former numbers. Figures for the present situation are not available, but it is not unlikely that the slaughter of cattle has been greater, and the slaughter of pigs has been smaller than last time. It is probable, however, that shortage of feed will be more of a limiting factor than shortage of stock. Pigs can very easily be replaced if there is plenty of feed, as they are so fertile, and Europe's cattle seldom are fed to the point of maximum production, even in normal times, so that additional feed might result in an increase in production (for example, milk) per head sufficient to counterbalance the decline in numbers. The decline in "dead" stock (ploughs, machinery, carts, and so forth) may be more serious, especially in the more highly-developed regions.

The decline in the exchangeable surplus

There is little doubt that the decline in the production of food will be aggravated by difficulties in distribution. During the war, the food supply of civilians is curtailed because of the large requirements of the armed forces. Soldiers eat more than the average civilian and their food supply is an absolute priority.

Both during and after a war, the food consumption of the agricultural population does not decline as sharply as the decline in food production. Hence, as we have seen, the decline in the supply of food available for the cities is greater than the decline in production. Then, finally, farmers are likely to hoard their food supplies when the cities have nothing to give in exchange. All these factors are bound to operate in the postwar period, and must be taken into consideration in any discussion of the problem.

Conclusion: Need for relief will last for several years

The lessons of experience in regard to relief are fairly clear. There is a desperate need for relief, which is likely to last for several years. The conditions that led to this state of affairs twenty-five years ago are for the most part operating today, and it is probable that the recovery period will be at least as long as it was then. In 1918 the governmental relief organizations, such as the American Relief Administration, were set up on the assumption that the relief program would be a matter of one or two years at the most. In fact, the recovery of Central Europe took much longer. It was not until 1925 or 1926 that the need for relief diminished sharply. Had it not been for the work of private agencies, such as the American Friends Service Committee, the situation in Germany, for instance, in 1923-1924 would have been even more desperate. There is little reason to suppose that recovery will be more rapid after this war; indeed, the extensive bomb damage may make the recovery period even longer. We should plan a relief program, therefore, that will cover at least five or six years.

Reasons for optimism

There is only one consideration which might lead to a more optimistic view. It is that the past twenty-five years have seen a remarkable development in what may be called the skills of government. This is a movement in which all countries have shared and is not particularly to be attributed to any unique diabolical intelligence on the part of the Nazis. Nevertheless, it seems to be true that the techniques of economic control are much more highly developed in Nazi-controlled Europe than they were in the Europe of the first world war. There seems to have been, therefore, a better use of resources in this war than in the last, and consequently the output of foods seems not to have declined so much, at least up to 1944, in spite of a highly comparable situation with respect to agricultural resources. It must be remembered, however, that the worst harvest of the last war period was in 1919, and that no amount of political and economic maneuvering can offset the long-run effects of a decline in resources. It is perhaps better, therefore, to err on the side of pessimism in making our prophecies, realizing that a large margin of error is inevitable, rather than to be too optimistic and find ourselves quite unprepared to deal with a desperate situation as a result.

The form of relief—shipping shortage

The next problem to consider is the form of relief—that is— what goods should be sent. In the first year or two, it is not unlikely that the principal limiting factor in the relief situation will be the scarcity of shipping space. As in 1919, the shortage of ships is likely to limit Europe's imports even more than any financial limitation. Bulk, therefore, may be almost as important a criterion as value in deciding what goods shall be sent. In this connection a significant development since the first world war had been the drying of foodstuffs. Not only milk, but vegetables and even meat and eggs can now be dehydrated with little loss of food value and can be shipped in the concentrated form. This innovation represents an enormous saving in shipping space and transportation cost; most foods contain from 50 to 95 per cent water, and there is no point in shipping water around the earth if it can be avoided. The more concentrated foods, therefore, are likely to be the first things sent.

Nutritional content of relief foods

The type of relief administered after the last war was open to some criticism from a nutritional standpoint, in that it consisted of too much cereal (especially wheat) and not sufficient fat and protective foods. The knowledge of nutrition was not, of course, so far advanced in 1919 as it is now, and greater attention should be, and no doubt will be, paid to the nutritional elements in the relief program. We must beware, however, of drawing up an elaborate program of nutritional requirements, only to find the requisite supplies do not exist or cannot be transported. It is probably true to some extent that if the staples can be supplied, the protective foods can be grown at home. The relief program should in each region be adapted to the pattern of foodstuffs that are grown in that region; more grain should be sent to dairying or fruit-growing regions, and more milk and fruit to the grain-growing regions. The technical study of nutrition has paid far too little attention to the economic side of the picture. The nutrition experts have not cast around sufficiently in the past for the cheapest and most available sources of the nutritive elements; being mostly middle-class people themselves, they have thought—and taught—too much at the level of a middle-class standard of life.

Relief in the form of feedingstuffs, fertilizers, and agricultural equipment

Food is the first thing that one thinks of in connection with relief. This no doubt is first on the program; as soon as the blockade is lifted, the immediate necessity will be to get as much food to the starving as possible. Nevertheless, the relief program should not stop there. It is probable that the shipment of fertilizer, feedingstuffs, and farm equipment would not only assist the food situation in the following years, and so speed recovery, but would actually help the food situation at the very time of shipment! We have seen that famines are due not only to a decline in food production, but are due to the "hoarding" and the undiminished consumption of farmers. This in turn is due to the fact that the cities have nothing to give the farmer in exchange for food. Shipments of fertilizer, feedingstuffs, and farm equipment, to be given to the farmers in exchange for food, would release supplies to the cities that otherwise would never get there, and would have an effect in persuading the farmer to restrict his own consumption. It is quite possible that a shipload of fertilizer or farm machinery, for instance, could be sold to European farmers in exchange for a volume of foodstuffs greater than that of the original shipment. Even from the point of view of conserving shipping space, the shipment of the less bulky and more valuable equipment, rather than food itself, might be desirable up to a point. Particularly is it important to resume shipments of phosphate from North Africa as soon as possible. There the shipping haul is short, and a relatively small tonnage should shift a lot of material. The relief agency might undertake to buy and ship the phosphate, and exchange it directly, through agents, for food from the farmers.[1]

The shipment of feedingstuffs should also form part of the relief program. The shortage of milk in Europe in 1919, as we have seen, was not due so much to the lack of cows as to a lack of feedingstuffs. It might be much better to ship concentrated feeds, such as maize and oilcakes, that could be turned into milk on European farms rather than to ship milk itself, even in the powdered form. The same is true in a lesser degree of eggs, though here there will be a scarcity of poultry as well as of feedingstuffs. In the case of pigs, the limiting factor is likely to be numbers as well as feedingstuffs, for the European pig population is decimated by the war. The prime necessity here will be to restrict slaughtering for a year or two in order to build up the numbers. Hence, shipments of pig meat would probably be more useful than shipments of feed for pigs. After the last war, the pig population recovered quickly in those countries that had access to imports (such as Denmark and Holland) and recovered much more slowly in Germany, where imports were difficult. Fuel for tractors and feed for horses might also be a proper part of the relief program, these also being exchanged for food now and assisting in the production of food in the next years.

Two stages of a relief program

In a well-planned relief program there would probably be two stages. As soon as permission is given for a relief program, food shipments should predominate. The relief program should

---

[1] Bertram Fowler (in *Common Sense*, June, 1943) has made the interesting suggestion that the "jeeps" of the American Army could be utilized in mechanizing Europe's farms. If these could be sold to Europe's farmers not for money but for foodstuffs, and the food thus obtained applied to relief, an important contribution could be made to the food supply of Europe's cities. In view of the small average size of Europe's farms, however, this would have to be done co-operatively. Whether the existing agricultural co-operatives could handle the matter is doubtful, but the experiment is well worth a trial.

advance as soon as possible into the second stage, in which food shipments are gradually replaced by shipments of fertilizers, feed, and equipment, designed to be exchanged for food in the countries to which they go. This in turn would pass over into a broader program of reconstruction. If fertilizer, feed, and equipment can be included in the relief program, they would not only make a substantial contribution to the immediate difficulties, but would also materially shorten the period for which relief would be necessary. We have discussed relief mainly in terms of food, but similar considerations apply to other necessities, such as clothing or medicines. In the early stages, it may be necessary to send clothes; but even then it might be better to send cotton or yarn or wool with which to start the spindles and looms that have been idle. The object of a relief program should not merely be the "handout;" it should be to produce as much as possible of the necessities involved in the recipient countries. In this way not only would a given volume of relief go further, but also the final reconstruction would be assisted. A relief program that is not at the same time a reconstruction program may actually hinder reconstruction; this is as true in international life as it is in personal life. There is a world of difference between the relief that pauperizes and the relief that reconstructs.

One further consideration in regard to the physical relief program should be noticed. Relief needs are likely to be very *localized* in character. Europe is not a homogeneous continent, and neither are the larger countries homogeneous in themselves. Hence the problem is not one of feeding the whole continent, but of finding the deficient regions. Northern France for instance, which normally has a high per capita production of foodstuffs, may be living fairly well while the south of France is starving. Eastern Germany might be living comfortably while the Rhineland is starving, and so on. Thus the problem of relief may be as much one of internal redistribution as it is one of outside supplies.

The finance of relief

The finance of the relief program after the last war was on the whole an unfortunate experience, and we are not unlikely to run into somewhat similar difficulties, though they will probably take a different form. After the last war relief to Germany was financed by the sale of almost the whole German gold stock to the United States—not a very wise procedure if the aim had been the reconstruction of the European economy along traditional lines. Relief to other countries was financed mainly by the aid of relief loans from the American government. This was a useful method of solving the immediate problem, but these debts proved to be a considerable embarrassment in the years that followed; along with other intergovernmental loans they were defaulted, with one or two exceptions, in the debacle of 1932. The European nations resented being saddled with obligations incurred at inflated prices in time of desperate need, and the formalistic attitude of the United States Government prevented any realistic solution of the problem. The situation of the European borrowers was not unlike that of the American farmers who borrowed heavily to buy land at inflated prices in 1919— except that Uncle Sam held no mortgage that could be enforced on the European debtors! The upshot was that the "loans" proved to have been mostly an unintentional gift. Indeed, it is not certain that the gift was unintentional, as many of the loans were made to shaky governments for political as well as for humanitarian reasons.

Relief in the "Lend-Lease" program

It was no doubt the unfortunate experience with the war debts after the last war that induced Congress to pass the Johnson Act of 1934, prohibiting the making of loans to defaulting countries. The act however had an unexpected consequence, as it proved indirectly to be responsible for the invention of "Lend-Lease." The act prohibited the lending of money, but not the lending of goods. It was easy to evade its intention therefore (when the Administration decided that the support of Great Britain was necessary), through the lend-lease policy, designed to "take the dollar sign off war debts." It would be possible to handle the relief problem in the same way. The recipient countries, instead of giving the United States a promise to pay definite sums of money in return for the goods supplied, would give instead certain rather vague economic or perhaps political obligations, to be determined at a later date. The purchase of goods would then be made directly by the United States with its own funds—as is indirectly the case in the first instance even when relief is financed by loans. The lend-lease philosophy has the advantage that it recognizes the supreme importance of goods and relegates finance to its proper secondary place. Nevertheless, it might cause trouble later on. The very vagueness of the obligations, which at the time is an admirable psychological device for overcoming certain political obstacles, may prove to be a serious source of future trouble. Vague obligations have this danger—that they are apt to be interpreted very differently by the two parties, and consequently may easily become the basis for misunderstandings and quarrels. It is all too likely that the beneficiaries of lend-lease interpret it more as a gift, while the benefactor is more likely to look on it as in some sense a loan. The opportunities for international friction which such a situation might possibly engender are not pleasant to contemplate.

Finance of relief by inflation

It should be noticed that an inflation of prices may play a part in the financing of relief. There is little doubt, for instance, that relief loans and relief purchases in 1919-1920 brought about a certain rise in the domestic price of American foodstuffs. The significance of this rise in the price of "relief goods" should not be overlooked. In an earlier chapter it was pointed out that the essential problem of "finance" is that of bringing about a restriction of consumption. The rise in price of the "relief goods" therefore is an important element in the financing of relief, in that it helps to limit the consumption of the consumers of the country that is the source of supply, and hence helps to *liberate* foods for relief purposes. If America is to send food to Europe, this can only be done through Americans producing more food than they consume. There must, therefore, be either an encouragement of production or a discouragement of consumption, or both, within America, if America is to export more than normal. The rise in the price of relief goods does just this—and did it in the years 1918-1920. It means in effect that some of the relief is financed through the "forced saving" ("forced abstention" would perhaps be a better phrase) of the American consumers, and some through "forced production" on the part of American producers. Because of the high price of foodstuffs from 1918-1920, consumers in America restricted their consumption in some degree, and producers in America increased their production—especially their production of wheat—far beyond what was prudent. Indeed, it is an odd paradox that the high price of wheat in 1919-1920, which looked at the time like a device to benefit the American farmer at the expense of the European consumer, in actual effect probably injured the American farmer, to the benefit of the European consumer. Under this stimulus, American farmers laid up for themselves troubles in the shape of surplus commodities and wasted land that were to plague them for years and decades to come, whereas the European consumer, while he paid a high price for his wheat, paid for it mainly with borrowed American money which he never repaid. The Central Powers and the neutrals, who had to pay cash for wheat at inflated prices, were perhaps the worst losers in the situation.

Sources of relief goods should be broadened

The final point to consider in connection with the relief program is the *sources* of relief goods. There can be little doubt that the need will be as great if not greater than in 1918-1919. On the other hand, the last twenty years have seen a noticeable shrinkage in international trade in foodstuffs and have been particularly characterized by a decline in the position of the United States as a food exporter. This is due, of course, to the increase in the industrial population of the United States and to a decline in its food production per head. The total production of basic foodstuffs in the United States has changed little in the past twenty-five years, whereas the population has grown. Hence the United States bulks much less as a world exporter of foods than she did twenty-five years ago. If Europe, and even more if other parts of the world, is to be fed on imported relief food, there must be co-operation between the United States and the other great food exporting countries—notably Canada, Australia, and Argentina. Indeed, it can only be done on the kind of scale which is necessary by a considerable restriction of consumption in these exporting countries, not only at the present moment, but also for several years to come. This restriction may be difficult to accomplish, not only because of the general difficulties of restricting consumption after a war, but also because the relatively large supplies of certain foods—mainly wheat and corn—may blind people to the necessity for restricting the consumption of other foods, such as meat, milk and eggs, which are in relatively short supply but are nutritionally of great importance. The situation that may arise is one requiring the utmost political tact and delicacy. The United States has made large promises to the peoples of occupied countries, claiming that they will be fed if and when they are liberated. There may, however, be some difficulty in fulfilling these promises, as the experience in Italy seems to show. Consumption of foods and of feeds in the United States has grown substantially during the war. The great stocks of cereals accumulated in the United States before Pearl Harbor turned out to be an important asset instead of the burdensome difficulty they were once thought to be. By the summer of 1944, however, the demands of lend-lease and of internal consumers had reduced these stocks to about half the 1942-1943 level.[2] It is evident that the provision of relief must be a matter for international collaboration. The establishment of the United Nations Relief and Reconstruction Administration was an important step in the right direction, though it is regrettable that political circumstances made it difficult to obtain the full co-operation of Argentina, one of the principal food exporting countries.

Long-run problems are as much political as economic

Turning now to the wider problem of reconstruction, we pass immediately into a field where political and financial factors are of such great importance that it becomes difficult to predict the course of events, or even the problems that may arise, with any degree of confidence. The problem of relief is largely a physical problem, because the need for relief is almost universally admitted and hence political and financial difficulties will not loom

---

[2] Stocks of wheat and corn in the U.S.A. on July 1st in each year were (million bushels):

	1941	1942	1943	1944
Wheat	385	632	621	316
Corn	965	857	818	583

so large. This is not to say, of course, that political factors do not enter into the distribution of relief. The very slogan "Food Will Win the War and Write the Peace" indicates that the United States regards food as a weapon. In the last postwar period American food was an important factor in limiting the spread of the Russian revolution; indeed, the Baltic countries could hardly have survived without it. There may, of course, be opposition to granting relief to enemy countries, as in 1919, though the professed statements of American and British leaders indicate that they feel a certain responsibility for the enemy peoples. Even here, however, the limiting factors in the first period of the relief program are likely to be physical rather than political. When human need is desperate, political considerations are apt to fall into the background. Patriotic hatred is, after all, a luxury that can be dispensed with in times of dire necessity.

When we turn to the broader problem of reconstruction, however, the political and financial elements of the problem loom much larger. Indeed, there is little to say about the physical problem. It is simply a matter of capital formation, through the restriction of consumption below the level of production in the world as a whole, and through "investment" in the "poor" areas by the "rich" areas—that is, by sending commodities from the rich to the poor areas without an immediate equivalent transfer of commodities from the poor to the rich areas. There is, of course, a question of *what* commodities to produce, to refrain from consuming, to import and to export; a "poor" area, for instance, will do better to import fertilizers and the services of teachers rather than perfumes and fur coats. There may be a case for governmental action here, on a national or an international scale. But even this question is secondary by comparison with the political question—what *kind* of reconstruction do we want?

Do we want to reconstruct?

There are people who wish reconstruction to be confined to areas of the correct political shade and who therefore do not wish the "wrong" areas to be reconstructed at all. There are those who wish to *prevent* the recovery of Germany, believing that the current enmity between Germany and their country is a permanent affair and that therefore the object of the war should be to disable Germany permanently. They see the recovery of Germany merely as a prelude to a new war, hence their interest in the reconstruction period is a purely negative one—how to prevent the building up of Germany's heavy industry, for instance, or how to make Germany dependent on foreign sources for her essential raw materials. Such a point of view, however, cannot properly be called a "reconstruction" point of view at all—rather does it envisage a perpetual state of warfare, with the same set of partners and enemies. The most casual acquaintance with history should reveal the unrealistic nature of such a viewpoint. It is true that there have been wars of extermination, such as the wars of Rome and Carthage. Even the most sadistic militarist, however, might well shrink from the prospect of exterminating the eighty million people of Germany or the seventy million of Japan. The only other logical solution to the problem is that of reconciliation—that is, the attraction of these countries into a world system of responsible government. If this is to be done, the problem of reconstruction must be looked at from a *world* point of view, not from the point of view of any particular nation. These problems must await fuller discussion in a later chapter. For the present, we shall assume that the problem of reconstruction is to be treated as a world problem, from a global point of view. The accidental friendships and enmities of the destructive monsters that we call "nations" may be important in their own right to the nationalist; but the scientist must be a servant of truth rather than of his nation, and as truth respects no political boundaries, neither must he.

How shall reconstruction-investment be financed?

Assuming, therefore, that no people is to be discriminated against in reconstruction and that investment in the "poor" areas is to be encouraged, the question immediately arises, should this be financed by private loans or by government loans? Again, however, it is difficult to give a direct answer without relation to political circumstances. There is no *a priori* reason why loans for reconstruction purposes should not be commercially sound. If the borrowers spend the money in the creation of enterprises whose value is greater than the loan and whose product is salable, there is every reason to suppose that the borrower will eventually be in a position to repay the loan with interest. The experience of much foreign investment has been of this sort— an old, rich country because if its great production is able to export commodities to a new country that as yet has no means of paying for them except through loans of money (that is, the issue of securities); these imports, however, enable the new country to develop its enterprises and capital equipment, until the time comes when its productive power is so great that it can in turn export more than it imports; this excess of exports is first used in the repayment of the old debts, and then the "new" country becomes "old" and becomes an exporter of capital rather than an importer. A devastated area is in the position of a "new" country relative to those areas which have not suffered so severely as a result of the war; hence, the rate of interest in it will be high, as capital is scarce, and investors in the "old" areas will be tempted to invest in it, provided that political conditions are stable enough to make the return reasonably safe. Once more we find political factors at the bottom of the problem; if property is reasonably secure in the area to be reconstructed, if its government is stable, and its money and exchange rates free from serious fluctuations, then quite a small differential between interest rates in the area to be reconstructed and the rest of the world may lead to a sufficient flow of loans to finance the reconstruction. If, however, political conditions are troubled, property insecure, and foreign exchange rates fluctuating, private outsiders will not invest in the area even at high rates of interest, and governmental loans may be the only way of financing reconstruction from outside.

Reconstruction is not restoration of the "status quo"

It is evident that reconstruction, even in a relatively short-run aspect, cannot be discussed except in a wide frame of reference. The problem of reconstruction is not simply that of restoring the *status quo ante*. Indeed, the whole reconstruction effort in the years following the war of 1914-1918 was hampered constantly by the desire to "return" to the golden age of 1913. This longing for the prewar world undoubtedly prevented men from seeing the significance of the changes that were taking place all about them and stood in the way of a realistic approach to many of the problems of the time. Thus, the return to the Gold Standard after 1924 was undoubtedly inspired not by any real understanding of the world's financial needs but by a pure rule of thumb logic—the gold standard had worked before the war, érgo, it should work now. Its advocates were oblivious to the fact that the circumstances which had enabled the gold standard to operate satisfactorily had passed away.[3]

Reconstruction is part of economic progress

Fortunately, this hankering for the past is less likely to plague us in the next reconstruction period—the fact that few people want to return to the insecurity and fear of 1939 is perhaps the one hopeful feature in the current situation. Nevertheless, we shall misinterpret the whole problem of reconstruction unless we see it not as a problem peculiarly set by the war, but as part of the whole drama of economic progress, in which the war is merely an interlude. The problems of reconstruction are in no way different from the problems of "construction" —that is, of human progress. In the next few chapters, therefore, we shall leave the narrow context of the postwar world and consider the broad problem of human progress—especially economic progress—viewed not merely as a matter of restoring certain devastated areas to a prewar level of productivity, but as a problem of raising the productivity of mankind as a whole. Seen in this light, the problem of reconstruction is not merely that of restoring the war-shattered buildings and fields of Europe or of Asia to their prewar condition: that is a task which can be accomplished in ten years. Rather is it the task of raising the standard of life of that three quarters of the whole population of the world that live on the edge of destitution—the half-starved, diseased, ill-equipped masses of the East, of South and Central America, of Eastern Europe and Russia, and even the

---

[3] These circumstances were first, the delicate and exact relationship between the gold stock of a country and its volume of bank credit, which had existed before the development of central bank control, and, secondly, a certain flexibility in money prices and wages which had been destroyed by the development of monopolies and trade unions.

submerged tenth—or is it third—in the richest countries the world has ever known. Here is a problem not of ten years, nor even of a hundred; yet beside it all other economic problems seem trivial, even the problem of the business cycle.

Part II

THE ECONOMICS OF REFORM

CHAPTER 5

The Principles of Economic Progress

√Reconstruction is merely a special case of economic progress.√ If we are to understand its problems thoroughly, we must examine what is meant by economic progress and try to discover how it comes about.

The reality of economic progress

Economic progress is not altogether easy to define and is even more difficult to measure. Nevertheless, the phrase clearly corresponds to a meaningful idea. We have only to contrast a savage society with our own. In a savage society, the same customs, the same techniques, the same ways of doing everything, from ploughing to praying, are maintained generation after generation, son following exactly in the footsteps of his father and daughter in the footsteps of her mother, without deviating an inch from the well-trodden way. In modern civilized society, on the other hand, there is constant change and flux; we are constantly improving on the methods of our ancestors, and indeed one of the surest ways to discredit anything is to call it "old-fashioned!" There are, indeed, cynical souls who see in this turmoil and bustle only change and not progress and who, perhaps, even sigh for the charm of a vanished day. But most of us, in spite of the terrors of modern warfare, would

73

not readily change places with the past; we look from our day of electric light and automobiles to the days even a century ago of candles and coaches with a sense of great technical superiority, touched only with a twinge of sentimental regret. Probably not even the staunchest medievalist, were he really to be plunged into the smells and filth and inconvenience of a medieval household, would willingly exchange it for the cleanliness and sanitation of the twentieth century. In spite of an uneasy feeling that spiritually and intellectually we may not cut a remarkably good figure beside our ancestors, we have a certain confidence that we excel them in economic matters; that economic progress is not a vague and unreal thing, but a real experience of humankind which can be experienced even within the lifetime of a single individual.

Economic progress consists of improved means and does not concern ends

There is good reason for this belief. Economic progress consists in an improvement in the efficiency of the use of means to attain ends. Whenever we discard an old method of doing something in favor of a new method that has proved its worth without doubt, then economic progress is taking place. Economic progress, therefore, means the discovery and application of better ways of doing things to satisfy our wants. The piping of water to a household that previously dragged it from a well, the growing of two blades of grass where one grew before, the development of a power loom that enables one man to weave ten times as much as he could before, the use of steam power and electric power instead of horse or human power—all these things clearly represent economic progress. This definition also enables us to account for our uneasy feeling that economic progress is not always progress in the noblest sense of the word. Economic progress is concerned solely with means, not with ends. It enables us to get what we want more easily than before, but it says nothing about the propriety of what we want. If we want the wrong things, then economic progress may enable us to damn ourselves all the more quickly and allow us to travel to hell at a hundred miles an hour instead of at ten. Indeed, economic progress makes a critique of wants all the more necessary, for the better we are able to satisfy our wants the more important it is that our wants should be "good" wants. We can see this clearly in the life of an individual. Increasing wealth is economic progress to an individual—for it gives him greater power to satisfy his wants. But the records are full of people who have been damned by a sudden increase in riches; whose wants were of such an undesirable character that while they did not have the power to satisfy them, they got along fairly well, but as soon as the power to satisfy these undesirable wants was granted, licentiousness, debauchery, and ruin followed. The same may even be true of nations and societies. Indeed, one may question whether it is not true of our own society; whether the tremendous increase in riches which has occurred in the last hundred years or so has not actually perverted our taste, debauched our cultural life, and permitted us to indulge in wars of a scale and extravagance which poorer ages never dreamed of. It is sobering to reflect that we seem to be turning all our surplus wealth and energies to destruction rather than to building up a nobler life for all, and one may be forgiven for wondering whether all our boasted economic progress has not merely enabled us to destroy one another rather more expeditiously than our grandfathers were able to do.

Is economic progress desirable?

In spite of the case against economic progress, however, it is a counsel of despair to advocate abolition. Rather should we be concerned to see that moral and spiritual progress go hand-in-hand with economic progress—that our ability to want the right things improves along with our ability to satisfy our wants. Otherwise, there is nothing to do but to sulk in our tents. There is something in the world that drives us forward, and in spite of all the cynics and the standpats, the faith in progress is a persistent part of our spiritual equipment. Even though progress in the fullest sense of the word must include both progress in the character of our wants as well as in the ability to satisfy them, economic progress is an essential part of this process and should not be despised simply because it is not the whole story.

Economic progress is important because our means are limited

If economic progress, then, signifies an increase in the efficiency of the use of means to satisfy our wants, we must know what those means are and why they are *limited*. It is the fact that our means are limited which makes economic progress significant—obviously, if we had unlimited means at our disposal, the efficiency of their use would be unimportant, as we could satisfy our wants completely no matter how inefficiently the resources were used. We must ask, therefore, what is the most fundamental limitation on our ability to satisfy our wants? The answer clearly lies in the fact that we each have only twenty-four hours a day to spend, and can never under any circumstances have any more time to spend than we have. The limitation of our natural resources—the "niggardliness of the soil" or of the sea or of mines—is also an important factor in preventing us from getting all that we want, but even this is secondary to the fundamental limitation of *time*. The scarcity or abundance of natural resources, or even of capital equipment, affects our wealth chiefly through its effect on the efficiency of the expenditure of man-time. When natural resources and capital equipment are plentiful, then we can do a great deal in an hour and produce a large quantity of satisfactions; when natural resources and capital equipment are scarce, we can only do a little in an hour, and can therefore produce only a small quantity of satisfactions. The fundamental quantity, however, is the "efficiency of the expenditure of man-time"—that is, the "output per man-hour"—output ultimately, of course, of want-satisfactions.

The measurement of economic progress

The measurement of economic progress is a difficult matter, owing to the difficulty of measuring want-satisfactions. Over relatively short periods, a fair measure could be obtained by an index of output of commodities per man-hour. Where comparisons have to be made over decades or centuries, however, the fact that the physical form of output changes makes it almost impossible to obtain a quantitative measure of economic progress. How, for instance, can we measure the change in want-satisfactions occasioned by the displacement of the horse and buggy by the automobile? Or how can we compare the output per man-hour of togas, chariots, and fibulas with the output of trousers, bicycles, and zipper fasteners? Even though an exact quantitative measure may be impossible, however, it may still be possible to define economic progress in a qualitative sense. Whenever one method of doing something displaces another, in the free operation of human choice, we may say after an interval of time long enough to ensure that the new method has had a proper trial, that economic progress has taken place. Thus the fact that the railroad displaced the stagecoach and the automobile displaced the horse and buggy indicates that these changes represent economic progress, assuming that the stagecoach and the railroad, or the horse and buggy and the automobile, represent alternative ways of doing the same thing. This broad definition avoids the difficulty which arises because most techniques do not have single ends in view, but are rather methods of satisfying a bundle of wants. Thus steam-trawling may be a much more efficient way of catching fish than the rod-and-line method, measured simply in the weight of fish caught per man-hour spent. Nevertheless, steam-trawling does not entirely displace rod-and-line fishing, because the latter method possesses a certain attractiveness in itself as a sport and thereby contributes to the satisfaction of wants other than the desire for fish. The fisherman with the rod catches not merely fish, but also the glints from the water, the excitement of the fight, the breath of the wind, and the freshness of the sunshine.

Progress measured by output per man-hour

In spite of the difficulties which are inherent in the measurement of economic progress, we can say with some confidence that it usually takes place whenever there is a rise in the amount of any commodity that can be produced with one man-hour of labor time. In counting the labor time necessary to produce a commodity, of course, we must include the labor necessary to replace the equipment that is used up in the process of production. A machine, for instance, may increase the speed of an operation, but this is not all a net gain in the efficiency of the expenditure of time, for the maintenance and replacement of the machine itself must be counted. A farmer with a combine harvester may be able to harvest four times as much wheat as he could with less elaborate implements, but this does not mean that the efficiency of the expenditure of man-time in wheat production is increased fourfold. A deduction must be made for the man-time necessary to replace the combines as they wear out, and a smaller deduction for the man-time necessary to replace the machines and equipment that make the combine, and so on.

Technical progress more significant in subsistence-goods industries

We have already called attention to the fact that technical progress, resulting in increased output per man-hour in agriculture, or, more generally, in the subsistence-goods industries, usually has a more significant effect on human welfare than similar technical progress in the luxury-goods industries.[1] The riches of a society are to be measured by the degree to which luxuries can be afforded; indeed, perhaps the best measure of the riches of any society would be the proportion of its total resources devoted to the production of nonsubsistence goods. The ability of a society to afford luxuries, however, depends in the first instance on the efficiency of the production of the subsistence goods and in particular on what may be called the "subsistence ratio"—that is, the number of people that can be supported by the product of one average worker in the subsistence industries. An improvement in the efficiency of production in the subsistence industries will not cause much expansion in output of these industries, but rather will cause a transfer of resources from the subsistence industries to the luxury industries and an increase in the output of the luxury goods.

The determinants of economic progress

Let us consider now what are the conditions under which economic progress becomes possible. It is evident that the rate of economic progress is very closely allied to the social and political environment of a society. Broadly speaking, where property is insecure, government arbitrary, and customs and

---

[1] See page 15.

manners conservative, economic progress may be slow, non-existent, or even negative—that is, there may be actual retrogression. On the other hand, where property is secure, government responsible and stable, and customs and manners highly flexible and subject to change, economic progress is likely to be rapid. The history of mankind is full of illustrations of periods of rapid progress, of slow progress, of stagnation, and of retrogression. Indeed, it seems as if there is a broad cyclical movement in history, with periods of progress alternating with periods of stagnation or of retrogression. Periods of progress, such as those that culminated in the age of Pericles, or in the age of Augustus, or that may be culminating now, have been characterized by relative political stability, freedom from long and destructive wars, and a spirit of adventure and enterprise, often characterized by the rise of a new class from obscurity to power and wealth. The periods of decline, on the other hand, such as the second and first centuries B.C., in Greece, or the second and third to the eighth or ninth centuries A.D., in the European-Mediterranean world, have been characterized by political anarchy, insecurity of life and property, frequent and costly wars, arbitrary and tyrannical government, and the maintenance of an elaborate caste system.

Security of property

The reasons for the close relationship between political security and economic progress are so obvious that they hardly seem worth stating. They all hinge ultimately on the question of the security of property. The property need not, of course, be individual property—it may be the property of some kind of collectivity, whether of the Manor, the Monastery, the Corporation, the Co-operative Society, or the Collective Farm. But unless property is reasonably secure in the possession of some individual, or of some group that is small enough or well-organized enough to permit a clear responsibility for its property to emerge, there can be no progress. For economic progress almost always involves the accumulation and administration of items of physical property, and unless that property is reasonably secure it will not be accumulated. Even where progress does not involve an increase in the total amount of physical property it always involves a change in the type of property which is used. Thus, one of the great technical advances was the domestication of the horse. Horsepower could not be used extensively in agriculture, however, unless the farmer was secure in the possession of the horse. If the peasant's horse was likely to be stolen by any marauding band of robbers, or requisitioned by an invading army, the peasant would prefer to dig his land with the less efficient, but more protectable spade rather than with a horse and plow. Theft is the worst enemy of economic progress—a fact which is enough to explain why war is so destructive to economic progress, for war is theft on a large and organized scale. Nothing renders property so insecure in the possession of its user than war, and especially civil war. It is no exaggeration to say that war, and not merely defeat in war, has been the cause of the downfall of all past civilizations.

The concept of property

The concept of property needs some elaboration in this connection, for it is complex and easily misunderstood. By "property" we do not, of course, mean physical goods themselves, although often in common speech we speak of "property" where the economist would speak of "physical capital." That is to say, we speak of land, or houses, or machines, as "property," meaning the physical things themselves. Actually, however, "property" means a certain *relationship* among men (as owners) concerning physical things; a relationship which implies that the owners have certain rights over the use of these physical things, or the benefits to be derived from their use. These rights are in some sense *exclusive*—that is, the fact that a thing belongs to Mr. A. implies that he has certain rights in it which other people do not. If I own an automobile, I have the right to drive it whenever I please, subject to certain important limitations, and as a necessary consequence, the right to prevent other people from driving it should I so desire. These "rights" are never absolute, but are always limited in some way by society and by law in the interest of general welfare. Thus, my ownership of an automobile does not entitle me to drive it down the wrong side of the street, or park it in front of a fire hydrant, or drive it at sixty miles an hour, or even, in 1944, to drive it much more than

600 miles every three months, if I happen to have an "A" ration card. This fact can be expressed by saying that property in any object consists of a "bundle" of rights concerning the object, a bundle which never includes all the possible rights that are associated with the object and which may be broadened or narrowed to include more or less of the possible rights as law or custom may decide.

The definition of property the main task of law

One of the great tasks of the social order is the proper definition of property, a definition that shall permit of economic progress on the one hand, and yet will not permit the exercise of antisocial "rights" on the other. It is hardly too much to say that social progress has been characterized by the progressive clarification and limitation of the concept of property; yet it is also true that where there are no property rights that are respected, economic progress is impossible. We see excellent illustrations of this principle in two very different orders of society.

Capitalism has been narrowing the rights of property

Capitalism, after a period in which the rights of property were very broad, has been engaged in narrowing these rights. We all recognize that property in human beings (that is, slavery) is illegitimate. Our "rights" as automobile owners are limited by the traffic laws, our "rights" as corporation promotors are limited by the Securities and Exchange Act, our "rights" as landowners are limited by zoning laws, our "rights" as stockholders by the law of incorporation, and so on. Even the "right" of one type of enterprise to force another out of business is now questioned, as in the Chain Store Taxation laws, which deliberately seek to penalize one form of business (the chain store) because it threatens to diminish the number of independent stores. Antitrust laws and tariff laws likewise limit the rights of property— of the would-be monopolist on the one hand and the importer on the other. Taxation also is a profound limitation of the right to property; it is indeed true that "the right to tax is the right to destroy," and nothing illustrates more completely the fact of the social nature of property than the right of the state to take it by taxation.

Communism has been broadening the rights of property

In the Soviet Union, on the other hand, there has been an irregular, but highly significant movement away from the dogmatic communism of its early days towards a modified recognition of limited property rights. As capitalism has moved from a system of wide property rights to a system of narrow property rights, so it might almost be said that the Soviet Union is moving from a system of no property rights to a system of narrow property rights. It would, perhaps, be too optimistic to suggest that both schemes of economic life may end up somewhere near the same point, but there is something profoundly significant in the fact that the two great economic systems of the world seem to be moving from opposite directions toward that which may be a common goal. Thus, the extreme "war communism" that followed the revolution of 1917 in Russia led to an insecurity of property and a consequent irresponsibility in the administration of property, which in turn led to a tragic decline in the production of almost all commodities. This decline in output resulted in the great famine of 1921-1922, forcing the authorities to modify the extreme Communist regime in the "New Economic Policy," under which a limited security of private property was allowed. Immediately, the economic system began to recover in an almost miraculous fashion, and production increased rapidly. This period was followed by the period of the "Five-Year plans" and of collectivization in agriculture. Here the same story repeated itself. In industry, the individual enterprise and the individual worker had a certain modified security of property; that is to say, if an individual plant made gains through increased economic efficiency, these gains were not immediately taken away by the state, and if an individual also made gains through economic efficiency, these gains also were allowed in part to remain with him. In agriculture, however, the collectivization was ruthless; the prosperous "kulaks" or middle peasants were cruelly "liquidated," and even the new collectives had no security of their property—if they worked hard and increased their output they were likely to find all their increase of output taken by the state. Under these circumstances, production again declined tragically, resulting in another famine—

that of 1932. In consequence, a limited security of property was granted both to individual peasants and to the collectives themselves and again the miracle happened, and production recovered.

Property in individual skills and abilities

The relationship between progress and security of tenure may also be observed in connection with the property that we have in our own minds and bodies. The acquisition of skills is, of course, an act of investment, and if the owner believes that he is unlikely to enjoy any fruits of this investment he is less likely to make that investment. Hence the importance of differentials between skilled and unskilled labor, and also the importance of a proper system of promotion according to merit. It is probable, for instance, that the restoration of Russian production after 1932 was due in no small measure to the development of a system of wage differentials and of promotions, both in industry and on the collective farms.

"Secure" property is not necessarily "private" or even "owned"

It must be emphasized that the concept of *security* of property, so essential to economic progress, is not quite the same as the idea of "private" property. It is not so much security in abstract ownership that is important, as security in the administration and in the usufruct of physical capital that really counts. Thus, technically the land of a collective farm may belong to the state, but if the farmers have security of tenure, this may have as good an effect on their agricultural progress as if they possessed the land in fee simple. Similarly, in capitalist society, the "magic of ownership" so frequently observed that can indeed make the desert into gardens, depends again on security of tenure rather than on legal title. With a poor tenancy law that leaves the fruits of the tenants' activity in the hands of the landlord, tenancy can be a curse greater than the plagues of Egypt. On the other hand, if the land laws permit the tenant to enjoy the fruits of his own improvements, tenancy is perfectly compatible with a progressive agriculture—as, for instance, in England.

Collective versus individual ownership

As a general principle, it may be stated that *collective* owner-ship is generally less likely to result in economic progress than individual ownership—unless the collective body is small enough to be organized like an individual, or unless the individual feels a deep sense of personal responsibility towards the group. Eco-nomic progress, as we have seen, involves change in the way of doing things. This change must be initiated by some individual. But change involves uncertainty, efforts, and sacrifices, and usually necessitates using existing physical capital in new ways, or the creation of altogether new kinds of physical capital. Where an individual holds no property of his own, but merely uses the property of some collective organization, it is almost impossible for him to initiate any changes in techniques. Thus, the private soldier, who possesses no property of his own and only very limited rights in his own body, and who is only a cog in a great machine, is only rarely capable of introducing changes in the techniques of war. The medieval peasant likewise, who was part of the collective organization of the manor, had a very limited property-right in his land implements and could not initiate improvements; the land of the manor was worked as a unit, by traditional methods, and it was impossible for any one man to deviate from what his neighbors were doing. It was not until the enclosure movement had broken up the old system and had given each farmer a "farm" within the boundaries of which he was fairly free to do as he wished, that there began the era of amazing progress in agricultural techniques in which we are now living.

Under collective ownership progress depends on leaders

The danger of collective ownership is that progress depends almost entirely on the *leaders* of the collective organization. Unless the effective unit of the administration of property is small, the creative abilities of the majority of people are likely to be wasted. No individual can initiate progress unless he has command over a certain amount of property. Where a society consists of a few administrators of large property and a mass of propertyless individuals, progress is likely to be difficult unless the propertied classes happen to be of a progressive and adventurous turn of mind. This however is not always likely to be the case, for large property produces conservatism in the individual. Hence we find that societies in which the effective unit of administration of property has been large have tended towards conservatism, but where the individual, or the small family, has been the effective unit of administration, the society has been progressive. Thus the great estates—the "latifundia"— of ancient Italy, or of modern Spain and Hungary, have on the whole been enemies to progress. The large family unit of China may also go far to explain the conservative character of Chinese economic life, for a man under such a system does not come into the effective administration of property until he is too old to wish to be an innovator. Even the great corporations of western capitalism, particularly when they become old and well-established, are often inimical to progress. Railroads are a noteworthy example, where labor and management frequently combine to prevent the fruits of technical improvement from reaching the public and where only the competition of the automobile and airplane produce any appreciable technical progress.

But this principle does not necessarily justify unlimited rights of private owners

The proposition that economic progress is most likely when the administration of property is widely diffused must not, of course, be taken to imply that unrestricted private property is the best possible system, or that there is anything necessarily evil about the extension of collective ownership of the means of production. As we have seen, it is security in the administration rather than in the legal ownership of property that is important, and the above proposition must not, therefore, be used to justify without qualification the existence of incomes from pure ownership, such as bonds and shares. This problem, however, will be reserved for a later chapter.

Collective ownership works best when there is collective responsibility

The adverse influence of collective ownership on economic progress is modified by the development of a sense of collective

responsibility on the part of individuals and by a sense of toler-
ance of innovations and of innovators on the part of the group.
It may almost be said that the most perfect "individual" is the
man who works not for himself, but for his family, and there is
no doubt that devotion to a group can call forth greater efforts
and sacrifices than devotion to one's individual self. The completely self-centered individual is rarely creative. Men introduce innovations in economic life not for reasons of self-interest,
narrowly conceived, but in the interest of their family, or their
country, or of the world at large, or even in the interest of
creative activity itself.

Is innovation its own reward?

Indeed, it can be argued that creative activity is so much
desired that no reward need be offered in order to induce it;
that the true innovator, like the true artist, will create whether
or not any financial reward goes with his creation. This is a
profound, and perhaps a rather dangerous, half-truth. When one
looks over the record of inventions, for instance, one is immediately impressed with the apparently fortuitous nature of many
of the discoveries that have contributed greatly to economic
progress. Invention indeed is an art as much as music, and the
greatest inventions, like the greatest music, have frequently
brought little reward to their creators. Nevertheless, the very
existence of the patent law and the copyright law shows that
we fear the springs of inventiveness might not flow quite so
freely if they yielded no financial reward. Furthermore, invention itself is not the only thing necessary to economic progress.
Inventions and discoveries must be applied before they can
pass into general use. The application of new discoveries on a
commercial scale is an art quite different from the art of making
discoveries and is usually practiced by a different set of people.
Discoveries, however, are barren unless they can be applied, and
the "exploiter" of inventions is just as important, from the point
of view of economic progress, as the inventor himself. The exploiter of an invention is usually actuated more by commercial
motives, and cannot operate unless he has the secure administration of his property.

"Imitative" and "original" progress

This very distinction between the original discovery of new methods (which may be called "original" progress) and the application, extension, and imitation of these methods (which may be called "imitative" progress) opens the possibility for an exception to the proposition that collective ownership is an enemy of progress. Where the problem is one of imitating the techniques of others rather than of originating new techniques, a highly centralized economy that happens to be blessed with good leaders may be a more effective instrument in bringing about technical change than an economy in which responsibility for property is diffuse. The past century has witnessed two or three remarkable examples of such "imitative" progress, initiated and forced on a somewhat unwilling people by a determined central authority. The industrial revolution in Japan that began about 1870 was the first great example of modern times. The Russian revolution is perhaps the greatest example of all time; the Turkish revolution exhibits the same phenemona on a smaller scale. All these revolutions on the technical side are examples of imitative progress. Their success, however, should not blind us to their essentially imitative nature, nor to the necessity for an extension of individual responsibilities and powers within these collective economies if progress is to continue and to pass from the imitative to the original variety.

Conditions of progress; encouragement of innovators

This brings us to another point of great importance in the interpretation of economic progress. As we have seen, progress must be done by somebody. If there is to be change, it must start somewhere, and a change in techniques always begins with a single individual or with a very small group of individuals, and then, if it is a successful change, spreads outwards through society by imitation and education. The capacity for genuinely creative innovation is rare, whether it be the capacity for new ideas, or the capacity for seizing upon the significance of new ideas and applying them in practice. The capacity for imitating the new methods is not particularly rare but may be greater or smaller, depending on the social customs that prevail. The condition most inimical to economic progress is a situation where those who have the natural ability to devise and execute new methods do not have the opportunity, while those who have the opportunity do not have the ability, and also where there is a generally conservative and traditional structure of social custom, so that change is regarded as an evil in itself. The condition most favorable to economic progress, on the other hand, is one in which the social arrangements permit those who have creative ability to express it, and in which there is a general feeling that change is desirable, that new things are apt to be better than old, and in which, therefore, there is a general willingness, even on the part of those who do not possess creative ability themselves, to follow the lead of the innovators.

Dangers of "progressiveness"

It is possible, however, for this "progressiveness" to be carried too far and for a society to be led into retrogressive steps simply through a restless desire for change. Where the desire for "modernity" is carried to the point where a society loses all sense of continuity with the past, it is likely to run into all manner of ridiculous excesses in its itch for novelty. Revolutionary Russia may be cited as an example. The ideal situation seems to be a balance between conservatism and progressiveness, in which there is a desire to test and prove new things to see if they are good, but not a desire to accept things as good merely because they are new. The view that anything must be good if it is new can be just as destructive to progress as the view that anything is good if it is old. Historically, however, mankind has been much more prone to err on the conservative than on the progressive side, and progress has been checked much more by the excesses of conservatives than by the excesses of radicals.

Why economic progress often follows political revolutions, especially when they are relatively nonviolent

This fact undoubtedly accounts for the remarkable economic progress which seems to follow thoroughgoing political revolutions, such as the French or Russian Revolutions, even when all the other circumstances—security of property and so forth—do not seem to be present. In French society before 1789, as in Russian society before 1917, power and property were concentrated in the hands of a small, pleasure-loving and irresponsible aristocracy. Consequently the creative abilities of the masses found no opportunities for expression, while those that had the opportunities usually had no creative abilities. In both cases, the revolution produced a social ferment in which much of the hitherto unutilized ability came to the fore, and in which the older, conservative classes lost property and power. Not only did the revolution tap reservoirs of unused ability, but also it created a frame of mind in which old things were suspected and new things welcomed, and in which, therefore, the masses were willing to follow the innovators.

It must not be thought, however, that violent revolution is of itself a cause of economic progress. A violent revolution is like an explosion that blows up a dam—the parched lands downstream do indeed get water, but they get floods as well that rob the water of much of its value. Where a revolution can be accomplished gradually and without serious violence, the results are greatly to be preferred. Thus the relatively bloodless revolution in England that began in 1688, and its American counterpart of 1776, led to an outburst of economic progress that has scarcely any parallel in history. In this case, the class structure of society was flexible enough to permit of a gradual replacement of an aristocracy by a commercial middle class. The relatively classless structure of American society in the nineteenth century was undoubtedly a major factor in America's astounding economic progress. The fact that there was little or no old-established "ruling class" meant that the new society could draw on practically its whole human resources for leadership. This was not true, however, in the ante-bellum South, and much of the economic backwardness of this part of the country may be attributed to its class structure. Even in old countries such as England and the Scandinavian countries, which inherited a fairly rigid class structure from feudal times, institutions have developed that permitted the rise of able people in the working class to positions of leadership. The co-operative movement, for instance, is a good example of a form of enterprise that has thrived by tapping hitherto unused sources of managerial ability in the working class.

Nonconformists as innovators

One remarkable fact concerning the "innovators" emerges from the study of economic history: that a very large proportion of them have been from the "nonconformist" element in society—that is, from those bodies which do not conform to the prevailing pattern of religious, social, or political ideas. The place of the Jews in economic history is well known; they have contributed far more than their share to the development of economic life, particularly in its financial aspects. The Christian nonconformists have played an even more important though less well-recognized part in economic progress. The Quakers, Methodists, and Baptists in England, for instance, were largely responsible for the industrial revolution. This was not only because their doctrines encouraged thrift, industry, and honesty, but also because there were so few opportunities open for members of these sects in the well-recognized professions and occupations. They were debarred from universities in England, for instance, until the beginning of the nineteenth century, and thus could not enter the more lucrative professions. Hence they moved into industry and trade, where the risks were greater and the work possibly harder, but where there was abundant opportunity for the exercise of their talents.[2]

The class structure may be too fluid for maximum progress

This historical fact suggests that a perfectly fluid or homogeneous class structure may not be the most conducive to economic progress. One of the problems of economic progress is that of encouraging people to become "innovators." Not only is the innovating ability a naturally scarce one, but even where it exists its possessors are frequently unwilling to exercise it, in view of the risks and troubles involved. If, then, the class struc-

---

[2] The development of the natural sciences was also in a surprising degree the work of nonconformists—for example, Priestley and Dalton. Their debarment from the "respectable" academic studies may have had something to do with diverting their interests into these unorthodox but immeasurably fruitful channels.

ture of society is completely fluid, so that there is equal opportunity for all to enter the easier-going professions, there may not be sufficient talent diverted into industry and trade to ensure a proper rate of economic progress. This is also likely to be the case where the prestige attached to political and bureaucratic occupations is great, and commercial occupations are despised. One of the things that hampers the economic progress of countries as diverse as Rumania and India is that the educational system tends to draw the best brains into politics, teaching, and the civil service, and consequently there is a lack of commercial and industrial personnel.

Conditions of progress: Frugality

Another trait of personality that is important in regard to economic progress is *frugality*. This is because economic progress almost always involves the accumulation of physical capital. But capital, as we have seen, can only be accumulated if production exceeds consumption. In poor societies especially, where production is small, a frugal disposition of the people is essential to capital accumulation, otherwise they will consume commodities as fast as they are produced. This is one more reason why the aristocratic, leisure class tradition is inimical to progress, for it encourages consumption and waste, and at the same time discourages productive activity. Frugality also fortifies the beneficial effects of religious nonconformity, especially in its more puritanical aspects, for there is no doubt that the puritan tradition, in its horror of waste and its emphasis on simplicity of life, materially assisted the creation of capital. Puritans worked hard and consumed little. A more perfect recipe for economic progress could hardly be found.

The praises of frugality must not, however, be sung too loudly. Frugality is important in societies where there is great need for accumulation, and where the meagerness of the stockpile is the main limiting factor on production. Even in this case collective frugality, whether by the state, as in Russia, or by private corporations, as in the United States, may be more important than individual frugality, though the willingness of the individual to be frugal, that is, his willingness to accept present sacrifices for the sake of accumulation, limits the accumulative power of even the most absolute state. But when accumulation has proceeded to the point where further accumulation becomes less and less necessary, frugality may become a positive vice. Under certain circumstances, it will result in unemployment, and may even lead to actual retrogression, as in the depression of the 1930's. There are few more dangerous confusions of thought, in the present era, than between frugality and economy. These are frequently identified in the popular mind, and frugality is therefore crowned with all the virtues that belong to economy. Economy is the efficient *use* of resources, of which accumulated wealth forms a part. Frugality is the *accumulation* of wealth through the restriction of consumption. Economy is always desirable; frugality is only a virtue when accumulation is needed—that is, when the stockpile is low, relative to existing techniques.

Conditions of progress: Competition

In conclusion, we must notice the importance of *competition* for economic progress. This is a fact which liberal intellectuals frequently dislike to face. Nevertheless, it remains true that superior methods must *displace* inferior methods if progress is to take place, and the operators of the inferior methods must therefore be driven out of business. The coming of the railroads inevitably led to the disappearance of the stagecoach; the coming of electricity led to a decline in the use of gas; the development of the oil industry led to a decline in the use of coal. Examples could be multiplied almost indefinitely. Unless the superior method is allowed to displace the inferior method, the fruits of economic progress cannot be enjoyed. Yet this displacement of inferior by superior methods is one of the meanings of that two-faced word "competition." This is not to say, though, that the competition of unrestricted private enterprise is necessarily the best way of achieving this displacement. It can be argued with some force that in certain cases governmental intervention is necessary in order to relocate displaced workers in other industries. But the fundamental problem of displacement remains as one of the major problems of economic life.

Some current fallacies: Chain-store taxation

Unfortunately, much present-day thinking on economic matters assumes implicitly that such displacement is unnecessary
and that a more efficient process should not be allowed to displace a less efficient. This is the logic of the taxation of chain
stores, on the ground that they can perform the retailing service
more cheaply than independent stores, and that therefore they
should be taxed in order to equalize the competitive advantage.
Such logic would have taxed the railroads to the point where
stagecoaches could have competed with them!

The "scientific tariff" and "parity prices"

The so-called "scientific tariff" is based on the same fallacious reasoning: if the tariff should be constructed so as to
equalize competitive advantages between domestic and foreign
industry, we could never benefit from any improvements in
foreign techniques. The same fallacy also underlies the "parity
price" formula for agricultural commodities. This formula sets
up as an ideal of agricultural policy the principle that the purchasing power of agricultural commodities should be constant.
If this policy were carried out strictly, the benefits from improvements in agricultural techniques could never be diffused
through society in the form of cheaper food. Normally, when
there is a technical improvement in the process of production
of a commodity, the production costs fall and its price relative to
other commodities—that is, its purchasing power per unit—also
falls. In this situation, there is no injustice to the producer, for
although one unit of his product buys less than before, because
of the technical improvement, he can produce more than before;
hence, his real income will be no less and may even be greater.
Suppose, for instance, that because of a technical improvement,
the average production cost of wheat fell from $1 to 50 cents.
In the normal competitive process, the price of wheat would fall
to somewhere around 50 cents, and everyone in society would
benefit from the improvement. If the "parity" party had its
way, however, and other prices did not change, the price would
be held up at $1 no matter what improvements were made in

the methods of production and nobody would benefit from improvements but the farmer.

Competition must not be too perfect

There is, however, another point of great importance in connection with the effects of competition on progress. If competition is too "perfect"—that is, if innovations are very easily imitated—it may not pay anyone to introduce them. Take again the example of wheat. Suppose that a new machine were invented which just about halved the cost of production of wheat. Those who first took advantage of this invention would reap large rewards, for while only a few used the new methods the output of wheat would not be greatly affected, and the price of wheat would therefore not be much changed. If, however, the new methods were easily imitated, more and more farmers would employ them, and it would become profitable to grow wheat by the new methods on land which previously had not been used for wheat. The output of wheat would increase and as it increased, the price would fall. The output would go on increasing until the price fell to about half what it was before, or perhaps a little more than half. Then all farmers would be producing with the new methods, for none could afford to produce by the old methods at such a low price. On the other hand, none of the farmers—not even those who had first introduced the new methods—would be making exceptional profits, for the new, low price would just about cover the new, low cost of production. If this process of imitation of new methods is too rapid, it will not pay anyone to introduce them, since the price of the product will fall almost immediately to the level at which, even with the new methods, production is just about normally profitable.

So we find ourselves in something of a dilemma: unless a new method can be imitated widely, it will not bear much fruit for society, but if it is imitated rapidly it will not bear much fruit for the innovator, and hence may never come into being. History seems to show, however, that it is a very rare situation where the imitation of new methods is too rapid to make it worth while introducing them. Almost universally, an innovator of a successful new method can make profits sufficient to justify the special risk he has taken in the few years that elapse before the rise of competitors eats away his special position. Particularly is this the case, of course, where patent and copyright laws protect the innovator from imitators for a certain period.

Occupational groups may be organized in opposition to progress

Nevertheless, there is a real danger from the other side: that where occupational groups are politically organized, they may use their organization to prevent technical improvements which might upset their established ways. It may easily be to the interests of the mass of wheat farmers, for instance, to prevent the more progressive and adventurous of their number from introducing improved methods. Labor unions also are guilty of many practices that prevent the introduction of improved methods, where these improvements will upset old established privileges. There is an alarming tendency in modern society for occupational groups to be organized in opposition to economic progress. The growth of agricultural protectionism and of the political power of the agricultural interest, is one sign of the attack on economic progress. In some phases of its activity, the labor movement also is more interested in the preservation of special privileges against the attacks of innovators than it is in improving techniques. Indeed, it might be said that the whole trend of governmental intervention today in the direction of more equal distribution of incomes may have a disturbing effect on the rate of economic progress. Even social security legislation may make people more unwilling to branch out on new lines of endeavor. It is indeed true, as one writer has said,[3] that there is a clash between security and progress. The price of progress is a certain amount of instability and insecurity, and while we are interested in obtaining progress at the lowest possible price, nevertheless we must beware lest our efforts to obtain security are not purchased at the price of stagnation.

Economic progress as a world problem

When we take a broad glance over the world, it is evident that from an economic point of view it falls into two rather well-

---

[3] Fisher, A. G. B., *The Clash of Progress and Security*. New York: Macmillan, 1935.

defined parts—the technically advanced and the technically backward. Among the technically advanced parts, we may reckon first the heart of Western Europe—roughly, an equilateral triangle with the points, let us say, at Rome, Belfast, and Riga, in Latvia. Then comes a broad band of North America, bounded roughly by the Missouri and Ohio rivers and the Mason-Dixon line on the south and west, by a line from Maine to Minneapolis or Winnipeg on the north, and by the Atlantic Ocean on the east, with enclaves on the Pacific Coast and in the mountain states. Outside these two main centers are a number of smaller sections: parts of Australia; New Zealand; a few enclaves in South America (for example, around Buenos Aires and Montevideo); a few coastal cities such as Cape Town. These areas are all characterized by high agricultural and industrial productivity, and a relatively high standard of life. Once we pass beyond them, the whole level of economic productivity falls rapidly, as we move, for instance, from Pennsylvania to Georgia, or from Germany to Rumania, or even from the north to the south of France. These regions of lower productivity in turn may be characterized as improving on the one hand, and stationary or declining on the other. Soviet Russia is the most notable example of a region that is still technically backward, but which has made enormous technical advances in the past twenty years. Turkey, Mexico, Brazil, and Japan likewise have been making substantial progress. India has progressed slowly, if at all; China as a whole may even have been retrogressing, though Western China (that is, Free China) has seen some progress.

Fundamental world problem is the backward areas

It is hardly an exaggeration to say that the most fundamental world economic problem is that of improving the level of technical productivity of the backward three quarters of the world. Until this is done, a genuine world unity cannot be achieved, and there will be constant sources of conflict, both economic and political. The magnitude of the task should inspire us rather than appall us. It is difficult; it may take one or two centuries, but it is not impossible. It will require large-scale investment on the part of the technically advanced regions, investment not only in equipment but in education. Indeed, it is probable that education is the most difficult part of the task, for it is easier to move mountains than to change the inherited patterns of peasant life. The first necessity is, of course, to improve techniques in agriculture. China, with between three or four hundred million farmers, produces no more food than the thirty or forty million farmers of the United States. There is little doubt that with modern techniques China could produce *more* food with a third as many farmers as she now has. The great problem is first, how to improve her techniques, and secondly, how to see to it that the displaced two thirds of her agricultural population are employed in producing clothing, houses, automobiles, and other necessities and conveniences of life. The same could be said in some degree of India, of Java, of most of Africa and South America, even of Poland and Rumania—and even of the state of Georgia. There is the basic problem; there is no physical obstacle to its solution that time cannot remove. It is the psychological and sociological obstacles: the lack of a feeling of world unity, the age-old conservatism of the peasant, the ancient systems of land tenure, the reverence for ancestors, the complicated structure of debt, the tangled beliefs and superstitions that keep us chained to poverty. It is a missionary enterprise of the first magnitude to break that chain.

Progress and population

We should not leave the subject of economic progress without some reference to the problem of population. It is clear that the standard of life of a people depends not only on its techniques and its natural resources, but also on the size of its population. After a certain point, any increase in the population which has to be supported with given resources and techniques must lead to a reduction in the standard of life. The more children there are around the table, the more difficult it is to feed, clothe, and house them. This is the basis of the "Dismal Science" of Malthus and Ricardo—dismal not so much because it was dull reading, but because its conclusions were so completely depressing. If nothing can stop the growth of population but starvation, then nothing can prevent the growth of the population till it starves.

There in a nutshell is the Malthusian specter. No amount of technical progress can do us any good in the long run, for though it enables us to live better for a while, the fact that we live better means that the population grows, and hence the standard of life will decline until it is down at the starvation level again, where the sickle of death keeps pace with the harvest of the womb.

The argument is logically flawless. It fortunately has a minor premise that is not necessarily correct. This is the assumption that only starvation can check the growth of population. Even Ricardo and Malthus recognized that this assumption might not be true, if people limited their families voluntarily. Now, in the technically advanced parts of the world, the voluntary limitation of families has reached the point where we have reason to fear not over-, but underpopulation. In hardly any Westernized country is the population reproducing itself; each generation as it dies leaves a smaller generation in its stead, and unless present trends are reversed, the technically advanced countries will suffer a fairly rapid decline in population before the end of this century.

This does not mean, however, that the Malthusian specter is finally laid. In the East, and to a smaller extent even in eastern Europe and southern United States, and in some parts of the tropics, there is real pressure of population on the means of subsistence. The disappointing results of British rule in India have been in large part due to the fact that the gain from improved techniques has been swallowed up in an avalanche of new mouths. The very density of population of China is the main physical obstacle to the reformation of Chinese agriculture. If only one could lift about 250 million Chinese up bodily, hang them in the air for a few years while tractors rooted out the old boundaries and while her pocket-handkerchief farms were consolidated into something on which a tractor could be used, and while factories and schools to receive the suspended Chinese could be built, then the problem of China would be easy! But if China is really to be reconstructed, millions must be driven off the farms *first* before the farms can be consolidated. How to accomplish this revolution painlessly is a problem that no country has yet been able to solve: England had her enclosures and "sturdy beggars," Russia her dispossessed Kulaks and starving peasantry. Perhaps it is not beyond the wit of man to devise a painless solution, or perhaps pain is the price of a new world.

Fertility falls as the standard of life rises

There seems to be a clear relationship between the fertility of a people and its standard of life: the higher the standard of life, at least up to a certain point, the lower the fertility. The causes of this phenomenon are imperfectly understood; everything from soap and hot baths [4] to contraceptives has been suggested as a reason. Probably the most important reason is the growth of economic consciousness and the clearer realization of the *cost* of children that comes about when the standard of life rises. Whatever the reasons for the phenomenon, it is as clearly established as any empirical fact can be. It is a fact of momentous significance, for it means that if a society can improve its techniques, and therefore its standard of life *fast enough,* the rise in the standard of life will be permanent, for the rising standard of life will inhibit the growth of population. If, however, a society improves its techniques too slowly, the old habits will persist and the rise in population will keep pace with the improvement in techniques, thus preventing any improvement in the standards of life. The only result of improved techniques in such a case would be that *more* people would be able to live in abject misery than before!—a dismal conclusion indeed. Yet, without outside help, the masses of the East may actually be in that position.

Improvements in techniques lead to rise in population

When a country first begins a rapid improvement of techniques, there is always a sharp rise in the population. This happened in the Western World between 1760 and the present day; it is just beginning in Russia, Mexico, and Turkey where the technical revolution has just started; it may still lie ahead for the rest of the world. The reason is plain: improvements, especially in the food supply and in medical care, lead to a marked fall in mortality, and particularly to a fall in the infant mortality. The fall in the birth rate however does not take place

---

[4] There does seem to be a remarkable relationship between dirt and fecundity.

for some time—perhaps not for a hundred years. In that interval death rates are low, birth rates are high, and the population grows accordingly. In Britain, for instance, the death rate fell dramatically between 1740 and 1760; the birth rate stayed up until about 1880. A similar course of events took place, or is still taking place, in all countries affected by the technical revolution.[5] Thus, we may expect a large growth in population in Russia, in Mexico, in Turkey, and in all rapidly developing countries during the next fifty years. The population of all these countries may be expected to double or treble in that time. If the technical revolution comes to India or China in an effective form, one trembles to think of the result. The very density of population of these countries, however, effectively prevents the technical revolution from spreading. It is significant that the most rapidly developing countries today are those with room to expand. The problem of China and India, of Poland and Java is therefore significantly different from the problem facing Russia. Russia, with her vast resources, can easily take care of an expanding population; she will continue to expand into Siberia, just as the United States expanded westward. Even now Sverdlovsk rivals Kansas City, and in another generation two great industrial-agricultural "heartlands" will face each other across the North Pole. But China cannot expand her population, or she will starve. Even if she utilized her land to the full, and doubled her yields (as technically she might do) even then she could only give a reasonably adequate diet to her 400 or 450 million people. She could not possibly support a billion people, any more than the United States could, no matter how chromium-plated her equipment. In her case, technical progress must go hand-in-hand with a vigorous program to check population growth and to shift people from the land. There is no other way for her. The same is true of the other densely populated countries.

Even migration in their case is of little use, unless it is carried out on a scale vaster than any we have hitherto con-

---

[5] It is absurd to call this the "Industrial revolution," as the most significant changes were made in *agricultural* techniques. The power loom was a much less important technical change than the four-course rotation, just as hybrid corn may ultimately be more significant than the radio or airplane.

ceived. The settlement of, say, 200,000,000 Asiatics in the Amazon Valley in 25 years might provide an answer. But anything much less than this would be useless. For every emigrant leaves food to support another child. Where infant mortality due to malnutrition is the main check on population growth, emigration then does nothing to solve the population problem. For every emigrant that leaves, one child—or perhaps even two children—grow up to take his place.

CHAPTER 6

Justice in Distribution

Maldistribution bulks large in liberal thinking

Although from a realistic point of view economic progress is the most important economic problem to the majority of the world's population, yet the question of justice in distribution probably bulks much larger in the thought of the politically conscious elements. It is a commonplace of political oratory that "we have solved the problem of production, and it only remains to solve the problem of distribution." This sentiment is not confined to soapbox radicals; it might almost be described as the hallmark of liberal orthodoxy. Thus Sumner Welles—who can hardly be accused of being an irresponsible radical—said in his Memorial Day speech of May 30, 1942, "The problem which will confront us when the years of the postwar period are reached is not primarily one of production. For the world can readily produce what mankind requires. The problem is rather one of distribution and purchasing power, of providing the mechanism whereby what the world produces may be fairly distributed among the nations of the world, and of providing the means whereby the people of the world may obtain the world's goods and services."

Unproductiveness is the more serious problem

It is of course true, as will be shown in this and in the next three chapters, that there is a very real problem of "distribution and purchasing power" to be solved. Americans in particular, who have bitter memories of a depression in which the paradox of "poverty in the midst of plenty" was all too apparent, and who observe great wealth and miserable poverty living almost side-by-side, may be excused for thinking that

102

distribution and purchasing power are the fundamental problems. When we look at the world as a whole, however, it is all too clear that the problem of productivity—that is, of economic progress—is really the most important. The black mass of grinding poverty under which a half to three quarters of the world's people subsist is not due primarily to exploitation, or to bad distribution of income, or to lack of purchasing power. It is due to the sheer unproductiveness of the mass of human labor. In those regions where the standard of life has been most spectacularly raised during the past two or three centuries, this improvement has come about not primarily through a redistribution of wealth or income, but through the increase of per capita productivity. The phenomenal rise in real wages which has taken place in the Western World in the past hundred years, for instance, has not come about by taking income from the rich and giving it to the poor. True, the rich have become richer. But the proportion of the national income that goes to wage earners, or to any other social group, has been remarkably stable. The rise in real wages—that is, in the standard of living of the workers—has come about through an increase in the *per capita* output of goods and services, through economic progress. It is not unfair, therefore, to regard economic progress—increase in output per head—as the prime desideratum and to relegate distributional justice to the position of an important side issue as far as the abolition of poverty is concerned.

Production and distribution are not separate problems

There is another error involved in the orthodox liberal assumption which is likely to lead to trouble. It is the assumption that "production" and "distribution" are *separate* problems; that society, as it were, cooks up the total product first in her capacious ovens and then distributes it in a quite arbitrary and haphazard way to the recipients who clamor around her table. In fact, production and distribution are not separate problems, but are merely different aspects of the whole economic process— not perhaps indissolubly wedded in all respects, but nevertheless connected by high degrees of kinship. The product and its distribution are mutually determined in the whole process of determining prices, outputs, and inputs. It is extremely important to know, therefore, what is the exact connection between production and distribution; how far can the state intervene in economic life in the direction of greater equality, for instance, without causing a decline in production? Is there indeed a clash between progress and security? Is there a conflict between the ideal of equal distribution and the ideal of economic progress, and if so, how far should we sacrifice the one in order to attain the other? These are questions of the utmost importance and are much neglected in contemporary liberal thought. This chapter does not propose to answer them completely, but to indicate some principles which are necessary to understand if an answer is to be found.

All income comes from property, even wages

The first principle of distribution is that the distribution of income depends on the distribution of property, that is, of capital, for in the last analysis all income is derived from property. It might seem at first sight that income from labor (wages and salaries) is not income from property. In fact, however, we only receive wages and salaries because we have property in our own minds and bodies. Wages and salaries are incomes derived from the sale of the services of our minds and bodies. If we did not own these services, and particularly if we did not own the source of these services, we obviously could not sell them. Wages, therefore, are income derived from our property in our own minds and bodies. This is quite clear in a slave system, where a slave receives maintenance, not wages, like a domestic animal, and anything that he produces over and above his maintenance belongs to his master. In a free society the fact is somewhat obscured because each man is his own slave, and consequently labor income is never capitalized; we do not, in our accounting (as in strict theory we should) place a capital value on our own bodies and minds, and hence we do not see our labor income as proceeding from this capital embodied in our bodies. A slave, however, does have a capital value placed on him, because he can be bought and sold. Hence, the labor income from a slave is clearly the result of investment, and the value of a slave depends on the anticipations of slave owners regarding the future labor income to be derived from him, just as the value of a house depends on the anticipations of house owners as to the income to be derived from houses. The fact that our property in our own bodies is not transferable to others—that we have an "inalienable right" to liberty—is responsible for our failure to set a value on our bodies in our accounts. Nevertheless, the economic principle remains, that all income is derived from property. The value of any particular item of property depends on the income which it is hoped will derive from it. Thus, a house that is expected to yield an annual income of $100 a year is likely to be twice as valuable as one that is expected to yield $50 a year. If our accounting system were perfect, therefore, and if we included in our accounts the value of our bodies and minds, the distribution of income and the distribution of the value of property would be approximately identical—a man who possessed a total net worth of $10,000 would always have twice as much income as one who possessed $5,000.[1]

Income is unequally distributed because capital is

The problem of unequal distribution of income therefore resolves itself into that of the unequal distribution of capital in the broad sense outlined above. The reasons for an unequal distribution of income lie in these historical forces which have led to an unequal distribution of capital. The remedy also for unequal distribution of income must be found in setting up institutions that will lead to a wider diffusion of capital and will discourage its concentration into few hands.

---

[1] This principle is true only as a rough approximation and would have to be modified in a more accurate statement. A man's net worth is equal to the present value of the future incomes which he expects to receive, discounted at some rate. The distribution of income and of capital would only be identical if the same rate of discounting were used in all cases. For many reasons—difference in risk, in insurability, in uncertainty, in time preference, in risk preference, and so on—these rates of discount differ from individual to individual. To put the matter in another way: an individual's income may best be defined as the *gross* absolute rate of growth of the value of his capital. Different individuals, however, will have different proportionate rates of growth—some may have an income that is 10 per cent per annum of their capital, some only 5 per cent per annum. These differences, however, are not likely to be so large as to vitiate the general principle above enunciated as a first approximation.

Inalienable and transferable capital

In this connection, we must distinguish between *inalienable* capital, of which almost the sole example is our bodies and minds, and *transferable* capital, ownership of which can be transferred from one individual to another, including almost the whole mass of *material* capital. There is a certain amount of inequality in the distribution of inalienable capital which is absolutely necessary and which cannot be destroyed without destroying the productive process. Certain abilities, for instance, are scarce, difficult to acquire, and perhaps troublesome to exercise. The capital value of the bodies of those individuals who possess these abilities must be high, or else these abilities will not be forthcoming. In the present state of human nature, at least, unless a skilled engineer is paid somewhat more than a common laborer, not enough people will go to the trouble and inconvenience of becoming a skilled engineer. It is true that the reward of skilled jobs and scarce abilities lies partly in the pleasure of skilled work and the prestige that is attached to responsible positions. But these things are not apparently enough to overcome the reluctance of mankind to acquire skills and to take responsibilities in quantity adequate to meet the needs of society. Nobody doubts that even if engineers and managers were paid the same real wages as common labor *some* people would be willing, even on these terms, to spend years of their life in training or to take on themselves the onerous load of managerial responsibility. But the fact that in a competitive society skill and responsibility nearly always command a higher monetary reward than common labor indicates that this higher reward is necessary in order to induce a sufficient quantity of these scarce abilities to be forthcoming. The experience of Russian Communism is a good confirmation of this principle. Starting with a pronounced equalitarian bias, the Russian system has been forced to introduce an increasing degree of inequality of personal incomes in the interest of productive efficiency.

Only transferable capital can be equally distributed, and then only in a slave state

Somewhat different principles apply to transferable capital, for in this case there is no absolute reason why everyone should not possess an equal amount. Nevertheless such radical changes in our social institutions would have to be made if the equal distribution of transferable capital were to be secured that we might well hesitate before setting up equal distribution as an end in itself. It is almost impossible to conceive of a situation in which individual ownership of capital is permitted and in which the historical process does not result in a certain inequality in distribution. This arises partly by chance, as fortune smiles on one individual and frowns on another, and partly through the differences in individual characters. Some individuals are of a frugal disposition and accumulate property; some are spendthrifts and dissipate what capital they have. Some individuals are able administrators of property, buying and selling wisely, so that the value of their possession continually rises. Others are careless administrators and their property declines in value. Inheritance also plays its part in creating inequalities; when wealthy families have few children, and intermarry, wealth becomes more concentrated. When the wealthy have many inheritors, and when the poor and the rich intermarry, wealth becomes less concentrated. As long as property is privately owned, therefore, and as long as the owner has a right to the income from his property, it is impossible to prevent the development of certain inequalities of ownership. Paradoxically enough, the most thoroughly equalitarian society would be a slave state, in which all individuals were slaves of the state and none owned property. It is the right of man to the produce of his own labor that results in the unequal distribution of property, for some will conserve that produce and some will squander it.

The state can and should intervene to make distribution more equal

This is not to say, however, that the state should not or cannot intervene to secure a more equal distribution both of property and of income than would ensue if events were left free to take their course. The principal weapons at the disposal of the state in this connection are the inheritance laws on the one hand and the system of taxation on the other. If primogeniture is the rule, so that the estate of a father passes unbroken to the eldest son, inheritance works in the direction of a greater concentration of wealth. If, on the other hand, it is customary to divide estates among many heirs on the death of the owner, there will be a tendency for property to become more equally distributed. The most powerful weapon in the hands of the state for creating a more equalitarian society is, of course, taxation. Inheritance taxes have an important effect in breaking up concentrated wealth. A progressive income tax has an even more important effect in nullifying the effects of an unequal distribution of property. The distribution of income, up to a point, can be made much more equalitarian than the distribution of property by penalizing those with large incomes through progressive taxation. If a man with large property has to pay 80 per cent of his income in taxes, while a man with small property pays nothing, it is clear that the relative advantages of large properties are much diminished.

Limitations on the distributive power of the state

Although the state by its tax system can modify considerably the distribution of incomes, its power in this respect is not absolute. There is some level of reward below which the owner of a factor of production will not feel it worth while to put his property to productive use. This level is usually called the "supply price" of the services in question. Thus, there is some wage below which a man will not work at a particular occupation; there is some rate of profit below which a capitalist would rather not hold his property in the form of productive goods, but would prefer to hold it idle in the form of money. This level of remuneration, however, is usually less than the income which the owner actually receives. Most men would be willing to continue at their present job even at a smaller wage and most capitalists would be willing to continue to hold goods at a lower rate of profit than they are now receiving.

The "economic surplus"

The *difference* between the level of income which is barely sufficient to induce the owner of property, whether his own person or some transferable capital, to use that property productively, and the level of income actually received may be called the "economic surplus" of the property in question. The importance of this concept lies in the fact that the economic surplus may be taxed away without interfering with the process of production. If, however, taxation cuts below this into the "supply price" of the service in question, production will suffer, for the owner of the factor so taxed will not feel it worth while to continue to use it productively or as productively as before. The economic surplus, therefore, is the only income that is available for redistribution. If we try to redistribute more than this economic surplus, the result is not the redistribution but the *destruction* of income as productivity is impaired.

Truth and error in Henry George

This is the truth that lies behind the errors of Henry George and the single-taxers. The economic surplus is what economists have called "economic rent," mainly because the theory was first worked out in the case of land and because also land provides the most striking single example of the phenomenon. If we assume with Ricardo that rent is paid for the "original and indestructible properties of the soil," then it is clear that the supply price of the services of land is zero, for being original and indestructible, they will continue to be forthcoming even if nothing whatever is paid for them. In that case, the whole remuneration of the landowner would be economic surplus and could consequently be taxed away by a hundred per cent tax without damaging in any manner the volume of production. This is, in a nutshell, the theory of Henry George. It contains, however, a serious fallacy: first, in supposing that there is something quite peculiar about land which distinguishes it from all other forms of property, and secondly, in supposing that "economic rent" is a phenomenon confined to land and not present in any other form of income. In fact, while land has certain peculiarities just as labor does, it falls into the general system of property relationships and is subject to the economic laws that govern property in general. It is not even true that the supply price of land services is zero and that the whole rent of land is economic surplus. The properties of land are *not* indestructible, as we are discovering none too soon in this country. Land must be maintained just as a machine must be maintained; it depreciates with use, and if not maintained, will decline in value and may even become quite worthless. In this respect land is exactly like any other capital good, and its supply price is usually not zero, even while it may be much lower than the actual rent. Just as not all of the rent of land is economic surplus, so part of the wages of most workers, the salary of most managers, and the profits of most capital are economic surplus and can be taxed away without harm.

Only the economic surplus is available for distribution

The economic surplus is all that a society has to dispose of, but it is available for any purpose that society collectively chooses. Economic surplus may be wasted in war or in the splendid extravagances of a court, or it may be used for the abolition of poverty. More than this surplus is not available, and if a society tries to spend, either in war, waste, or welfare, more than its economic surplus, its production will shrink, its capital will decline, and its ruin will inevitably follow. The fate of the Roman Empire is a case in point: it fell because it tried to maintain a superstructure of city life and imperial warfare greater than the economic surplus could stand.

What determines the surplus?

It is extremely important, therefore, for the whole problem of distribution policy to know what determines the economic surplus. If the only thing that determined the volume of production was the physical subsistence of men and the physical replacement of equipment, the economic surplus would consist of all that part of the total produce of society in excess of "maintenance"—that is, that part of the product required to maintain the physical health and numbers of the population, and the quantity and quality of the total stock of goods. This concept is not unlike that of Marx's "Surplus Value." In fact, however, the part of the total product which is necessary to maintain production is much greater than the amount required for physical subsistence, for psychological motivations are important in determining how much an individual will produce. A man may have enough food, clothing, and shelter to maintain life and health. but if he is unhappy, or disgruntled, or even ignorant, he will not be as efficient a producer as he might be. This fact makes the whole concept of the economic surplus a flexible one, for it means that the amount necessary to maintain production depends very much on the general psychological and political atmosphere of society. The modern world is driven more by psychology than by physiology. As we shall see later, this fact is of great importance in connection with possible remedies for maldistribution.

Only rich societies can afford to be equalitarian

The fact that the economic surplus is equal to the *difference* between the total product and the amount needed for maintenance underlines once again the great importance of economic progress, even in solving the problem of distribution. The economic surplus which is available for redistribution can be increased in two ways only—by increasing the total product, or by diminishing the amount needed for maintenance. It is much easier to increase the total product than to diminish the amount needed for maintenance. Hence, the very solution of the problem of distribution, which depends on the development of a large economic surplus, hangs on the increase of the total product— on economic progress. It is literally true that only a rich society can afford to be equalitarian. Indeed, as we shall see in a later chapter, we can go even further, and say that a rich society *must* be equalitarian or it will spill its riches in unemployment.

Wide distribution of property may hinder its administration

There is a further point of great importance to the problem of the interrelations of production and distribution. Where ownership and administration of property cannot be separated, the wide distribution of property may be a hindrance to its administration and hence a drag on economic progress. We have seen earlier that one of the main tasks of the financial system is to permit a separation of ownership from administration of property, so that the capable administrator can control property that he does not own. Where the financial system is not well developed—as, for instance, in European agriculture—the equalitarian ideal may well clash with the ideals of economic progress. Property cannot be properly administered if it is broken up into too small units. Thus under the European system of peasant proprietorship, in which the ownership of land is widely dispersed, each owner possesses only a very small plot or plots, and finds it difficult to acquire more by rental or purchase. Under these circumstances, economic progress in agriculture is very largely inhibited. What the French call *parcellement*—the division of the land into innumerable tiny plots—is the curse of European agriculture. It is not only that the total amount of land worked by each farmer is too small for full productive efficiency, but frequently his twenty acres may be split up into twenty or more little plots, scattered all over the landscape. Consequently, he is forced to waste a great deal of time simply in passing from one plot to another, and each plot is too small to permit the use of modern methods. *Parcellement*, however, is the result of deliberate policy in the direction of equality; it is the most direct expression of the *Egalité* of the French Revolution.

Equality versus productivity

Here there seems to be a real and difficult dilemma. If we try to disperse the ownership of land in the interests of equality, we run into inefficiency and poverty. As we have seen in the previous chapter, agricultural progress is an absolutely essential part of general economic progress; hence, the serious nature of agricultural inefficiency can hardly be overstressed. On the other hand, if we aim to have farms of a size which will permit the use of modern techniques we run into the danger of creating an agricultural proletariat and also a socially undesirable distribution of income. There may be a solution to this dilemma somewhere along the lines of collective ownership and co-operative operation, but the long line of failures of co-operative farm enterprises and the profound modification which the collective farm system is undergoing in Russia indicate that the problem is more easily solved on paper than in life.

The criteria of distributional justice

Before we can draw any conclusions as to distributional policy, it will be necessary to examine a little further what we mean by "distributional justice," or "social justice." What criteria can we set up to test the justice of any system or arrangement? Immediately we find ourselves in the presence of conflicting ideals. On the one hand, "justice" implies the rendering to each of his "deserts." The simplest and most practical expression of this criterion of justice would be "to each according to what he produces." On the other hand stands a rival criterion, the criterion of need. "To each according to his need" sounds as plausible, or even more plausible, than "To each according to his contribution."

Distribution according to contribution

Neither of these criteria are altogether satisfactory. The narrow ideal of justice that is based upon deserts leads us into hopeless contradictions. In the first place, how can we know what each deserves? "Use every man after his own desert and who should 'scape whipping." It is a dangerous ethical assumption to identify "desert" with "contribution." Yet this identification seems to be the only solid ground in the midst of a bog of tentative opinion and groundless judgments. Who is to judge between "happy, undeserving A" on the one hand, and "wretched, meritorious B" on the other? The only concept of justice which permits of any objective solution on the criterion of desert is "reward according to contribution." The impersonal dictates of the market set prices for the services of the various factors of production, and the contribution to the total product made by any factor can be estimated by multiplying the price of these services by the quality rendered. This may be called the "pure capitalist" solution of the problem. If the market price of the services of my body is 40 cents an hour and I work 2400 hours in the year, both the contribution that I make to the total value of the product, and the value of the reward that I receive for this contribution are equal to $960 a year.

The "pure capitalist" solution is unsatisfactory

For all its apparent logic, the "pure capitalist" solution fails to satisfy us. In the first place, if we assume the rights of private property in transferable goods, it is likely to lead to a degree of inequality that we feel to be dangerous. We also have a strong feeling that income from material property, or from loans and bonds, is in some sense "unearned" in a way that income from personal exertion is not. Even our income tax law used to recognize the distinction, and "unearned" income was taxed at a higher rate than "earned income." The pure capitalist criterion, however, would treat all income alike, whether it was derived from property in our own bodies and minds or from property in stocks, bonds, and real estate. Finally, we are forced to recognize that society has certain obligations towards nonproducers, particularly towards children, old people, the sick, the insane, and the involuntarily unemployed. We must break down the criterion of "reward according to contribution" in some cases; hence, it loses its validity as a general formula. The reason for this seems to be that there is a certain sense of kinship that binds us all together and makes us feel in a measure responsible for the welfare of all. We must relieve the unproductive elements of society because in some sense they "belong" to us, just as a limb belongs to us. A craftsman does not deny his feet shoes because he earns his living with his hands. We cannot be pure individualists because we are not pure individuals; we are bound together in a social web that permits none of us to be either completely independent of others or completely nonresponsible for others. It is on this rock that the pure capitalist criterion splits.

The "pure communist" criterion is also unsatisfactory

Should we, then, go to the other extreme and adopt what may be called the "pure communist" criterion—"from each according to his abilities, to each according to his needs." There is much that is superficially attractive about the idea of distribution according to need. Nevertheless, on examination it turns out to be full of difficulties, both theoretical and practical. Just as it is impossible to judge the deserts of another, so it is impossible to judge his need. The criterion of need, therefore, breaks down on two grounds: theoretically, because it is essentially mechanistic; practically, because it presents an administrative problem of impossible complexity.

Difficulties of distribution according to need illustrated by rationing

Nothing illustrates these difficulties better than the problem of rationing scarce supplies. The simplest method of apportionment is, of course, to give everyone an equal share. This has been done—in wartime, for instance—in the case of sugar and coffee. Equal distribution, however, is clearly inequitable, for needs are not equal. Some like sugar, some do not; some bake cakes, some do not; some are diabetic, some are not. Hence, rationing means no hardship for some, and considerable hardship for others. The equal rationing of coffee is even more inequitable—a household where only one member drinks coffee feels no pinch, whereas a household of heavy coffee drinkers is sharply restricted. Gasoline rationing is even more difficult. With the same ration, A is happy, B is not; for A the car is a luxury, for B it is a necessity. Even for the simplest needs, therefore, equal rationing is hopelessly unjust. Hence, there must be graduated rationing; special food rations for heavy workers, special gasoline rations for heavy drivers, and so on. The attempt to ration for individual needs, however, results in a piling of board on board and application on application until red tape engulfs everybody. Even in the case of such basic "need" as food, rationing cannot be applied as a universal principle. If all food were rationed, no matter how carefully the ration is graduated according to age, sex, and occupation, some would starve and some would be relatively comfortable, for nutritional requirements differ markedly from person to person. It is a basic principle of food rationing in wartime, therefore, that some important source of calories must be left unrationed—such as bread in England or potatoes in Germany.

The "point price" system

It is significant that as the technique of rationing develops it tends to approximate more and more to a price system, using the criterion of effective demand rather than of need. Point rationing is a partial return to a price system; what is, in effect, a supplementary money is issued (the ration tickets), and demand is equated to supply by adjusting "point prices" rather than the regular money prices. But whereas money prices can adjust to every local situation, rising to accommodate a temporary scarcity and falling to relieve a temporary glut, "point prices" have to be fixed by the rationing authority at regular intervals. Errors in the setting of point prices therefore lead to large wastages of perishable products before they are adjusted. Any "administered" price system is bound to run into these difficulties, and as the control of distribution necessarily involves control of prices, controlled distribution likewise runs into a similar administrative impasse.

Difficulty of estimating "needs"

If the criterion of need is so difficult to apply even in the case of basic necessities, how much more difficult would it be to apply it to the luxuries and conveniences of life! The thought of distributing phonograph records, books, travel, and the like according to individual need by some rationing authority is one before which the stoutest communist might quail. It may be objected that we can still permit goods to be allocated through the price system, so that there is a certain amount of consumers' choice, and yet ration *incomes* according to need. But what standards could we follow in such a case? Should we give all university graduates double the income of high school graduates, because presumably a college education breeds expensive tastes? There is simply no administrative solution to the problem of allocation according to need, once we get away from the barest necessities, and even there the administrative problem is almost insuperably difficult and can only be solved by rule-of-thumb methods.

"Needs" and "abilities" do not correspond

There is, however, an even more fundamental objection to the pure communist criterion. It is that abilities and needs are not likely to correspond. The things we most want to do (the activities miscalled "leisure") do not in general produce a sufficient quantity of the commodities that we need. This is the fact which makes necessary the whole system of economic values and institutions. Suppose, for instance, that we had a society in which everybody liked fishing and had great ability in the art, but in which nobody liked fish, and in which, to make the case even stronger, fish did not agree with the people so that they had to live mainly on bread. It would require a remarkable act of chemical magic to transform the fish which the abilities produced into the bread that the needs demanded! Such a society would be forced to do something to make fishing unattractive relative to breadmaking. The price of fish and the wages of fishers would have to be low, and the price of bread and the wages of breadmakers high, even though the needs of the two groups might be identical. The logic of valuation would force the authorities to abandon any attempt to distribute solely according to need; they would have to distribute in order to encourage some lines of production and discourage others. This is what has happened in Communist Russia, where the desire for increased production continually thwarts the desire for equalitarian distribution.

The abolition of exploitation and discrimination

There is another ideal which is continually present in the discussions of distributional justice—connected perhaps with those mentioned above and yet important enough to deserve independent consideration. This is the ideal of the abolition of exploitation and discrimination. Even the most *laissez-faire* of economists have always recognized that the pure capitalist ideal of distribution according to contribution was thwarted by the presence of monopoly, ignorance, and the consequent exploitation. It is not altogether easy to define exploitation in the evil sense of the word. To the Marxian, of course, the whole capitalist system is one of exploitation, and the whole income of the nonlaboring classes is gained by the exploitation of the working class. We shall consider this criticism in a later chapter and will give reasons for supposing that the Marxian definition is much too broad.

Exploitation a consequence of monopoly

In ordinary speech the word "exploitation" usually bears the sense of paying workers less than they are entitled to. This is likely to happen where the employer is in a position of monopoly with respect to the workers. A good example would be that of a one-factory town, or a one-mine town, in a rather isolated situation. It might be very difficult for the workers to move away, and as there is only one employer and many workers, the employer would be able to get as many workers as he wanted at a wage that was lower than the wage prevailing elsewhere for that particular kind of work. Even where the number of employers is large, as in agriculture, or in the clothing industry, it may be possible for an individual employer to exploit the ignorance of his workers and pay them less than the prevailing wage. Where rates of wages are secret and are determined by individual bargaining between employer and employed, there is always an opportunity for exploitation of this sort. The remedy for exploitation is the development of a strong trade union organization, or failing that, a judiciously administered minimum-wage law. As far as wages are concerned, indeed, the main function of trade unions is the elimination of what we may call "hole and corner" exploitation. As we shall see later, the power of trade unions to raise wages in general has been much exaggerated, but there is little doubt that they have performed a most valuable function in the elimination of individual cases of exploitation. The principal justification of a minimum wage law is also that it can help to eliminate individual exploitation.

Discrimination is also a result of monopoly

Another aspect of the same problem, and unfortunately much further from solution, is the problem of discrimination. Discrimination occurs whenever different individuals in the same locality are paid different wages for the same work. In a broad sense, of course, all individual exploitation is an example of discrimination. It is most difficult to deal with, however, when the discrimination is directed against groups and classes of individuals, rather than against single individuals. There are several groups that suffer from discrimination. Racial discrimination results in Negroes, Mexicans, Chinese, and certain immigrant groups receiving lower wages for a given job than native white Americans. Sex discrimination results in women receiving lower wages for a given job than men. Age discrimination results in the exploitation of children and old people. Caste discrimination results in lower wages for people with "inferior" language and manners.

It is a general economic principle that discrimination exists only in the presence of monopoly. If two different prices exist for the same commodity in a competitive market, all the buyers will rush to buy from the venders selling at the lower price, so that their price will rise, while the lack of buyers forces the high-price sellers to lower *their* prices, until everyone is selling at the same price. If the labor market were perfectly competitive, with large numbers of both workers and employers, and open knowledge of the wages and abilities offered, there could not be different wages for the same work, for employers would all rush to employ the low-wage workers, thus bidding up their wage, and would not employ the high-wage workers until their wage had come down to the general level. If the labor market were perfectly competitive, for instance, it would be impossible to maintain a higher wage rate for whites than for Negroes, in identical jobs, for in that case employers would rush to employ Negroes, and any employer who employed white only would be forced out of business.

Monopoly may be on the side of employer or workers

Discrimination can exist only where there are elements of monopoly, either on the side of the employer, or on the side of organized labor. If, for instance, we have a situation in which a single employer is faced by two groups of employees, one of which is prepared to work for a lower wage than the other, he may be able to make greater profits by paying the less-favored group a lower wage, provided that he is in something of a position of monopoly. Or, on the other side, an organized labor group may be able to get higher wages for its members by the process of shutting out certain groups, classes, or races from its ranks. This again is really an exercise of monopoly power, and the story of trade unions is full of examples of it. The discrimination of many unions against Negroes and against women, is a good example. If a union can keep Negroes or women out of a particular employment, a higher wage can thereby usually be ensured for the members. This is simply an example of the general method of exercising monopoly power—through the restriction of the supply of the monopolized commodity.

Taken alone, not one of the three ideals of distributive justice is satisfactory. Nevertheless, a synthesis may be suggested. All three are valuable mainly in a *negative* form. Thus, while it is impossible to justify a strict system of distribution according to productivity, it is not unreasonable to propose as an ideal that no factor of production should receive *less* than its supply price; otherwise, the process of production will suffer. Similarly, while it is impossible to justify a strict system of distribution according to need, nevertheless common humanity demands that nobody in a society be allowed to fall below a *basic minimum level* of subsistence. This is an old principle; it is involved in any "poor law." The practical problem—and the one that is likely to cause most controversy—is that of deciding where this minimum level should lie. The English Poor Law of 1834 decreed that it should be at the barest minimum necessary to sustain life. As society becomes richer, however, the basic minimum it can afford can be raised. The level of the basic minimum which a society can afford depends, of course, on economic surplus; the larger the surplus, the higher the basic minimum can be. We have good reason to suppose that, in the Western World at least, we can now afford to set a basic minimum much higher than we have been accustomed to in the past, because of the rise in productivity and in the economic surplus. A flat basic minimum could only apply, of course, to a fairly homogeneous region. Over a large and heterogeneous area, it would be necessary to set lower basic minima in those areas less technically advanced and more accustomed to poverty.

It remains to consider the conclusions for economic policy which follow from this discussion. They may be summarized as follows:

1. Although the problem of distribution is in reality less important than that of economic progress, the state has an obligation to intervene in this matter in order to prevent exploitation and discrimination and in order to prevent anyone in the society falling below a basic minimum standard of life.

2. There are several methods available for the elimination of exploitation and discrimination. As this is always due pri-

marily to a monopolistic situation, it is important that all such conditions, where they cannot be broken up by law, should be regulated by law. Labor unions have an important function in preventing the exploitation of individuals. Minimum wage laws may also accomplish this end. It is more difficult to prevent the exploitation of groups. Particularly is this true where the exploiters are not the employers, but the organized workers. A tight craft union with restricted membership is as much a monopoly as the old Standard Oil Company and needs regulating just as much. A degree of regulation aimed simply at preventing unreasonable obstacles to membership, and eliminating obstructions to economic progress would probably be adequate. Direct legislation aimed against discrimination is also possible, and is a little-tried field. The Fair Employment Practices Committee is an example of something that could be made much more general and permanent. Many political and sectional interests stand in the way of a federal antidiscrimination law; nevertheless, it is a completely logical development of the American ideal and should not prove impossible to put through.

3. The state has an obligation to see that nobody falls below a certain basic minimum standard of life. The level of the basic minimum which a society can afford depends on the economic productivity of society, and in particular on its "economic surplus." If the problem of distribution is to be solved, then, it is extremely desirable to develop a large economic surplus. There are two ways of achieving this end. The most important is the direct encouragement of economic progress. Not to be neglected, however, is the development of a social pressure against riches and the display of wealth, and in favor of simple and frugal standards of life. This is of particular importance in countries where productivity and the economic surplus are low, for under these circumstances it is impossible to achieve a reasonable rate of economic progress unless consumption can be forced below the meager level of production, so as to permit of accumulation. Even in rich countries, however, provided that monetary and fiscal policies are devised that will ensure full employment, it is highly desirable to educate the people in favor of simple standards of life. In the richest of contemporary societies, and still more if we take into account the

world as a whole, the abolition of poverty will require a considerable restriction of consumption on the part not only of the well-to-do but of the middle classes. In time of war it is all too clear that unnecessary consumption withdraws resources from the war effort. It should be, but alas is not, equally clear in time of peace that unnecessary consumption withdraws resources from the "peace effort"—the attempt to provide a decent standard of life for all. Assuming full employment, the food that the upper brackets consume needlessly is literally snatched from the mouths of the underfed, their fine houses built at the cost of slums, their unnecessary clothes taken from the backs of the ill-clad. A social taboo on high standards of consumption—which are in any case desired not so much for their own sake as for the prestige which goes with them—would make it perceptibly easier for any society, rich or poor, to achieve a decent minimum standard. Our slogan for the postwar world in the field of distribution should be "it's ridiculous to be rich!"—the natural corollary being, in the field of full employment, "it's ridiculous to be poor."

4. The principal instrument in the redistribution of income is, of course, the system of public finance. By taxing the rich and giving benefits to the poor, a society can materially change its distribution of income, provided that its taxes do not dig below the economic surplus. One of the more difficult problems in this connection is how far the benefits should be in cash and how far in kind. Some of the benefits, of course, must be in the form of free services—for example, education, public health, and so on. Some of them should probably be in the intermediate form of insurance benefits. There is, however, a large debatable ground between, say, the advocates of relief in cash and the advocates of relief in kind. There is also a difficult problem concerning the recipients of benefits. Every member of a society, rich and poor alike, might be regarded as sharing a potential property right in the economic surplus, and therefore entitled to a money income from the state—an income which would, of course, be taxed away again in the case of the rich. There is a certain attractive simplicity about this idea of a "social dividend." If it were much above a bare subsistence, however, it might have a detrimental effect on productivity, for many would

not wish to supplement this income by working. The alternative solution of a complex system of social security benefits is probably more desirable, though less elegant. In this connection, the special position of children deserves notice. A large proportion of "primary poverty" is due to the existence of large families. A wage that supports two in comfort brings starvation to a dozen. If we admit the logic of public education, we must also admit the logic of public responsibility for the nutrition, health, and clothing of the child, for it is absurd to give a child education which he cannot absorb because of his poverty and malnutrition. These problems, however, lie rather in the field of sociology than in economics, and are somewhat outside the scope of this work.

CHAPTER 7

Unemployment: The Problem

Will peace bring new depressions?

Will there be another great depression? That is one of the big questions in the mind of the average man as he looks at the prospects for the postwar world. In spite of the fact that wartime economic discussion is concerned with inflation rather than with unemployment, it is not so long ago since unemployment was the problem that seemed to dominate all others. Men in the prime of life today will remember vividly two serious depressions: the short but very severe depression that broke in the middle of 1920, and the long and disastrous depression that began in 1929. Even the prosperity of the later twenties was by no means universal; in Great Britain, for instance, the volume of unemployment in 1928 was so large that almost everyone regarded the situation as one of depression—only to find by 1932 that by contrast it had apparently been a boom! It is no exaggeration to say that Great Britain experienced a continuous depression from 1921 to about 1938. There is little wonder that men are turning to the prospects of peace with some anxiety and are wondering whether the years to come will not bring equally severe or even more heartbreaking depressions than those of the interwar period.

Depressions must be prevented for political and economic reasons

It must be pointed out that in one sense, if we look at the economic life of the world with a truly world-view, the depressions of western capitalism are of secondary importance. Even at the depth of depression, the standard of life of the industrial nations of the west is so far above that of the rest of the world, that a Hindu or a Chinese peasant might well be amazed at our concern over the problem. For most of the world, the fundamental problem is that of economic progress. The very existence of depressions is a sign of a high standard of life—only the rich and technically advanced societies can afford to have depressions! Nevertheless, there is not the slightest excuse for having them if they are avoidable; and the consensus of students of the subject is coming to be that they *are* avoidable through appropriate governmental action.

Even if the economic importance of depressions tends to be overemphasized, their political and social effects are enormous. It is not the realities of economic life that matter in the political realm, but the fantasies; it is what people think and dream about their condition, rather than their true condition that matters to the politician. During a depression, the Western World does not thank its lucky stars—or its fortunate history—that even at the lowest ebb of its production its standard of life is so far above that of primitive agricultural peoples, but rather does it look back to its rosier past and curses the lot—and the government—that is seemingly responsible for the ebb of its fortunes. It is scarcely an exaggeration to say that the depression which followed 1929 brought about a revolution of some sort in almost every country in the world: the New Deal in America, the National Government in England, the Popular Front in France, the Nazi Revolution in Germany, and so on. The depression was mainly responsible for the breakdown of the war-debts and reparations system, and helped to set in motion the forces of extreme nationalism that culminated in the present war. It is not, perhaps, true to say that the present war would not have happened had there been no depression, for the underlying political disunity of the world would have brought it about sooner or later. But almost certainly had it not been for the great depression, the war would not have come as soon as it did. Depressions are good soil for political weeds to grow in, and the demagoguery of Hitler would have fallen on deafer ears had his hearers been employed and prosperous. The mass of Germans have been prepared to swallow many things that they detested in the Nazi regime because of its undoubted success in dealing with unemployment. For political as well as for economic reasons, therefore, it is of vital importance that the scourge of unemployment should be brought under control.

The abolition of depressions is possible: The "New Economics"

Fortunately, there is evidence on the intellectual horizon, at least, that the possibility of preventing depressions is at last within sight. One of the most important things that has happened in the past twenty years—more important, perhaps, for the long-run welfare of humanity than the foamings of dictators or even the fortunes of war—has been the development of a body of thought on the subject of depressions which at last is commanding general acceptance among economists and which seems to provide an adequate basis for public policy. This is the theory that has grown up around the name of Lord Keynes. Not that all Keynes's views are necessarily sound, nor are the views of his followers (often *plus royalistes que le roi*) to be taken at their face value. But in the last twenty years, there has been accomplished a revolution in economic thought, of which most people outside the circle of the experts are only dimly aware, that transcends in importance anything that has happened in economics since Adam Smith. Not a little of this revolution has been stimulated by the attempts of economists to answer the criticisms of the "monetary cranks," such as Silvio Gesell, Major Douglas, and Foster and Catchings. Although these writers are full of errors as far as their systems as a whole are concerned, they undoubtedly perceived a fragment of truth that had been unrecognized by the orthodox economists,[1] although it fits very easily into the general line of development of economic doctrine. This neglected truth was that under certain circumstances there may be a deficiency of purchasing power or of consuming power, in the sense that the public is not willing to buy, at existing prices, the total volume of goods that are offered for sale. When this happens, the level of prices and incomes, expressed in money, is bound to decline, and for reasons that will be shown later, unemployment is bound to follow.

---

[1] With the notable exception of Malthus.

Nonmonetary factors in depression: The "Bathtub Theorem"

Before we go on to examine in detail the monetary mechanism, it will be desirable to consider the nonmonetary factors that underlie the unemployment problem. The key to the understanding of this problem is the proposition that we have already encountered in considering the problems of reconstruction: the rate of accumulation of the stockpile of goods is equal to the rate of production less the rate of consumption. This may not inaptly be called the *Bathtub Theorem*: just as the rate at which water accumulates in a bathtub is the difference between the rate at which it runs in from the faucet and the rate at which it runs out through the drain, so the rate of accumulation of goods is equal to the difference between the rate at which goods are added to the stock and the rate at which goods are drained away. Production is the act of adding to the stockpile: when a farmer produces wheat, for instance, or a factory a machine, something is added to the total stock of goods which was not there before. Consumption is the act of subtracting from the stockpile: when we eat a loaf of bread, or wear out an automobile, something is subtracted from the total stock of goods. If production (the flow from the faucet) is greater than consumption (the flow down the drain) it is clear that the water in the economic bathtub (the total stock of goods) must rise.

The great accumulation of the past two centuries is unlikely to continue

For the past two hundred years we have been accustomed to an enormous increase in the total stockpile [2] of the Western World. So accustomed to this have we become that it seems to be in the natural order of events, and we can hardly conceive of a situation in which the stockpile is not increasing rapidly. The great increase in the stockpile in the past two centuries has been due, however, to a peculiar combination of factors which are not likely to recur again, at least not in the same degree. One

---

[2] By the "stockpile," of course, I mean all goods, not merely goods in storage: it includes all buildings, machines, railroads, inventories, furniture— everything that is a physical commodity and has value. It should also include such nonmaterial assets as skills and abilities.

has been the enormous increase in population, which would have necessitated a proportionate increase in the stock of clothes, furniture, houses, roads, and so forth, even if there had been no changes in techniques and no rise in the standard of life. Another has been the opening up of vast empty lands for settlement. If we visualize the great empty American continent of 1745, or even of 1805, and visualize it today, studded with great cities and innumerable towns and farms, crisscrossed with roads and railroads, we see what an immense amount of *accumulation* has gone on in the past few generations. Another factor has been the development of new capital-using inventions, such as the railroad and the steel frame building. None of these factors is likely to operate as strongly in the future as it has in the past.

It is now becoming clear, therefore, that the size of the economic bathtub is limited; that the opportunities for accumulation are not indefinite, and that a point must come, as accumulation proceeds, when the rate of accumulation must decline. Eventually, of course, net accumulation must stop altogther, when the bathtub is full—that is, when the total stockpile is as large as it can usefully be, given the techniques of production and the standard of life. This is clearly seen in the case of a particular commodity, such as wheat. A great advantage is to be gained from having a year's supply of wheat in the warehouses. There is probably some advantage in having two years', or even three years' supply of wheat in stock. But there is no conceivable utility in having ten years' supply of wheat in storage. The same is true of any other commodity, and ultimately of commodities in general, though we are, of course, still some way from the point where no further increase in stock can be of any use.

The unreal dilemma of our time—war or unemployment

Now, there are only two ways of bringing about a decline in the rate of accumulation. One is to shut off production. The other is to expand consumption. Faced with an overflowing bathtub, we can turn off the faucet or we can pull out the plug —or, of course, we can hack a hole in the side. Here lies the fundamental explanation of the crisis of our time. Our modes of thought do not permit us to do the sensible thing—that is to pull out the plug, or to expand consumption. Consequently, we are faced with a horrible, but completely unreal and self-manufactured dilemma: to stop the monstrous accumulation of goods either by turning off the faucet of production, which is accomplished through depression, deflation, and unemployment, or by hacking a hole in the side of the bathtub by war, and allowing the stockpile to flow out in a flood of waste and destruction. In the absence of a constructive policy for the encouragement of consumption, then, we are forced to make the choice between peace and unemployment, or full employment and war, and in fact oscillate miserably between the two evils, peace leading to an unmanageable flood of plenty, which is subsequently dissipated in war. This is not to say that war as such is the result of these economic forces: as we shall see later, war as an institution is primarily a result of political rather than economic forces, and wars have gone on even in periods when the economic forces were ranged rather on the side of accumulation than on the side of destruction. But the peculiar ferocity and destructiveness of modern war and perhaps the very institution of "total war" may be attributed at least in part to the necessity for consumption—war being the only acceptable way of consuming things on a very large scale!

Why the stockpile cannot grow forever

We must now ask ourselves in more detail exactly how the capacity of the economic bathtub is limited and what is the machinery by which an overflowing stockpile leads to unemployment and a decline in production. We can see, of course, that there are technical reasons why the stockpile should not grow forever. The economic pressure that prevents the growth of the stockpile comes, however, from its *owners*. Somebody, it is clear, has to own the goods which constitute the stockpile. In a capitalist society, these goods are owned, for the most part, by private individuals and private corporations. As the stockpile grows, these owners get less and less willing to hold goods; they become, therefore, more anxious to sell goods (to exchange them for money) and less anxious to buy them (to exchange money for goods). The result is a fall in *prices*. Indeed, beyond a certain point it becomes impossible to increase the *value* of the stockpile because each addition to the physical stock of goods leads to a proportionate, or more than proportionate, fall in their price. Thus, if an increase in the stock of wheat from 500 to 550 million bushels led to a decline in the price of wheat from $1 a bushel to 90 cents, the *value* of the stock of wheat would fall from 500 to 495 million dollars. Under these circumstances it would be impossible to invest in wheat—that is, to raise the value of the total stock of wheat by adding to its physical volume. A situation may easily arise where the same is true for commodities in general.[3]

How a rise in the stockpile causes unemployment

The most fundamental cause of unemployment is the rise in the stockpile to the point where people are not willing to own further accumulations. This force may operate directly. Thus most purchases are made and most orders are given in order to replenish a depleted stockpile. When the consumer finds that the shirts in his drawer have become unwearable and must go into the rag bag, he goes out and buys shirts. When the retailer

---

[3] There is a simple formula connecting the price of a commodity with its total stock when the commodity is storable and has a competitive market. Let P be the price of the commodity, Q the total physical stock ("bushels"), M the total stock of money in the hands of the marketers. Let r_m be the proportion of their total assets which the marketers wish to hold in the form of money, and r_q be the proportion of their total assets which the marketers wish to hold in the form of the commodity. We may call r_m the "preferred liquidity ratio" and r_q the "preferred commodity ratio." Then if T is the total value of the assets of the marketers, by definition

$$r_m = \frac{M}{T} \text{ and } r_q = \frac{PQ}{T}$$

Eliminating T between these two equations we have:

$$P = \frac{M r_q}{Q r_m}$$

This equation holds not only for any particular commodity but also for the price level of commodities in general. If P is the price level and Q the quantity of all assets, r_q becomes $(1-r_m)$, for if we wish to hold, say 10 per cent of our assets in the form of money that is the same thing as wishing to hold 90 per cent of our assets in the form of commodities in general. The equation then becomes

$$P = \frac{M(1-r_m)}{Q r_m}$$

From this equation, it is clear that the total value of assets (PQ) cannot increase unless there is an increase in the quantity of money or a decline in the preferred liquidity ratio.

finds that the purchasers of consumers have depleted his shelves, he orders shirts from the wholesaler. When the wholesaler finds that his warehouses are emptying, he orders shirts from the manufacturer. When the manufacturer receives orders from the wholesaler, he buys cotton and sets men to work. When the consumer's closet is·full, and the retailer's shelves are full, and the wholesaler's warehouse is full, there are no orders and there is no work. But the effects of an overstuffed stockpile also work themselves out through the decline in prices and in money incomes. In order to understand how this operates, we must digress a little to examine some ideas about the monetary system.

The monetary system. Expenditure is income

Perhaps the greatest obstacle to the understanding of the monetary system lies in our tendency to think by analogy from our own experience. We are now concerned with the whole economic system, and the whole flow of money, incomes, and outputs. In such a closed system, many things that are true of the experience of individuals, or even of groups, within the system are not true of the system as a whole. It is often misleading, therefore, to argue by analogy from our individual experience and to treat the whole society as if it too were an individual; for the individual exists in the environment of society, he is surrounded by society, as a drop is surrounded by the sea. But the whole society has no environment—it is its own environment. Hence what is true of the drop is often not true of the sea. We find one of the most striking examples of this truth in our concepts of money income and expenditure. To an individual, his money income flows into his pocket, again rather as water flows into a bathtub, and his money expenditure flows out of his pocket just as water disappears down the drain. The amount of money in his pocket (or his bank balance) obviously depends on the relative sizes of income and expenditure; when he is getting money faster than he is spending it, the amount of money in his pockets increases, just as a bathtub will fill up if water is running in faster than it runs out. Similarly, the amount of money in his pocket will decline if his expenditure outruns his income. To an individual, then, money income and expenditure are obviously different, and to some extent unrelated things; there is nothing to prevent his income being greater than his expenditure, or his expenditure being greater than his income. When we look at our whole society, however, and add up *all* the incomes of all people, and add up all the expenditures of all people, it is clear on a moment's reflection that not only must these totals be equal, but that they are simply different ways of looking at exactly the same thing! For my income is always somebody else's expenditure, and my expenditure is somebody else's income; every item of income figures, therefore, as somebody's expenditure, and every item of expenditure as somebody's income. From the point of view of society as a whole, therefore, income and expenditure are exactly the same thing, for every *transfer* of money is at the same time income to the person who receives it and expenditure to the person who gives it. This truth is so obvious, once it is stated, that it seems almost impossible that it could be misunderstood; nevertheless, the Keynesian revolution in economic thought consists essentially in the explicit recognition of this truth and its incorporation into the body of economic principles.

If expenditures stop, incomes stop

The next essential step in the argument is the realization that if people stop spending, other people stop receiving incomes, so that the total income of society in any one period (say a "week") depends on the amount that everybody decides to *spend* in that week. If people decide to spend more, money incomes will increase; if people decide to spend less, money incomes will decline, simply because money incomes and expenditures are the same thing over a whole society.

Three groups of getters and spenders

The next step in the development of the argument is to classify the money-getters and money-receivers into three groups, which we may call the public, business, and the government. Each of these receives income from, and makes expenditure to, the other two, and also may receive incomes from and make expenditures to other members of the same group. Thus, the public buys consumers' goods: food, clothing, and so forth. These payments represent expenditure to the public, but they are income to business. Business buys labor, and pays wages; buys the services of property and pays rents and dividends. These payments are expenditure to business and income to the public. The government likewise buys commodities from business and labor, and property-services from the public, and pays out money which is expenditure to the government, but which is income to the recipients. The government collects money from the public and from business in the form of taxes; this is expenditure to the public, but income to the government.

Depressions mainly due to a decline in business expenditure

Now, the total of incomes depends on the total of expenditures. In particular, it depends on the expenditures of these three groups—the public, business, and the government. If the expenditures of any one of these groups decline, the total income of society will likewise decline, unless there is a corresponding increase in the expenditures of the other two groups. What happens in a depression is a decline in *expenditure*, mainly on the part of business. The principal reason for this, as we have seen, is the failure of consumption to prevent an overaccumulation of the stockpile. There are additional reasons, connected with the age distribution of the stockpile and with the psychology of business: these, however, are less important and will be discussed later. There may also be a decline in the expenditure of consumers, due to the accumulation of consumer goods in their possession. This decline in expenditure leads to, and is, in fact, exactly the same thing as a decline in *income*— the income of the people who receive the expended money.

How a budget deficit creates incomes and a surplus destroys them

Whether the activity of an individual creates, destroys, or has no effect on the income of society depends on whether he has a "budget deficit," a "budget surplus," or a "balanced budget." This is true not only for individuals, but for business enterprises and for governments also. If any such economic organism has a "budget deficit"—that is, if it is currently spending more than it is receiving, the net effect is likely to be a rise in incomes elsewhere in the system. If, for instance, I receive $100 in a week and spend $150, the $150 is income to those who receive it, and increases directly the income of society by $150: the $100 that I receive, assuming that it would have been spent anyway, represents a loss of $100 income to the rest of society. The net effect of my actions would therefore be immediately to increase the income of society by $50. If, however, I have a "budget surplus"—if, for instance, I received $100 and spent only $50, I would decrease the income of the rest of society by $50. If my budget is balanced, if I both receive and spend $100, the net direct effect on the income of the rest of society will be nil.

How investment produces incomes

These principles apply to business enterprises as well as to private individuals. When a business enterprise has a "budget deficit"—that is, is currently spending more than it is receiving from the public or the government, the result is a rise in the incomes of the public. The "budget deficit" of a business, however, is its net investment during the period—the amount by which it has increased its nonliquid assets.[4] When investment takes place, a business will be spending larger sums than it is receiving, and hence incomes will be created elsewhere in the system. The direct effect of investment is to transfer money from the possession of businesses to the hands of the public. The income-raising effects of investment depend largely on how the investment is financed—on the source of the money which the business spends. If the business raises money by borrowing from the public, the effect of investment on income is likely to be small, for the increase in incomes which results from business expenditures is to some extent offset by the decline due to the fact that the public cannot now spend the sums which it

---

[4] When a business spends money, it exchanges a liquid asset (money) for a nonliquid asset (the thing bought.) Similarly, when a business receives money from the sale of its product it exchanges a nonliquid asset (the thing sold) for a liquid asset (the money received.) Economists generally use the word "investment," or the "rate of investment," thought of as a *process*, to mean the rate at which the nonliquid assets are growing. In ordinary speech, "investment" sometimes means the total amount invested, as when we say that a building "represents an investment of $100,000." This meaning should not be confused with the one used above.

has lent to business. It may be, of course, that the public would not have spent these sums had they not been borrowed; in that case, the inflationary effect of business borrowings on income will be greater. Business may also invest out of previously accumulated liquid funds. This indeed is likely to be the case after the war; during the war, the highly inflationary public finance has been offset to some extent by a great increase in bank deposits held by business. If these are spent for reconversion after the war, the effect will be strongly inflationary—so much so that it may become desirable to offset this expenditure by a deflationary federal budget surplus. Business may also finance investment by borrowing from the banks. This method is also highly inflationary, since it results in the creation of liquid funds (bank deposits) which did not previously exist.

If business expenditure is made either from accumulated funds or as a result of borrowing from the banks it produces a direct effect on incomes just about equal to the amount of expenditure.

The "multiplier effect"

The direct effect of expenditures on incomes is only part of the story, however. When the individuals who have received the expended money find that their incomes are larger, they too will increase their rate of expenditure; this in turn will increase the incomes of those who receive the new expenditure, and these people will also increase their expenditure, creating new incomes. So each increase in expenditure results indirectly in an increase in income larger than itself, provided, of course, that the increase in expenditure persists. The ratio of the final increase of income to the initial increase of expenditure is called the "multiplier." Thus, if the multiplier is 3, an initial increase of expenditure of $100 will cause an increase in income of $300.

Why does a decline in money income lead to unemployment? It disrupts relative values

The next point to make clear is why large changes in money income are undesirable, and particularly, why a decrease in money income is likely to lead to unemployment. Economists have recognized from the days of Adam Smith that the absolute level of prices and incomes is a relatively trivial quantity, and that what is really significant is *relative* prices and incomes. We can see this immediately if we suppose that Congress passed a law which said that wherever the word "dollar" had been used before, the words "two dollars" must be used now. Then all prices, all wages, all rents, all debts, all taxes—everything reckoned in dollars—would double in numerical value, but apart from the fact of our having to do a little more arithmetic, nothing of importance would have been changed. Everyone would be just as well off as before, enterprises would yield the same rate of profit as before, the purchasing power of all communities would be the same as before, real wages would be unchanged, and the rate of interest would be no different. It was perhaps because this fact was recognized so clearly that economists for a long time overlooked another equally significant fact: that *changes* in the value of money—in the level of prices and incomes—produce violent and usually undesirable effects on the economic system. This happens for two reasons. The first is that a change in the value of money cannot be accomplished in fact without disrupting the *relative* values of different prices and incomes. Some prices and some incomes are "sticky"—that is, they do not change easily. Others are highly flexible. Consequently, when there is a general downward movement, the flexible prices and incomes fall more than the inflexible prices and incomes, and so there is a fall in the purchasing power of commodities with flexible prices while there is a rise in the purchasing power of commodities with inflexible prices. One of the inflexible elements in the price system is industrial money wages, which are difficult to revise downwards, especially where labor unions are strong. When the general level of prices and incomes is falling, money wage rates lag behind the general fall, and unemployment results; "real" wages become too high for the profitable employment of all workers.

Deflation makes profits disappear

The second reason why deflation results in unemployment is even more fundamental. The reason is that when prices are falling, it is almost impossible for business to be profitable, and unless business is profitable, men will not be hired. Even more, when prices are falling, the holding of idle money is itself a profitable investment. If I hold $100 in my stocking for a year and during that year prices have fallen ten per cent, in terms of real purchasing power, my $100 has risen in value ten per cent— I can buy ten per cent more with it at the end of the year than I could at the beginning. The operations of business, on the other hand, require the businessman to hold most of his resources in the form of commodities. When the price of commodities is falling, the holding of commodities involves their owner in loss. Thus, if I hold a hundred bushels of wheat for a year, and at the beginning of the year the price of wheat was $1 whereas at the end of the year it was 80 cents, the value of my holding has fallen from $100 to $80 and I have made a loss of $20. The act of hiring a man, however, of necessity involves the employer in the holding of commodities of one kind or another. An employer, in fact, is a man who gives up money for the product of labor. In the very act of giving employment, the employer changes the form of his assets from money to the *commodity* which is the product of the labor of the man that he has hired. When prices are falling, then, it is folly to engage in business, folly to try to make profits, and folly to hire people; it is much wiser, from the standpoint of personal gain, to sell as much as possible of one's possessions and then sit back with folded hands waiting for one's hoard of money to increase in value as prices fall.

The expectation of rising prices leads to larger expenditures

Conversely, when prices are rising, it becomes unprofitable to hold money, and profitable to spend it. Consumers find it better to spend money now than later, when prices will be higher. Businessmen find it better to spend money now in wages, rather than to wait until wages are higher. It is easy to make profits, for the commodities that businessmen are holding are continually rising in value. We see, therefore, that the *anticipation* of rising prices is likely to lead to large expenditures, and to large incomes, and to large demands. If people expect prices to rise, they will be anxious to buy things (including labor) and will be disinclined to sell. This state of mind, however, inevitably *results* in a rise in prices. Similarly, if people expect prices to fall, they will be disinclined to buy things or to hire people, and will be anxious to sell. This will result in a fall in prices. So we have the law of self-justified expectations, which says that what enough people expect, will happen whether it was going to happen or not!

The instability of the price system

Because of the law of self-justified expectations the *whole* price-income system is profoundly unstable. Indeed, it may be wondered why prices are not perpetually increasing or perpetually decreasing, since every increase seems to strengthen the forces making for a rise, and every decrease seems to strengthen the forces making for a fall. The oscillations of prices have been described, very appropriately, as being not like that of a pendulum which swings about a central point, but like a billiard ball bouncing between two parallel cushions; once it is moving in a certain direction, there is nothing to bring it back again until it hits up against something that reverses its direction. Indeed, were it not for three facts, the remarkable (though unfounded) human belief in the ultimate stability of the value of money, the inflexibility of certain prices and wages, and the inelasticity of the supply of money, the price system might easily swing even more dizzily than it does. Suppose that we had a system in which the supply of money were perfectly elastic, so that the quantity of money increased in proportion to every increased demand; in which also people had lost faith in the stability of prices, and in which wages and prices were all easily adjustable. In such a society there would be nothing to prevent prices rising indefinitely. Indeed, this has happened on more than one occasion in history, the last being the great German inflation of 1923. The opposite of the unlimited inflation—the bottomless deflation—has never actually happened, mainly because it is more difficult to decrease the quantity of money than to increase it. Nevertheless, there is no absolute reason why it could not happen, given the appropriate monetary institutions. If, for instance, all money was bank money, and if money prices and wages were highly flexible, any decline in money prices and incomes would tend to perpetuate itself almost indefinitely. If everybody anticipated a fall in prices, all money demands would shrink, no one would be willing to buy at existing prices; all supplies would rise, as everyone became anxious to sell, and hence if prices were flexible they would fall with almost inconceivable rapidity. What usually brings this fall to an end fairly soon in practice is that as prices fall, the existing stocks of money become more and more valuable in terms of purchasing power; since we have an insufficient appreciation of the possibilities of earning "value" by doing nothing under these peculiar circumstances, we eventually get to the point where old habits reassert themselves and we start buying things again, even though this may be quite foolish if we still expect a fall in prices. The monetary system then may be compared not inaptly to Alice in Wonderland—the slightest impulse sends it shooting skyward until its feet are quite out of sight, or sends it shrinking until its chin bangs violently up against its toes. The more flexible are money prices and wages, the more violent are these fluctuations likely to be.

Conclusions

The argument of this chapter is beginning to lead to some fairly definite conclusions. It is clear that under a system of unregulated private enterprise the monetary system is profoundly unstable and is in constant danger of plunging the economy into deflation, with consequent unemployment, or into inflation, with consequent injustices and dislocations. It is also clear that no agency other than the government is powerful enough to deal with this problem. It looks, therefore, as if government has an inescapable responsibility to insure a reasonable stability of money incomes and to protect society against both deflation and inflation. In the next two chapters it will be shown that no method of dealing with this problem is adequate except the adjustment of the deficits and surpluses of the government to meet the changes in money income of the rest of society. When businesses and individuals collectively have budget surpluses, so that income is declining and unemployment rising, the government should offset this by having a budget deficit. When business and individuals collectively have budget deficits and an inflationary situation threatens, the government should offset this by a budget surplus. The neglect of this prime economic responsibility of government has been one of the main causes leading to the deplorable situation in which the world now finds itself.

CHAPTER 8

Some Proposed Remedies for Unemployment

Before we proceed to consider what must be the nature of an adequate policy for full employment, it will be desirable to examine some proposed remedies for unemployment in the light of the analysis of the last chapter, to see how far they can be considered satisfactory.

Price and wage flexibility is no cure for unemployment

A remedy which has been popular among economists has been the proposal to make prices and wages more flexible, and especially more flexible in a downward direction. It is argued that if commodities cannot be sold, or if labor cannot find employment, then that is a sure sign that the price of commodities or the price of labor (wages) is too high, and should come down. It is argued further that monopolies, whether of business or of labor, prevent these adjustments by keeping their prices too high. The remedy would seem to be a combination of exhortation, regulation, and "trustbusting" designed to permit the downward adjustment of prices in times of depression.[1] The practical men of affairs have never thought much of these proposals, and it now seems likely that their practical instincts have been nearer the truth than the economists have believed. The argument for price flexibility rests, in fact, on a logical fallacy—the fallacy of composition. It is true that if we could assume that the demand curve for a commodity or for labor were fixed, then it is highly probable that a fall in price would lead to a rise in sales and a fall in wages to a rise in employ-

---

[1] This point of view is expressed in the many publications of the Brookings Institution, Washington, D. C.

ment. Hence, it might be thought that if all prices were lowered there would be a rise in total sales, or that if all wages were lowered there would be a rise in total employment. Such, however, is by no means necessarily the case. The demand for any one commodity, or for any one kind of labor, depends on the incomes of other groups in the society, which in turn depend on the demands for their product and the prices at which it is sold. Hence, it cannot be assumed that demands remain the same when prices and wages are lowered. A fall in wages of carpenters, for instance, may increase the employment of carpenters; but if it diminishes the incomes of carpenters, the effect will also be to diminish the expenditures of carpenters and hence diminish incomes and employment somewhere else in the system.

There is another, and perhaps even more fundamental, reason why flexibility of wages and prices is no answer to the problem of unemployment. The demands for commodities or for labor depend very much on the expectations of future prices. If we expect prices to fall, we shall be likely to postpone the purchase of commodities, where that is possible, and demands will fall. If employers expect wages to fall, they are likely to postpone the purchase of labor as much as they can until it is cheaper, and this of itself will bring about a decline in the demand for labor. Insofar as people base their expectations of the future on what is happening in the present, a fall in prices may lead to a decline in demand and to an actual shrinkage of sales, while a fall in wages may likewise lead to a decline in employment. This is particularly likely to be true of general reductions in prices and wages, which, as we have seen, are all too likely to lead to further deflation.

Nor is flexibility a cure for an inflationary situation

The fallacy of the "flexibility" argument can be seen perhaps even more clearly if it is applied to an inflationary, rather than a deflationary, situation. Just as a deflationary situation is the result of overaccumulation, so an inflationary situation is usually the result of a short stock of goods resulting from the vast consumption of war, and a large stock of money resulting from war finance. If prices are inflexible—if they are prevented from rising, either by law or custom, the result is the disappearance of stocks and the development of "shortages." A "shortage" of commodities or of labor is the opposite of the "glut" or "unemployment." Just as in deflation people have commodities and labor which they want to sell at existing prices but for which they cannot find buyers, so in inflation people wish to buy commodities and labor at existing prices but cannot find sellers. According to the "flexibility" argument, the remedy would seem to be to allow prices and wage rates to rise; this would discourage the consumption of commodities and the employment of labor until a new equilibrium was reached. It is almost universally agreed, however, that this remedy is fallacious: that if prices and wages are allowed to rise in the face of shortages, this rise by raising incomes and by encouraging speculative demand will "create its own draft" and will tend to perpetuate itself. Hence, we develop price control, rationing, and such devices as substitutes for price equilibrium. That is, instead of allowing prices to perform their supposed function of equating production to consumption, we use direct methods for allocating the scarce supplies and hold prices down. In practice, therefore, we affirm what theory has been loath to concede until very recently—that there is *no* natural equilibrium level of prices and that in relation to general money prices, the "law of supply and demand" does not work. It is only for a particular commodity that price can perform the task of equalizing the amount offered to the amount demanded. The price system, unassisted by outside interference, is incapable of performing this task for commodities as a whole. Just as a general rise in prices is no cure for a situation of shortages, so it should be equally obvious that a general fall in prices is no cure for a situation of glut.

Particular wage and price adjustments may be desirable

This does not mean, however, that particular wage and price adjustments are of no value in diminishing unemployment, or raising incomes in times of deflation, or in relieving labor shortages and lowering incomes in times of inflation. A fall in a price or in a wage rate can be inflationary or deflationary in its total effect, depending on the response of sales or employment in the particular case—that is, on the elasticity of demand. The more inelastic the demand in any particular case, the more likely is a fall in price to have a net deflationary effect, both on incomes and on employment. Suppose, for instance, that the demand for bricklayers is rather inelastic, so that a fall in wages from $60 to $50 a week only raised employment from 100,000 to 105,000. The lowering of the wage would then lower the total income of bricklayers from $6,000,000 to $5,250,000 a week. The expenditure and consumption of bricklayers would be likely to decline with a consequent decline in incomes and employment elsewhere in the system. If this secondary decline in employment was more than 5000 men, as is quite likely to be the case, the net effects of the reduction in wages would be unfavorable. If, however, the demand for bricklayers was relatively elastic: for example, if employment rose in the above instance from 100,000 to 125,000 men, the income of bricklayers would rise from $6,000,000 to $6,250,000, and the secondary effects on employment would almost certainly be favorable. The same argument can be applied to prices: if the price of wheat is reduced, the general effect will be inflationary and favorable to employment only if the demand for wheat is fairly elastic; otherwise, the incomes of wheat farmers will be reduced, and the reduction in their expenditures will lower incomes and employment elsewhere in the system.

Wage and price adjustments not desirable as a general solution for instability

At any one moment, therefore, it should be theoretically possible to divide all prices and wages into two groups: those in which a fall in the price or wage will increase employment, and those in which it will diminish employment. If in times of deflation we could lower prices and wages in the first group, and raise them in the second, employment and incomes would be increased. Similarly, in times of inflation it would be advantageous to raise prices and wages in the first group and lower them in the second. There may be a case for some adjustments of this nature. Nevertheless, as a general solution to the problems of deflation and of inflation, it is woefully inadequate. In the first place, it is virtually impossible in practice to distinguish between the two classes of prices and wages and to know whether any particular price or wage should be lowered. In the second place, even if this practical difficulty were overcome, the procedure would not necessarily be desirable, for it would be achieving the end in view (a rise in employment) by clumsy and indirect methods when, as we shall see, there are more direct and efficient ways of tackling the problem. Not only that, but a readjustment of relative prices which might be most desirable from the point of view of lessening unemployment might be quite undesirable from other points of view—such as justice in distribution. There is no reason to suppose that the adjustments in relative wages and prices which would most effectively raise employment are at the same time those readjustments which would best conform to our sense of distributional justice. Indeed, as high wages and prices are more likely to be found where demands are relatively inelastic, it is quite likely that increasing the wages of the well-paid and lowering the wages of the poorly-paid would have a favorable effect on employment, when from the point of view of equitable distribution, it would be vicious. Similarly, in time of war-inflation a manipulation of prices and wages in the interests of preventing inflation might well move them in a direction opposite to that which was required for diverting resources into war industries.

Central bank policy

Another remedy for depressions that found more favor with economists in the past than it does today is the control of the monetary system through the operations of a central bank, such as the Federal Reserve Banks or the Bank of England. There is no doubt that the operations of the banking system affect money incomes, and that also the government, or the monetary authority, operating mainly through the central bank, has a certain power of control over the banking system. The main criticism of such control is that it is not powerful enough and that also it is much more efficient in suppressing booms than it is in assisting recovery. Although central bank policy is important, therefore, as a supplementary weapon in the fight against unemployment, it is not powerful enough, especially in modern circumstances, to be used as the single instrument. It is, however, important that banking policy should be co-ordinated with other policies—it would be absurd, for instance, to have the tax policy directed at the expansion of money income, when banking policy was directed at its contraction.

The mechanism of central bank control

The control of the banking system by a central bank depends on the fact that the *reserves* of the member banks consist of *deposits* at the central bank. Hence, any action which tends to increase central bank deposits, tends to increase the member bank reserves and hence may be expected to increase the member bank's loans and deposits. Similarly, any action which tends to decrease the central bank's deposits will lower the member banks reserves and lower their loans and deposits. Thus, when a central bank buys securities, the seller of the securities receives in return a deposit at the central bank; as the central bank does not usually carry on a private banking business, the seller transfers this central bank deposit to his own bank—say the First National—in return for deposit in that bank. The First National Bank thus comes into possession of a deposit at the central bank, which means that its reserves are augmented by that amount, and it will be in a position to expand its loans and thereby expand its deposits. If, on the other hand, the central bank sells securities, the buyer pays with a check on his deposit at, say, the First National; the central bank clears this check with the First National and as a result the deposit of the First National with the central bank falls by the amount of the check; its reserves will therefore have fallen, and it may have to contract its loans and deposits. This is the mechanism known as "Open Market Policy." The central bank may also affect the member bank's reserves directly by raising or lowering its rediscount rate (in England known as the "Bank Rate")—that is, the rate of interest at which the member banks can borrow from the central bank. If the "Bank Rate" is raised, this will discourage borrowing, lower reserves, and induce a deflationary movement. If the "Bank Rate" is lowered, borrowing is encouraged, reserves are raised, and an inflationary movement is started.

Central banks have lost control over member banks

For a variety of reasons the mechanism described in the preceding paragraph has largely ceased to operate in the world of today. An essential link in the mechanism is the relationship between the volume of member bank reserves and the volume of their loans and deposits. As long as the reserve ratio is constant, any increase in reserves will lead to an expansion of bank loans, and therefore of deposits. If the fear of losing reserves, then, is the main factor which inhibits a banker from expanding his loans and investments, a rise in his reserves is sure to make him expand his loans and investments. If we suppose that a banker regulates his policy so as to maintain a constant ratio of reserves to deposits—say of 10 per cent, then with reserves of $1,000,000 he would expand his loans until deposits rose to $10,000,000. If his reserves rose to $1,100,000, his deposits would expand to $11,000,000. Any change in reserves thus results in a tenfold increase in deposits. This condition was approximately true of the old National Banking system of the United States before 1914, and of the British system before the depression. In recent years, however, the main factor restraining the expansion of bank loans and investments has not been the banker's fear of losing reserves but his sheer inability to find suitable borrowers or securities. The volume of private securities suitable for bank assets has declined substantially, in part due to the increased tendency for corporations to hold more liquid assets and hence to be in a position to finance expansions from their own resources, and in part due to the generally pessimistic expectations of the return on investment.

In this situation the central bank virtually loses all its power to control the volume of member bank deposits. It may continue to regulate the volume of member bank reserves, but this is now no guarantee of corresponding changes in deposits. The result of an increase in bank reserves under present-day circumstances may simply be a rise in the reserve ratio, not an expansion of loans and investments. This is because the scarcity of suitable investments, coupled with a high preference for liquid assets on the part of the bankers, has raised the reserve ratios far above the legal limit, and the legal limit is therefore inoperative as a restrictive force. The situation changed temporarily during the war, because of the enormous volume of government obligations issued to cover the budget deficit. These government bonds provided banks with a suitable form of investment in large quantity, and in consequence a fall in the reserve ratio brought it by mid-1944 close to the legal limit.[2] In a war situation, however, it is clear that the main inflationary stimulus comes from the budget deficit, and not from anything peculiar to banking policy. The experience of the depression proved that as long as the banks have reserves in excess of the legal minimum, an expansionist policy on the part of the central bank will have very little effect of itself.

How central bank policy can stop a boom

In peacetime a contraction of credit by the central bank is much more likely to lead to a contraction of the member bank's loans and deposits than it is to a reduction in their reserve ratios. This is especially likely to be true in time of boom, for then the reserve ratios of the banks are likely to be as low as they care to get, and a reduction of reserves will almost certainly plunge them into a deflationary policy. This explains why central bank policy seems to be so much more effective in preventing or in killing a boom than it is in lifting us out of a depression. It is, of course, a most undesirable state of affairs, for "stabilization" by central bank enthusiasts might easily result simply in chopping off the booms and in exposing us to the delights of one continuous depression.

Need for a high legal reserve ratio

There is one obvious remedy for the flaw in the banking system: it is to require a *legal* reserve ratio which is well above what the bankers, if left to themselves, would wish to have. Thus if the bankers themselves tend to want a reserve ratio of 30 per cent, a legal reserve ratio of ten or even twenty per cent is simply useless; it means absolutely nothing. All the talk about "excess reserves" in recent years is something of a commentary on the way our minds run in legalistic rather than realistic

---

[2] The excess reserves of American banks fell from about six and one-half billion in 1940 to under one billion in 1944.

channels; "excess reserves," of course, means reserves in excess
of those required to fulfil the legal reserve ratio. They are a
purely legal concept, with very little economic significance, apart
from the indication which they give that central bank control
has broken down. "Excess Reserves" can, of course, be abolished
overnight by the simple expedient of raising the legal reserve
requirement to a point where it is at least equal to what bankers
wish to hold of their own free will. Indeed, in 1936 and 1937 the
Federal Reserve Board raised the reserve requirement, doubling
it in these two steps. This immediately abolished the bulk of
"excess reserves" but still did not solve the problem.

The "hundred per cent reserve" plan

These considerations, among others, have prompted some
economists to draw up a plan known as the "hundred per cent
reserve plan" which deserves some attention.[3] The proposal
briefly is that banks should be compelled to carry a hundred
per cent reserve against deposits—that is, that the legal minimum reserve ratio should be 100 per cent. In support of this
proposal it is pointed out that, in effect, the banking system has
usurped one of the principal prerogatives of the government—
the issue of money. The fluctuations of the business cycle, it is
argued, are augmented by the fact that the banks pursue an
inflationary policy in time of boom and a deflationary policy
in time of depression. They are enabled to do this only because
of the fact that they do not hold 100 per cent reserves against
deposits. If they were compelled by law to do this, then for
every dollar of reserves there would be only one dollar of deposits, no more and no less. The volume of bank money would
then be entirely under the control of the government. It is
argued, by way of historical justification, that this is essentially
the same principle, extended to bank deposits, that the English
Bank Act of 1844 applied to bank notes.

The trouble with this scheme is that it seems to be much
more drastic than is actually necessary. If the commercial banks
had to hold a hundred per cent reserve against deposits, it would
virtually deprive them of all their earning assets. They could

---

[3] See Fisher, Irving, *100% Money*. New York: The Adelphi Company, 1935.

only continue to exist by imposing heavy bank charges for checking and other services, charges so heavy that they would of necessity greatly restrict the use of the checking system, and force us back to more primitive methods of transferring money. At present, the checking system is subsidized by the interest earned on bank assets, whether loans or government securities; indeed, a considerable proportion of the interest on the national debt really serves as a subsidy to the checking system. The lending functions of banks would largely have to be taken over by other institutions, such as savings banks and dis- count houses—institutions which do not at present exist in sufficient number. Altogether the disruption which such a scheme would cause in our whole financial mechanism would be ade- quate reason for rejecting it even if the benefits were very large. The benefits, however, are extremely doubtful. There is nothing in the hundred per cent plan which would ensure continuous prosperity or a stable money income. It is not so much changes in the quantity of money that are important, but changes in the rate of expenditure, or in its velocity of circulation.[4] Even if we had a completely inflexible quantity of money, there would still be great opportunities for variations in money income; for the faster money is spent, the more money income there will be. The 100 per cent reserve plan, therefore, does not get at the root of the matter of monetary instability and would yield no benefits commensurate with its cost.

A legal reserve of 35-40 per cent might be advisable

Nevertheless, there is much to be said for fixing reserve re- quirements at a substantially higher level than they are now, in order to force banks to keep their reserve ratio approximately constant. As we have seen, only under these circumstances could central bank control be really effective. A legal minimum reserve ratio for commercial banks of, say, 35-40 per cent, would not disrupt the banking system, as the banks could hold suffi- cient earning assets to cover most of the cost of the checking

---

[4] If M is the quantity of money, and V is the income-velocity of circula- tion, that is, the number of times in a year that a dollar appears as income, then the total amount of income or expenditure is MV. Even if M remains constant, there can be, therefore, large changes in MV due to changes in V

system. It would almost certainly insure a close correspondence between the total of reserves and the total volume of bank credit, sufficient to enable the central bank to regulate the total volume of bank credit by controlling the volume of reserves.

Depreciating stamp money schemes

We now pass from schemes to regulate banking to schemes for regulating *currency*. It has long been recognized, especially in rather unorthodox circles, that in a time of unemployment it is highly desirable to increase the velocity of circulation of money, or what is practically the same thing, to increase the rate of spending. Several devices have been proposed to this end, one of the most interesting being that called "depreciating stamp money." The interest of this scheme lies not only in its theoretical implications, but also in the fact that it has been tried in practice; on a small scale in the village of Wörgl, Austria, and on a larger scale in the province of Alberta, Canada. The principle of the scheme is that money should depreciate in value as it is held. This is insured by making the holders put a stamp on the back of bills at regular intervals. Thus, in the Alberta scheme the back of the scrip dollar notes had 52 spaces, one for each week of the year. A two-cent stamp had to be stuck on each space up to the one representing the week in which the money was spent. Whoever held the money for four weeks would have to buy 8 cents worth of stamps to stick on it before the note could be spent. At the end of 52 weeks the fully stamped note would be redeemed by the state government. The theory was that for each dollar note issued, the public would have to buy $1.04 in stamps, and at the end of the year the state would have enough money to redeem the note, with four cents profit. It is obvious that such money would circulate with extreme rapidity, for no one would be anxious to hold it, especially towards the end of a week. It might get to the point, in fact, where nobody would accept it at all, except at a discount; then it would virtually cease to be money. In the Alberta experience the state government was, of course, forced to accept the scrip in payment of taxes and other obligations due to it, and hence almost as soon as the money was issued, it came right back to the state. The difficulty was that the Dominion money circulated side by side with the Alberta scrip, and naturally was preferred.

Stamp money schemes fail because of money substitutes, and are too inflexible

These "depreciating stamp money" schemes are not quite as crazy as they may sound, although they have one fatal flaw. One of the principal reasons for unemployment, as we have seen, is that in time of falling prices it becomes profitable to hold money, which is rising in purchasing power, rather than to hold goods, which are falling. If we can make the holding of money actually unprofitable, then the deflationary effect of an expected fall in prices will be much smaller; people will prefer to employ labor and to hold goods in process, even though this is unprofitable, rather than to hold money, if the holding of money could be made even more unprofitable. One trouble with the depreciating stamp money scheme is that it does not take sufficient account of money substitutes. The depreciating stamp money schemes that have been tried broke down because there was actually a substitute *currency* (the national money) available. But even if a completely autonomous country tried such a scheme, if it merely introduced a depreciating stamp currency, but left bank deposits unaffected, people would simply shift to the use of bank deposits. Even if bank deposits were taxed, other substitutes might be found; commodities might begin to serve as a medium of exchange. A more fundamental flaw in the scheme is that as usually proposed, at least, it is quite inflexible. It might serve very well in a time of extreme deflation. But the moment the scheme was successful, it would become a grave danger, for in an inflationary period an increase in spending is precisely what we want to avoid. Most of the advocates of these schemes are obsessed by the evils of deflation, and while a small dose of this obsession might be a good thing for our orthodox bankers, it can go much too far and blind us to the opposite, but equally significant, dangers of inflation.

There is a case for a flexible tax on bank deposits

Nevertheless, it may be possible to learn something from these proposals. Depreciating stamp money in itself is a clumsy and inconvenient method of achieving an increase of money income, and also a highly inaccurate and insensitive method. But there may be a case for applying the same principle to bank deposits, where it takes the much simpler form of a weekly, monthly, or annual tax—or better still, a constantly accruing tax. The tax should not be too high—probably 2 or 3 per cent per annum would be ample to drive "idle money" out into investment. It should be flexible; the rate should vary with the degree of deflation; the more severe the deflation, the greater should be the rate of tax. In the form of a negative tax, or subsidy, it could even be used as a weapon against inflation, that is, as soon as inflation threatened, instead of paying a tax on bank deposits the depositor should receive a 1, 2, or 3 per cent per annum subsidy. There would remain the possibility that the tax on bank deposits would induce depositors to exchange their deposits for notes and cash—the "money substitute" problem would come up here also. Theoretically, this could be solved by making all notes "depreciating stamp" notes. Possibly a simpler way to deal with the situation would be to impose a legal maximum on the amount of notes and cash possessed by any individual or corporation—that is, to "ration" notes and cash. This legal maximum could be enforced quite easily by making everyone turn in his notes for notes of another color every year, "last year's notes" then becoming invalid.

Although there is much to be said for these proposals, it is doubtful whether in themselves they would be sufficiently powerful to maintain stability. If used at all, they would have to be used as an adjunct to more fundamental policies, and the question arises whether they are *necessary* as an adjunct. If these schemes are not, then they would hardly seem worth while, as they would cause a certain amount of inconvenience, and in a conservatively minded society might be difficult to introduce without undesirable loss of confidence.

"Social Credit" plans are also too inflexible

Another proposal which is closely linked with the depreciating stamp money plan is that of the "social dividend," or "social credit" as Major Douglas calls it. In essence, this plan proposes that the government shall give a certain sum of money to each individual each week. Like the depreciating stamp money plan, however, its weakness lies in its inflexibility. Although in times of very severe deflation there is something to be said for such a proposal, in time of inflation it would be ridiculous. The "Townsend Plan" is subject to the same criticism, quite apart from its effects on distribution and its fantastic tax proposals.

Reform of the monetary standard. Bimetallism and symmetallism

A scheme which has a much greater weight of authority behind it than either the depreciating money or the social dividend plans is that known as the "commodity reserve standard" plan. The essence of this scheme is the return to something like a "gold" standard, with the important difference that the standard should not be a single commodity, or even two commodities, but a whole group of important raw materials. This scheme is really a development of the bimetallism controversy of the late nineteenth century. Then also, in a period of deflation, it was argued that the base of the monetary standard should be widened to include both gold and silver. The essence of the gold standard is that the government (or central bank) offers to buy and sell gold at a *fixed legal price* in unlimited quantities. Under a bimetallic standard the authorities offer to buy and sell gold *and silver* at fixed legal prices. In practice bimetallism has proved impractical, although France, the Latin Union, and the United States have had experience with it at different times. The difficulty is that the relatively plentiful metal tends to drive the less plentiful metal out of the monetary use. Thus, the great gold discoveries of the 19th century made it profitable to sell gold to the bimetallic governments and buy silver from these governments until they were forced to abandon the free coinage of silver. In order to remedy this defect, Alfred Marshall proposed a new scheme which has been called *symmetallism*.[5] Under a symmetallic standard a government would offer to buy and sell gold and silver in *fixed proportions:* for example, the government might offer $30 for every ounce of gold plus ten ounces of silver, and offer an ounce of gold plus ten ounces of silver for every $30. Under such a regime the market prices of

---

[5] Alfred Marshall, *Official Papers*, p. 14.

gold and silver would fluctuate with conditions of supply and demand, but the weighted average price of gold and silver in the market would be constant. Thus, if the standard were as shown above, the price of an ounce of gold and ten ounces of silver in the market would always be around $30; if it were more, it would pay bullion dealers to buy gold and silver from the government and sell it in the market, which would reduce their price in the market: if it were less, it would pay bullion dealers to buy gold and silver in the market and sell it to the government; this would raise the price in the market. It would be perfectly possible, however, for the market price of gold and silver to fluctuate separately. Thus, gold might be $20 per ounce and silver $1; or gold might be $25 per ounce and silver 50 cents.

The multiple commodity reserve standard

The multiple commodity reserve standard is essentially the symmetallism proposal extended to include not only gold and silver, but tin, rubber, cotton, wheat, and a large number of other commodities. Under the scheme proposed by Mr. Graham,[6] the government would not actually buy and sell the commodities themselves, but would buy and sell warehouse receipts, giving title to definite quantities of these commodities, in fixed proportions. The proportions would be determined roughly by the importance of the commodity concerned, as measured by the value of world stocks. Thus, if the average world stock of wheat is four times as valuable, in dollar terms, as the world stock of coffee, the warehouse receipts bought and sold by the government would give title to four times as much wheat as coffee. Under this scheme, as under symmetallism, the weighted average price or the price level of the composite commodity in the market would be practically constant. If the price level of the composite commodity group fell below the standard level at which the government stood ready to buy and sell, it would pay dealers to buy up commodities and take the warehouse receipts in appropriate bundles to the government in return for money. If the price level of the commodity group rose above the standard, it would pay dealers to buy the warehouse receipts from

---

[6] B. Graham, *Storage and Stability*. New York: McGraw-Hill, 1937.

the government and sell them in the various commodity markets. In the first case, the average price of the composite commodity group would tend to rise; in the second case, it would tend to fall, until it reached the standard price.

Stabilizing influence of the multiple commodity reserve

It is argued that such a composite commodity standard would act as a stablizing influence not only on the prices of the standard commodities but also on all other prices and on money income. If a deflationary movement set in, with a reduction in all or most money incomes and prices, the prices of the standard commodities would fall likewise, but this would immediately make it profitable to sell the commodities to the government. The government would increase its holdings of commodities, and the quantity of money in the hands of the public would rise. Both these movements are inflationary in character, for the public will hold fewer commodities and more money. Similarly, if an inflation is threatened, prices—including the prices of the standard commodities—will rise; it will become profitable to buy the standard commodities from the government to sell in the market; this action will not only raise the prices of the standard commodities, but will take money out of circulation and so will have a generally deflationary effect on all prices and incomes. Furthermore, in deflation the price of the standard commodities will remain relatively high, and so the production of the standard commodities will be profitable; their production will increase, and more and more commodities will be offered to the government in return for money; as long as the prices of other (nonstandard) commodities remain low, therefore, there is a strong force in operation making for an increase in money and in money incomes. Similarly, in a period of inflation, the prices of the standard commodities will be relatively low, consequently production of the standard commodities will be unprofitable and will fall off; the government stocks of these commodities will be withdrawn and consumed and the money used to buy these stocks will pass out of circulation; incomes in the standard-commodity industries will fall, and through the multiplier effect incomes in other industries will tend to fall also, and the inflation will be stopped.

The effect exists, but is too slow under the gold standard

It should be noticed that somewhat the same effect takes place under the gold standard. If the quantity of gold runs short and there is a deflation, the value of gold in terms of commodities will increase, and gold mining will become unusually profitable. The output of gold is likely, therefore, to increase, and prices and incomes will rise again. If, on the other hand, there is a large output of gold, leading to a rise in prices, the production of gold will become unprofitable, since the price of gold cannot rise along with other prices and wages, because of the gold standard. Hence, gold production will decline, and prices will tend to fall again. There is little doubt that this mechanism operated to some extent during the nineteenth century. However, it operates slowly and hesitantly, with a period of perhaps a generation or more between the initial stimulus and the final result. Moreover, the output of gold is subject to chance fluctuations due to accidental discoveries quite unconnected with the movement of prices. On these grounds, therefore, it may be concluded that gold, by itself, is a most unsuitable standard. The multiple commodity standard, however, would operate much more rapidly and with much less danger of accidental variations in output.

Objections to the multiple commodity standard: difficulty in maintaining standard

There is much to be said, therefore, for the multiple commodity standard. Nevertheless, there are certain objections which must be faced. Under the gold standard, as it has operated in the United States in recent years, there has been an enormous accumulation of gold, without apparently setting in motion sufficient of the inflationary forces which would bring these gold flows to a stop. It may well be asked whether there would not be a similar danger under the multiple commodity standard; whether, for instance, in times of severe deflation, the stocks of commodities owned by the government would not increase almost indefinitely, as the gold stock has increased under the gold standard, until the sheer impossibility of expanding storage capacity forced the collapse of the standard. An immense value of gold can be housed in a relatively small space at Fort Knox, but imagine the consequences of trying to house similar values in wheat, coffee, cotton, rubber, and the like! At the other extreme, a series of short harvests in the agricultural components might easily result in the depletion of the whole government reserve and in the consequent breakdown of the standard. The maintenance of a gold reserve under a free gold standard presented difficulties in many cases; the maintenance of a composite commodity reserve might even present more difficulties.[7]

Difficulties in foreign exchanges

Troubles would arise also in the international sphere. The greatest advantage of a universal gold standard is the stability of foreign exchange rates which it brings about. If a single country were on a multiple commodity standard, that by itself, of course, would no more insure stability of the exchange rates than a single-country gold standard. Even if two countries were on an identical multiple commodity standard, there would still be opportunity for rather wide fluctuations in the exchange rates. Gold has the advantage over a multiple commodity unit as a standard in that it is easily transportable; it would be much more difficult for the multiple commodity group than for gold to move from country to country. Hence, the multiple commodity would be much less efficient in the settlement of international balances.[8] This difficulty, however, is not a serious ob-

_____

[7] It might be possible to prevent too great accumulations or decumulations of the commodity reserve if the standard rate of purchase were adjustable— i.e. if the official price of the "standard bundle" was raised when the reserve was threatened by withdrawals, or lowered when it was threatened with too great accumulations. This however would be tantamount to an abandonment of the standard as such, and would destroy the stability of the price level. This does not mean of course that adjustments in the composition of the "standard bundle" might not be made from time to time, as new commodities rose to importance and as old commodities declined.

[8] When two countries are on a gold standard, the rate of exchange of their currencies cannot vary much above or below limits set by the cost of transport of gold between their respective financial centers. Thus, if New York is on a gold standard at a rate of $5 = ¼oz. gold, and London is on a gold standard at a rate of £1 = ¼oz. gold, and it costs 2 cents to transport ¼oz. gold between New York and London, then the foreign exchange rate will not vary much outside the "gold points," $5.02 = £1 and $4.98 = £1. Under a bilateral multiple commodity standard, there would be "multiple commodity points" like the gold points, depending on the cost of transport of the multiple commodity group

jection to the multiple commodity standard, for there are direct methods of maintaining stability in the foreign exchange rates—for example, by means of the operations of exchange equalization funds—which are probably superior, in flexibility at least, to the method of the standard commodity or commodities.

Of all the purely monetary devices which have been proposed, the multiple commodity standard seems least open to objection. Nevertheless, there are grave doubts whether this proposal would work if not supplemented by fiscal policy. The fundamental objection to it is that it is an *indirect* method of attack on a problem which is susceptible of direct attack through government expenditures and receipts. It is, however, not capable of automatic working, as the quantities and kinds of commodities in the standard would have to be changed from time to time if it was to be successful. This would open the door to political maneuvering on the part of the various commodity pressure groups—cotton, wheat, corn, silver, and so on—which might lead to competitive depreciation of the standard, each group pressing for a high price for the composite commodity and a larger proportion of its own commodity to be included. Nevertheless, the proposal has the merit of being close enough to orthodox thinking so that it has a fighting chance of acceptance. The more direct solutions to the problem that will be outlined in the following chapter require a revolution in thought which may not easily be accomplished. The multiple commodity standard has the virtue of not only being fairly sensible, but also of *sounding* fairly sensible to more timid minds. As such, it may well prove to be the next step in the development of economic policy.

---

between the financial centers. This cost of transport, however, is high in proportion to the value of the commodities. The same multiple commodity might be obtained in New York for $5 or in London for £1. If however the cost of transport of this unit was $3, the exchange rates could theoretically fluctuate between the "multiple commodity points" of $2.00 and $8.00 to the pound sterling.

CHAPTER 9

A Full Employment Policy

Conclusions of the preceding argument

From the argument of the two previous chapters, certain very important conclusions can be drawn, and at least the outlines of a full employment policy can be sketched. These conclusions can be outlined as follows:

1. In times of peace, the productive powers of our technical civilization have a strong tendency to outrun the consumptive powers, leading to a situation where the rate of accumulation of the stock of physical goods is greater than the rate at which capitalists are willing to increase their holdings.

2. In the absence of governmental intervention, this condition leads inevitably to a downward movement of prices and incomes and to unemployment. Because of the fundamental instability of the price system, this downward movement tends to perpetuate itself and is the cause of further unemployment and economic distress.

3. It is, therefore, a direct responsibility of government, a responsibility which no other agency in society can assume, to prevent large fluctuations in the volume of unemployment and in the level of money income.

4. The control of the banking system and the manipulation of the monetary standard may be of some assistance in attaining this end, but by themselves they are not powerful enough to prevent general depressions. They operate only indirectly and do not strike at the root of the trouble.

5. There would seem to be only one agency in society powerful enough to accomplish these ends: that is the fiscal system. Only by appropriate manipulations of governmental expenditures and receipts can money income be stabilized and general depressions abolished.

How government deficits and surpluses can stabilize income

Let us consider first the problem of the regulation of money income. This is not quite the same thing as the abolition of unemployment, for it would be possible to have some unemployment even if money income were held constant. Nevertheless, the stabilization of money incomes would be an important accomplishment. It would prevent monstrous dislocations such as the 1929-1933 deflation, when the national money income of the United States almost halved. Left to itself, the system produces intolerable and meaningless fluctuations in money income. These great fluctuations must be and can be avoided. We have seen in Chapter 7 that for any economic organism a budget deficit has an income-increasing effect on the rest of society, and a budget surplus has an income-decreasing effect. If, therefore, consumers and enterprises have budget surpluses, so that income is declining, the obvious answer to the problem is for the government deliberately to create a budget deficit. Similarly, if consumers and enterprises have budget deficits so that income is increasing too rapidly, the government should offset this by having a budget surplus.

The "Adjustable Tax Plan"

The budget surplus or deficit is equal to the difference between current receipts and current expenditures. Any desired surplus or deficit, then, can be attained either by adjusting receipts or by adjusting expenditures. There are some occasions, as we shall see, when expenditures should be adjusted. The main burden of income control, however, should fall on government receipts from taxation. There is no reason why these adjustments should not be made automatically, under an "Adjustable Tax Plan."

Thus the tax system should consist primarily of a broad-based income tax, deductible at source wherever possible, and payable at frequent intervals.[1] The rate of tax should

[1] The accounting period does not need to be as short as a month, but should probably be shorter than a year, as large inflationary or deflationary movements can take place in twelve months. If monthly adjustments proved to be inconvenient, quarterly or bimonthly adjustments could be tried.

depend on the *movement* of money income during the past
month. Thus, if money income has risen during the past month,
beyond an amount designated, the rate of tax in the next month
should be increased in order to prevent inflation. If the money
income has declined during the past month, the rate of tax
should be lowered in order to counteract this decline in income
and so to prevent deflation and unemployment.

The sensitivity of tax adjustments

The best ratio between the change in the tax rate and the
change in national income would have to be determined by
experience. If the ratio is too small, the adjustments will not
be sensitive enough to counterbalance fluctuations. If the ratio
is too large, the adjustments would be supersensitive and might
of themselves lead to instability. The proper ratio depends on
the degree to which a change in the tax rate changes income.
If a change in the tax rate causes expenditure, and therefore
income, to change by an equal amount, a decline in income
could be offset by an equal absolute decline in the amount of
the tax. It is probable, however, that a change in tax causes
a smaller change in expenditure and income: thus, if I discover
that instead of paying $100 tax I only have to pay $90, I may
increase my expenditures by $5 but am unlikely to increase
them by the full $10 reduction in the tax. If income declines
by, say, $1,000,000, there must, therefore, be a greater reduction
in the tax, say of $2,000,000—in order to offset the decline in
income. Similarly, if income rises by $1,000,000, there should
be a greater increase in the total tax—say of $2,000,000 in order
to check expenditures. As the total tax yield is only a small
proportion of the total income, the proportionate change in the
tax rate must be greater than the proportionate change in
income. It should be observed that within limits the exact sensitivity of the adjustment is not very important. The exact
sensitivity of a governor on an engine is not important, as
long as it "governs"—that is, as long as it brings into play a
speeding-up process when the engine is running too slow and
a slowing-down process when the engine is running too fast.
The tax system should be the "governor" of the monetary sys-

tem, and its exact sensitivity is not important as long as it brings into play inflationary forces when the system is running into deflation, and deflationary forces when the system is running into inflation.

Why adjust taxes rather than governmental expeditures?

There are important reasons for selecting government *receipts* as the balancing item rather than government expenditure. The total of government expenditure that is not self-financed should be determined mainly by social and political considerations, not by monetary considerations. If the government decides to build dams, roads, houses, schools, and so forth, and to go in for the development of public works, these expenditures should be determined on their own merits, and not with a view to their effects on money income. Otherwise, "boondoggling" is inevitable, with the resultant waste of resources—a waste that is inexcusable when other and cheaper means are available to produce full employment. Likewise with social security schemes; these too should be considered with regard to the ideals of distributional justice; they should not be treated as a means of avoiding or of recovering from depressions. If, for instance, the government decides that a basic minimum standard of life must be and can be provided, this decision will have a profound effect upon the total of government expenditure. In times of deflation, expenditures under such a scheme would have a desirable effect; in times of inflation, an undesirable effect, from the point of view of the stability of money income. They must, therefore, be justified on their own merits; otherwise, the whole system of distributional justice will be thrown into confusion by the constant adjustments necessary to keep money income stable.

It is unfortunate that the exponents of the deficit-spending method of increasing money incomes have concentrated so much in their propaganda on the expansion of government *expenditure,* which is often difficult and subject to grave abuses, when exactly the same result could be achieved, with much less difficulty, by the contraction of government *receipts.* The tax system, especially when the basic tax is an income tax, is highly flexible, as is shown in time of war. The rates of income tax can easily be raised or lowered; every rise in the rate will have a deflationary effect in incomes, for it will reduce people's expenditures, every fall in the rate will have an inflationary effect on incomes, for it will increase people's expenditures. If income tax is collected on a "current" basis, adjustments could be made quickly and easily without disrupting the long-period character of governmental expenditures.

The possibility of negative taxation

It may be objected, with some force, that under ordinary peacetime conditions the total of government receipts is not large enough to control the total national money income. Consider, for instance, what happened between 1929 and 1933— a reduction of the national money income from about 90 billion to about 45 billion dollars. If the "multiplier" was only equal to 1, it would have required a budget deficit of 45 billion in 1933 to bring national income back to the 1929 level. In fact, a deficit of some 20-30 billion would have been enough, but as government expenditure then was only about 5 billion, even the complete abolition of all taxes would not have produced a sufficient budget deficit. Of course, in 1943 a budget deficit of 45 billion seemed quite small, but in peacetime it appears undesirable to have a volume of governmental expenditure equal to what is accepted in time of war. It would seem at first sight, therefore, as if the adjustable tax plan necessarily assumes a volume of governmental expenditure equal to a substantial proportion— say 25 per cent—of the national income. This is not the case, however, if we once admit the possibility of *negative taxes*. There is no particular reason why tax rates should stop at zero, if it is necessary to counteract a large deflationary movement of incomes. A negative tax rate would mean, of course, that the government would pay money to the taxpayer instead of taking money from him. There is nothing inherently ridiculous or unsound in this idea, however shocking it may sound by reason of its unfamiliarity. In fact, of course, if an adjustable tax plan were in operation, it is likely that the adjustments that actually had to be made would be relatively small, for if people *knew* that deflation or inflation would both be prevented, they would not expect deflations or inflations, and as we have seen, it is the expectation of price and income movements which is the main factor in causing them. It is highly unlikely that under an adjustable tax plan deflation would ever be allowed to proceed to the point where negative taxes were necessary, especially with postwar budgets running around 20-30 billion dollars. Nevertheless, the possibility should be allowed.

The adjustable tax plan under zero government expenditure

The essential nature and purpose of taxation under an adjustable tax plan can be seen very clearly if we suppose that governmental expenses were nil, so that the average rate of taxation would be zero. Then the tax rate would fluctuate between positive and negative levels, accordingly as inflation or deflation threatened. Once we get out of our heads that the *primary* purpose of taxation is to "raise money for the government to spend," we can see the true purpose of taxation, as the most powerful weapon in our hands for the stabilizing of money prices and incomes.[2] On the one hand the tax system would have a vital function to perform in society even if there were no governmental expenditure at all, and on the other hand the tax system is not even necessary to enable the government to make expenditures. The government, by virtue of its power of creating money, is the principal organ of society that can make expenditures without getting receipts. Through the operations of the banking system, business as a whole may also be in this position, but the government is the only agency large enough to use its money-creating and money-destroying power to prevent fluctuations. Because it is the only agency that has the power, it is the only agency that can accept the responsibility.

---

[2] This proposition applies strictly only to the tax systems of sovereign national states, which have the power of creating money. It does not, of course, apply to local governmental units, such as cities, counties, school districts, or states. For such units taxation must always be primarily a means of raising revenue, and the conventional canons of orthodox finance (for example, balancing the budget, borrowing only for capital investment, and so on) are more likely to apply. A strong case can be made however for the integration of local taxation into the over-all system, so that changes in local taxes at least do not counteract the efforts of the national government to stabilize incomes.

Criticisms of the adjustable tax plan: Effects on distribution

Our next task is to anticipate certain criticisms of the adjustable tax plan and to point out certain difficulties that may be encountered. One difficulty is that the tax system, as well as the expenditures of government, is part of the system of redistribution of income. A progressive income tax is rightly regarded as one of the principal means available to a capitalist government whereby a more equitable distribution of income can be achieved. Under the adjustable tax plan, if the adjustments were all made in *rates,* in times of deflation, when taxes were lowered, the rich would gain proportionately more than the poor. In a period of deflation so extreme that the plan called for negative taxes, the rich would presumably be paid more than the poor, for the payments from the government would be calculated exactly as income tax payments are calculated now. The problem is not perhaps so important as it may appear, for situations in which large reductions in taxes are necessary are unlikely to occur very often, while the rich will suffer proportionately higher taxation in periods when inflation threatens. However, it is not impossible to devise a system which will permit wide fluctuation in the total volume of tax receipts and yet will not destroy the progressive nature of the income tax. This can be done by setting up a standard schedule of taxation, based on the volume of normal government expenditure. Then the adjustment necessary to maintain stability could be made in the form of an *absolute* addition or subtraction from income above the desired minimum. In this way, the progressive character of the tax structure could be maintained even though the basic yield of taxes fluctuated.

Effects on the national debt: Financing the budget deficit by borrowing from the public

Perhaps the most important criticism of the adjustable tax plan is that it would involve an apparently endless increase in the national debt. This point is of such importance that it will be well to examine it in some detail. There are three possible ways of financing a budget deficit. One is by borrowing from the public. The second is by borrowing from the banks. The third is by printing money—greenbacks. The effect of a budget deficit will depend very much on the method adopted to finance it. Borrowing from the public has a direct deflationary effect which may in large part counterbalance the inflationary effect of the deficit. It is, therefore, a wholly inappropriate method of deficit financing when the purpose of the deficit is to prevent deflation. The method is, however, desirable when the deficit is due to a large and sudden increase in government expenditure, such as that due to war. In that case the danger is inflation rather than deflation, and if for political reasons, or even for economic reasons, the deficit cannot be met by taxation, borrowing from the public is one way of helping to prevent inflation. In the case of a very expensive war, such as World War II, it is virtually impossible, quite apart from political difficulties, to devise a tax system which will be adequate to finance it, for when taxes up to 50 per cent or more of the national income are required, it would be necessary to tax each individual strictly according to his capacity to pay. This plan would be administratively impossible, so part of the public's surplus funds must be siphoned off by voluntary lending.

Borrowing from banks

Government borrowing from the banks has a much more directly inflationary effect. When the government borrows from the public the first result is to reduce the public's holdings of money; even when the borrowed money is spent, and so comes back to the public, there is no net increase in the public's holding of money; there is merely an increase in its holding of government securities. When, however, the government borrows from the banks (that is, sells government securities to them) the banks pay for these securities by giving newly created bank deposits to the government. In the first instance, there is no withdrawal of purchasing power from the public, unless the bank is forced by the government borrowings to call in some private loans, which is not usually the case. When the government spends the bank deposits so acquired they come into the hands of the public. The net result of government borrowing from the banks is an increase in the total of bank deposits in the hands of the public. This makes people more willing to spend, and has a directly inflationary effect. In time of war it is, therefore, an undesirable method of financing a deficit; in time of deflation, however, it is more suitable than borrowing from the public.

Government borrowing from the banks has one undesirable consequence. Government securities come to occupy a larger and larger place in the assets of banks, and hence the stability of the banking system comes to depend in an alarming degree on the price of government securities. If the process went on long enough, we should find almost the whole of bank assets consisting of government bonds. A fall in the price of government bonds in that case would render many banks insolvent. Even today many banks have something like 60-70 per cent of their total assets in the form of government securities. A mere five per cent fall in the price of these securities would wipe out the whole capital of some of the most respected banks in the country. Where these securities are very short term, with maturities of under a year, the likelihood of such a fall in their value is not great, for the prospect of the repayment of the bond within a short period makes it unlikely that there will be any great fall in its value. It is quite possible, however, for long-term government bonds to fall sharply in value; indeed, they will do so if there is any rise in the rate of interest. As banks are increasingly looking to long-term government securities for their earning assets (as short-term bonds pay very low interest) the danger to the banking system of a fall in the price of government bonds is not to be dismissed lightly.

The ownership of great quantities of government securities by the banks also has the effect of weakening the already weak control of the Federal Reserve System over the member banks, particularly in regard to an inflation of credit. As long as the bank's portfolios are swollen with government bonds, it is impossible for the Federal Reserve Board to pursue an anti-inflationary policy. If the Federal Reserve Banks raise their rediscount rate, or if they sell government securities, the result may be a fall in the price of these securities which will seriously endanger the financial position of the member banks.

Issue of greenbacks

The third method of financing a government deficit is by the issue of paper money ("Greenbacks"). This has the advantage over the other two methods that it does not entail any interest payments. A greenback is, in fact, a noninterest-bearing government security, redeemable in payment of taxes and hence so liquid that it is indistinguishable from money, and circulates from hand to hand in the payment of all debts. Nowadays, virtually all our money has this "fiat" character, as neither silver certificates nor federal reserve notes are redeemable in silver or gold by the general public. Even silver dollars and our subsidiary coins (quarters, nickels, and so forth) are not really "hard money", for the value of the metal which they contain is less than their face value. Our coins, that is to say, are "bills" printed on rather expensive material. The issue of greenbacks is likely also to have the effect of increasing bank deposits. There is a certain ratio of notes ("pocket money") to deposits which the public normally wishes to hold. If more notes are issued, the people who receive them will pay most of them into their bank accounts—that is, will exchange them for bank deposits. Suppose, for instance, that people wish to hold 10 per cent of their money (their liquid funds) in the form of notes-in-the-wallet, and 90 per cent in the form of bank deposits. Then, out of every million dollars of notes issued to the public, $900,000 will be paid into the banks in exchange for bank deposits. The banks will in turn pay the bulk of these notes over to the Federal Reserve Banks in exchange for a Federal Reserve·deposit. This will increase the *power* of the banks to lend, and hence may result in a still further increase in deposits. It does not, however, force the banks to expand their loans and thus may not lead to a further increase in deposits if the banks prefer to allow their reserve ratio to rise.

Each method has its place

All three of these methods of financing a budget deficit may be used, depending on the circumstances. In time of war, the adjustable tax plan would result in a large increase in taxes, in order to combat inflation, but it might not be possible to finance the whole budget by taxation, and borrowing from the public would then be the most desirable method. In time of normal government expenditure and threatened deflation, a combination of finance by borrowing from the banks and by issuing notes would probably be most desirable. Which method predominates depends on the rate at which we wish to increase the national debt. In times of severe debt-deflation when private debt has diminished greatly, there is something to be said for increasing the national debt. There is a certain demand for bonds and similar debt-instruments, and if the issue of private bonds is not sufficient to satisfy this demand on the part of investors, the price of bonds will rise—that is, the rate of interest will fall. If the rate on bonds falls too low new funds may be diverted to stock speculation. This could be checked by the issue of government bonds, which of itself would have an effect in lowering the price of bonds and raising the rate of interest. If, on the other hand, the volume of private debt was very large, bond prices were low and rates of interest high, it would be desirable to finance deficits by the issue of notes. This would have the effect of bidding up bond prices and lowering the rate of interest.

No need to fear an uncontrolled increase in the national debt

In any event, there is no reason to fear an uncontrolled increase in the national debt as a result of the adjustable tax plan. It would be perfectly possible to finance the plan in times of threatened deflation without any recourse to government borrowing at all, by the issue of paper money. Under the plan, it would be possible to regulate the national debt as part of the general debt structure and to increase it or to diminish it as conditions in the private debt market require. There is no real reason to fear that the growth of the national debt will make it more difficult to achieve a just system of distribution. It is true, of course, that insofar as the debt is held, directly or indirectly, by the richer half of the population, it has the result of diverting income from the poorer to the richer part of society. But this effect could easily be counteracted by a system of progressive taxation. It may be argued, of course, that for political reasons this will not be done, and that therefore the growth of the national debt will have a retroactive effect on the distribution of income. There is, however, no economic necessity for such to be the case.

Government spending and business confidence

Yet another argument against any type of deficit finance program is that government spending impairs business confidence, and that the income-creating effects of government deficits are more than counterbalanced by the resulting decline in private spending, and growth in private budget surpluses. The point is an important one. There is little doubt that in the era of deficit spending from 1933 to 1939 the income-increasing effects of government expenditure were offset to some degree by the income-decreasing effect of the decline in private, and especially in corporate expenditure, a decline which was in turn due to fears engendered by the radical behavior of the government. Nevertheless, the experience of the war shows that it is all too easy to expand the budget deficit in times of grave emergency far beyond the rate that is necessary to maintain full employment and into the danger-zone of inflation. Is it too much to hope that the abolition of unemployment, or even the abolition of poverty, can be a task at least as inspiring as the destruction of an enemy? For it is literally true that the only thing that prevents us abolishing unemployment and extreme poverty, in the Western World at least, is the lack of will to do it.

The "Hang-over Theory" of depressions

One final argument may be considered in criticism of any scheme that proposes to do away with unemployment. There is a school of thought (called by Dr. Wernette [3] the "Hang-over School") that regards depressions as necessary in order to liquidate the bad investments made in time of boom. This school regards all attempts to alleviate depressions as likely actually to prolong them, by preventing the liquidations, bankruptcies, and economic adjustments which it is the depression's business

---

[3] Wernette, J. Philip, *The Control of Business Cycles*. New York: Farrar & Rinehart, 1941.

to effect. On this view the ideal depression is a short, sharp one, and if governmental intervention is to be applied at all, it should be in the direction of accentuating rather than alleviating the depression, on the ground that a quick death is better than a lingering illness. There is something to be said for this view on the side of historical evidence. It seems to be true that the worst depressions—those of the 1870's and the 1930's—occurred in periods of "easy money," and depressions such as those of 1920-1922 or 1857, in which the decline in prices was precipitous and unalleviated, proved to be short, their bottoms were soon reached, and recovery soon began. If this view were true, it would indeed strike at the very foundation of the adjustable tax plan. It therefore deserves our most serious consideration.

Nonmonetary causes of depressions

The problem resolves itself into two questions. The first is whether fluctuations in trade and income can be traced to causes outside the behavior of money—that is, are there causes for depressions operating from the side of commodities rather than from the side of money? The answer to this question is undoubtedly in the affirmative—indeed, the most fundamental causes of economic fluctuations are found in the structure of real capital. So much must be conceded to the "hang-over" school. The second question is whether a deflation of prices and incomes is necessary in order to make the necessary readjustments in the capital structure which depression accomplishes. The "hang-over" school seem to think that this is necessary—that all must suffer vicariously for the excesses of a few investors during a boom. This last question, however, I should answer firmly in the negative. There is nothing in a *general* deflation which assists in correcting economic maladjustments; its effect is simply to multiply and to spread over the whole economy what should have been confined to a small sector.

Too rapid investment

There are three main forces operating on the "commodity" or "real capital" side to bring about depressions. The first is that rapid investment in particular forms of capital goods, especially those with long life, leads to a distortion in the age distribution of these goods which in turn leads to an abnormal demand for their replacement every so often—the period of the cycle depending on the length of life of the commodity. Suppose, for instance, that houses have a period of active use of 25 years. If there is a big building boom in a new town, the town may become supplied with fairly new houses; when there are enough for the population, building will almost cease. Then in another twenty-five years the original group of houses will have become obsolete and will have to be replaced, and there will be another building boom, to be followed by another twenty or twenty-five years of very slack building activity.

Bad investments made in boom

The second non-monetary force operating to bring about depressions is the fact that in periods of business optimism at the height of a boom, rising prices lead the judgment of business-men astray and investments are made which in fact cannot be profitable. It is hardly an exaggeration to say that a boom is a time when bad investments are made, the crisis is the moment when this sad fact is discovered, and the depression is the time when these investments are slowly liquidated. In Detroit in 1928, for instance, many new office buildings were started under the rosy illusions of the "new era." By 1929 it was painfully apparent that these could not possibly be profitable, and work on many of them ceased overnight.

Impossibility of accumulating physical capital for ever

The third non-monetary factor is the fact, already noted, that as capital is accumulated and as the total stock of all goods grows with the process of investment, it becomes increasingly difficult to find new profitable opportunities for investment. It is obvious in the case of the simpler commodities, such as wheat or cotton, that there comes a point in the accumulation of stocks beyond which investment in stocks of these commodi-ties becomes impossible, for any increase in the physical stock leads to so great a fall in the price of the commodity that the value of the stock actually declines. This is also true of com-modities in general, and accounts very largely for the difficulties of our present time.

The futility of deflation

In none of these three cases, however, is a deflation of money incomes and prices any help in solving the fundamental problems which they raise. In the first case, a depression in one industry can easily become a general depression through the "multiplier effect" if steps are not taken to prevent it. A decline in building, for instance, causes a decline in the incomes of the building trades, and the subsequent decline in expenditure of individuals whose incomes come from building is reflected in a decline in incomes all through the system. In the second case also, where industries have been built up through faulty investments that cannot be maintained, the results of the fall in incomes in these industries is again to cause a fall throughout the system. The process of "readjustment" that is so often talked about consists really in getting people and resources out of the overexpanded industries into others. A general deflation and depression *prevents* this from happening; the fluctuations in building, for instance, actually cause depression and unemployment in other industries, which cannot possibly expand to meet the decline in building under these circumstances. If money income could be held reasonably stable, this would not prevent depressions from occurring in particular industries and localities, but it would prevent these depressions becoming universal. *Local* depression is a necessary result of economic progress—the development of railroads undoubtedly caused a depression in the stagecoach industry! But *general* depression is inexcusable, for it prevents the transfer of resources out of declining into expanding industries and even reverses the desirable movements. Thus, in the course of economic progress, resources always have to be squeezed out of agriculture; but during a depression, the unemployment in the towns actually causes a return to the farms— a sure sign of economic retrogression. If, then, money incomes can be held fairly stable through the adjustable tax plan, a depression in one industry, due to any cause whatever, can be counterbalanced by prosperity in others, and resources can fairly easily be moved from declining to expanding industries.

Other elements of a full employment policy: The encouragement of investment

The adjustable tax plan would in itself be a guarantee against the worst consequences of general deflation or inflation. It must be remembered, however, that both deflation and inflation are themselves only symptoms of deeper diseases in the economic body. In constructing a well-rounded policy for full employment, therefore, these deeper causes should be taken into consideration and some direct remedies applied. We have seen that the fundamental cause of deflation and depression is that the rate of consumption lags so far behind the rate of production that capitalists are not willing to increase their holdings (that is, "to invest") fast enough to keep pace with accumulation. There are two lines of action which attack the problem. The first is to encourage consumption, so that the gap between production and consumption narrows and the rate of accumulation falls to that which capitalists are willing to countenance at existing price and income levels. This is the main object of the adjustable tax plan: by lowering taxes, or even making them negative in times of great deflationary pressure and rising unemployment, consumption would be encouraged and accumulation diminished. It may also be possible to encourage consumption directly, by direct subsidy or gift—for example, the distribution of milk to children, school meals, free education, the food stamp plan, and the like. However, there is also a second line of attack—to encourage investment, that is, to increase the willingness of capitalists to hold the increased quantities of goods which accumulation creates.

The danger of overconsumption

The importance of giving encouragement to investment is easy to underestimate, as well as to overestimate. On the one hand are those who seem to think that only by encouraging investment can unemployment be prevented, and who therefore advocate subsidies to the capitalist, or failing that, vast programs of public works. Presumably the flood of accumulation is to go on until the whole earth is covered with concrete! It is obvious, however, that beyond a certain point investment.

is stupid, and that the encouragement of investment is no *permanent* answer to the problem. Ultimately, we cannot avoid the necessity of enjoying the fruits of our labors, if we do not wish merely to destroy them. Nevertheless, at the present moment we are still an appreciable way from that idyllic time when further investment will be unnecessary. There are hundreds of millions of people to be equipped with the houses, furniture, tools, and machinery that modern techniques make possible. It would be folly to try to accumulate forever, but it would be equal folly to pursue a policy that would expand consumption in the present to the point where accumulation stops now, and the existing underequipped state of the world is perpetuated. We do not want to raise the standard of consumption to the point where full employment was only obtained at the price of a steady decline in the quantity and quality of our equipment, and therefore in our productive powers. This might happen, even under the adjustable tax plan, if the results of the plan were to make čapitalists wholly unwilling to invest. Thus, suppose that each fall in the tax rate led not only to an increase in consumption but to a decline in the willingness to invest, no matter to what irrational beliefs this decline was due. Then the deflationary pressure would continue even under substantial budget deficits—indeed, the deficit would be filling a gap that would continually grow as it was filled. Eventually, as deficits were increased, the increase in consumption would catch up with the decline in the willingness to invest and further deficits would be unnecessary, but this point may not be reached until capital is actually *decumulating,* with consumption exceeding production. Such a state might be worse than unemployment itself.

Defects of a property tax

In the present state of the world, therefore, it is important that we should reach a state of full employment while there is still a marked amount of investment going on. One method of doing this, as we shall see in the next chapter, is by the encouragement of foreign investment. In devising its general tax policies, however, government should take into consideration the effect of the *method* of raising taxes on the general willingness of capitalists to hold their resources in the form of goods, that is, to invest, or to conduct enterprises, and should reject methods of taxation that discourage enterprise. Thus, property taxes as such are much open to criticism—it is much better to base the amount of tax that an individual or a corporation has to pay on its income rather than on its property. Property taxes are not important in national taxation, but they are important at the local level. To what extent the system of local taxation is responsible for our slums and the generally backward state of housing is not known, but would be worth inquiry. There may be a strong case for shifting local taxes from a property to an income basis.[4]

Defects in the annual income tax: The penalizing of risk-bearing

There is a serious defect in our present income tax which militates against enterprise and investment, and should be rectified. It lies in the fact that income is reckoned annually and that no account is taken of the fluctuation of incomes from year to year. This is of great importance when the income tax is steeply progressive, since it means that an individual or enterprise with sharply fluctuating income in reality pays a higher rate of tax than an individual with a steady income. Thus, an individual who received $100,000 in one year and nothing for nine years after that would have to pay, in surtax, $59,140 under the 1943 schedule. On the other hand, if he received $10,000 every year for ten years, he would only have to pay $2,020 each year or a total of $20,200. Thus, an identical income, spread over ten years is liable for only about 40 per cent of the tax that would be incurred if the income were bunched into one of the ten years. This cannot fail to have an adverse effect on the willingness to bear risks and to make risky investments. The receipts of the capitalist are by their very nature subject to fluctuation, and a tax system which discriminates against risk cannot help but discriminate against investment.

---

[4] Such a shift would have to be accompanied by a "capital levy" on the rise in property values due to the removal of the tax, in order to prevent an unearned increment going to the existing property holders.

The remedies: cumulative tax base

The real problem here is the fallacy of identifying "income" with "net receipts." The receipts of the man who gets $100,000 in one year and nothing for nine years therefore should obviously not all be counted as "income" in the first year: if the rate of interest were zero, only $10,000 of his $100,000 should count as "income" and the rest as a capital asset that gradually depreciated during the next nine years. Capital accounting, however, especially as applied to human assets such as abilities, bodies, and minds, is in so primitive a state that it is virtually impossible to construct a satisfactory workable definition of annual income which can be used as a basis for an income tax. A simple remedy, however, seems to be available: to permit the cumulative averaging of taxable income over an indefinite number of years in the computation of the tax. Provision is made in the tax law of the United States for the averaging of the income of a corporation over three years, but this is a quite inadequate period and the privilege is not extended to individuals. If the tax liability were to be reckoned on the average of all receipts since the individual began paying taxes, or even since some date reasonably far in the past—say ten years—and if past tax payments could be credited against present liabilities, much of the inequity in regard to fluctuating incomes would be removed. Thus, the man who received $100,000 in one year would pay his $59,140 tax, but if he received nothing in the next year his tax liability would be reckoned as $50,000 for two years, and a refund would be in order.[5]

An expenditures tax

Another possible solution to this problem is to base tax payments on *expenditure* rather than on income. The administration of such a tax would probably be more difficult than that of an income tax, though there is no reason why it should be impossible. Difficulties would arise, however, in cases where there was a large expenditure on durable goods. Unless some allowance were made to enable the expenditure on durable goods to be

---

[5] On this point see Groves, Harold M., *Production, Jobs and Taxes*, Chapter IX. New York: McGraw-Hill, 1944.

spread, for tax base purposes, over the length of life of the goods, an expenditures tax would penalize investment, especially in durable consumers goods, and would therefore be undesirable. An expenditures tax, also, is apt to be less "progressive" in its upper brackets than an income tax. It seems likely that the modifications in the income tax suggested above would be sufficient to take care of the problem of discrimination against risk.

Subsidies to enterprise

Another interesting question in tax policy is whether the tax system could encourage investment directly by subsidies or rebates. It is a familiar proposition in the theory of taxation that a "franchise" tax—that is, a fixed sum independent of the quantity of output—is not likely to affect the output of an enterprise, since it reduces profits at each output, but does not change the output at which profits are a maximum. On the other hand, a subsidy or a rebate of taxation whose magnitude varied directly, or even progressively, with output would have a stimulating effect on production. One might expect a combination of a fixed tax with a rebate on high levels of production to have a favorable effect on production and employment. The administrative difficulties in the way of such a plan are considerable, but not insuperable, and the possibilities of a plan to encourage the expansion of output and penalize contraction are at least worth investigation.

Corporation income tax. Difficulties of "soaking the rich"

A feature of the existing tax law which has come in for much criticism is the corporation income tax. It is argued that the corporation stockholder pays income tax twice—once when the corporation pays it and again when he pays his personal income tax. There is much justice in this criticism, and there is little doubt that the corporation income tax acts as a hindrance to investment. There arises here as we have seen elsewhere a certain rivalry between the various ends of economic policy—in this case the end of distributional justice on the one hand and of full employment on the other. From the point of view of distributional justice, there is everything to be said for "soaking the rich." From the point of view of full employment, however, it is a regrettable fact that it is the rich who own most of the stockpile, and if they are "soaked" too much they may refuse to perform this function of "holding the stock," in which case full employment could only be attained at the cost of disinvestment and the running down of the stockpile. The only escape from the dilemma seems to be to penalize the rich in ways which will not discourage their willingness to hold and to increase their holdings of capital goods. The possibility of taxes on liquid funds, noted in the previous chapter, might be an important instrument of policy in this connection.

Public investment

There is yet another element in an investment policy besides the encouragement of private investment, and that is public investment. If private individuals are not willing to increase their holdings of capital goods, then it may be necessary for the government to increase its holdings. This is the basis of the "public works" path to prosperity, and while it may easily lead to unproductive employment and the building of unnecessary dams, monuments, or pyramids, it nevertheless has its place. There is a large field of investment where, for various reasons, private investment cannot assume responsibility. The building of roads is one of the best examples: the provision of education, libraries, museums, playgrounds and the like also seems to fall largely into this category. It is becoming increasingly apparent that the field of housing is also one where there is a strong case for a good deal of public investment. In general, the longer the length of life of the investment, and the more important are those non-monetary benefits derived from it which cannot be collected by the investor, the stronger is the case for public as against private investment. It must not be thought, however, that public and private investment are mutually exclusive. In some fields they may be; but even in such a field as housing, the European experience and the British experience have shown that it is quite possible for public investment, for example, in housing, not only to co-exist with, but even to stimulate private investment of a similar kind.

Conclusion: The shadow of the stationary state

When everything has been said about the desirability of stimulating investment, however, it remains true that the most important long-run problem of Western society is that of raising the standard of consumption.

The institutions of nineteenth century capitalism were admirably adapted to a society in which investment was proceeding at a rapid pace. It is no exaggeration to say that capitalism found an empty world, and filled it—filled it with roads and railroads, steamships and automobiles, grain elevators and factories, skyscrapers and state capitols. For nearly two centuries the economic world has been an "expanding universe"—expanding geographically, expanding in population, expanding in capital equipment, expanding in the total value of its wealth. We are now somewhere within sight of an era in which *income* can rise but *capital* will not; in which there will be no necessity for net investment, except as new discoveries occasionally shake up the existing structure, and in which, therefore, the rate of production will have to equal the rate of consumption. It is the shadow of the classical "stationary state" that hovers over our day, and though it may be postponed by wars, by new discoveries, and by the opening up of new geographical areas to investment, yet these things only seem to be a postponement. It is true that the devastation of Europe will open up a great field of investment; but in twenty years we shall hardly know there has been a war. It is true also that if a stable political system can be established in Asia, there are great potentialities for investment there. But all these things but postpone what Keynes has called the "day of judgment" when no more new investment will be necessary. In that day also there can be no saving; no increase in the aggregate of private net worths, and the problem before us will be—shall this be accomplished by an increase in consumption, or by a decline in production through desperate unemployment; shall we enter this period with triumph and thanksgiving, as the manifold labors of mankind now yield their long-awaited fruit, or shall it be a day of wholly unnecessary unemployment, when the fruits of the ages shall be spilt on the ground and men shall starve out of their very abundance? Upon our courageous and intelligent handling of the monetary and fiscal system the answer depends. Deflation attempts to solve the problem by restricting production until we are so poor that we are forced to consume all the pittance we produce. War attempts to solve the problem by a vast, indiscriminate, and costly destruction of wealth. There is no reason in the world, apart from ignorance, why this should be; why we should not direct our fiscal and monetary policies toward an ultimate expansion of consumption commensurate with the capacities of a technical age, and our political policies towards the speedy abolition of international anarchy and war.

CHAPTER 10

The Reconstruction of International Trade

International trade in its prime

Among the economic problems which troubled men's minds between the two world wars that of restoring international trade and investment loomed large—perhaps disproportionately large. By the beginning of the twentieth century a world-wide system of international trade and investment had grown up under the protection of a well-nigh universal gold standard. The achievements of this system were substantial. The prosperity of the Western World, and especially of Western Europe, seemed to be closely bound up with it. The immense merchant fleets of the Western European countries—England, Norway, Holland, France, Germany—carried on a world-wide exchange of products on a scale larger than history had ever known. The tropical products—spices, fruits, nuts—which once had been luxuries became commonplaces of working-class consumption. Tropical oilseeds produced the milk of Britain and Denmark. Tin and rubber from Malaya, copra from the South Seas, coffee from Brazil, whale oil from the Antarctic, flowed to Europe to raise the standard of living there. More important still in volume, a flood of manufactured products flowed among all nations. The rails and rolling stock of the two Atlantic seaboards spread around the world to open up great new areas to western techniques. The hardware and textiles of Europe entered into the consumption of the whole world.

The finance of international trade and investment

Parallel with these developments in trade and consumption went the growth of a complex financial structure, largely centered on London. The ultimate economic purpose of the international financial structure is, of course, that of the financial structure in general—to permit the separation of the ultimate ownership (equity) of physical things from their administration and use. In international trade this has two aspects: there is the problem of the finance of things in transit—that is, the finance of "trade" in the narrow sense of the term, and there is also the problem of the finance of permanent improvements and equipment, that is, of "investment." This distinction must not be pressed too far, for all trade involves investment; but it corresponds to the broad distinction between "short-run" and "long-run" finance.

The problem of the finance of "trade" concerns the ownership of commodities in transit—for example, on trains, on the high seas, and in temporary storage. The financial system, through the issue and acceptance of bills of exchange, permits a specialization to take place between the "trader" who organizes and administers the transit and storage of goods and the "financier" who really "owns" them—that is, who holds the equity in them. That is to say the trader, by discounting a bill of exchange—by borrowing from the financier—is able to ship goods in larger volume than his personal capital would allow. This specialization evidently results in an increase in trade, for it enables the skilled trader to organize a much larger volume of trade than would be possible if he were limited to the value of goods in transit represented by his own capital.

In like manner the issue of long-term securities on an international scale permits poor, undeveloped countries to increase their equipment by importing a greater value than they export, while the rich, highly capitalized countries are enabled to export a greater value than they import, the difference representing the equity in the equipment and new developments abroad. By this means, the technical advances of the Western World were diffused through the less technically advanced quarters of the globe, and while the record of foreign investment is stained with many examples of exploitation and corruption, there is little doubt that on the whole it deserves a credit balance in the moral ledger.

The decline of international investment

The whole international economic order ·was disrupted by the first world war and never really recovered. ·Particularly was international investment in durable goods destroyed; trade recovered to a substantial extent in the twenties, though the depression of the thirties brought about a spectacular decline. The decay of international investment is not difficult to understand. No capitalist will invest in foreign securities unless he feels reasonably sure of his future returns. But the risks of foreign as opposed to domestic investment are greatly increased by political instability and by instability of the exchange rates. A New York capitalist will not invest in Brazil unless he feels fairly sure that there will be neither a political upheaval leading to the expropriation of his property, nor a violent shift in the ratio of exchange between Brazilian and American currency, for his future payments will most probably have to be transferred from milreis to dollars. In the twenties and thirties not only was the world political situation uncertain in a high degree, but the gyrations of the exchange rates, especially from 1918 to 1925, were such as the financial world had never before experienced.

Can the "good old days" return?

It was little wonder that the financial advisers of·the twenties saw the problem primarily in terms ·of a return to the "good old days" of a universal gold standard, reasonably ·free trade, and extensive foreign investment. In spite of many sincere attempts to follow the orthodox advice, however, it became clear in the thirties that the old recipes, however well they might have worked before 1914, were quite inadequate to deal with the new world situation. Those countries, such as Czecho-Slovakia and Great Britain, which followed the path of financial orthodoxy, balancing their budgets and returning to the gold standard, did so at the cost of severe internal depression and unemployment. It is true that from 1924 to 1929 there was a period when it looked as if the old gods were to be re-throned; the gold standard was revived, exchange rates were stabilized, trade revived, even international investment, especially in German securities, revived; the reparations problem seemed to have been solved, production revived, and unemployment diminished;

Germany joined the League of Nations, the international political situation stabilized itself, and it looked almost as if the good old days were to come again. But the world deflation of 1929-1933 broke the whole structure in pieces; the gold standard as an effective international system disappeared, protectionism increased by leaps and bounds, using not only the old methods of tariff raising but newer and more destructive methods such as import quotas, exchange control, and competitive currency depreciation; international investment dried up almost completely, and the international political situation deteriorated to the point where a second world war became inevitable. We may well wonder, therefore, what the future has in store for us in this field; shall we see a repetition of the chaos of 1918-1939, or shall we see an attempt to solve the problem along new lines?

International trade as a sample of total trade

The great lesson that emerges from the experience of the past generation is that international trade is not a special problem to be solved by itself, but that it is part of the great body of total trade, and reflects the movements of trade in general. The tendency is for international trade specialists to treat "nations" as if they were economically homogeneous individuals trading around a table. The truth is quite otherwise; international trade is merely that part of the total web of trade which happens to cross international boundaries. Anything that affects the total movement is likely to affect that part of it which happens to cross frontiers, and while the existence of national frontiers, national currencies, and national trade and migration policies introduces certain complications into the movements of trade, these are only modifications of the total pattern and are not the pattern itself. Thus, a movement of goods from New York to Montreal is in no way fundamentally different from a movement of goods from New York to Washington; yet, because the former happens to cross an international boundary, the spotlight of interest is focused on it, and because the latter does not cross a national boundary, it often escapes even the notice of the statistician. The highly arbitrary character of our "international trade" statistics may be observed when national boundaries change. When the old Austro-

Hungarian empire split up into a number of new countries the "volume of international trade" was thereby raised merely by the creation of new frontiers; if the flows of trade had continued exactly as before, the volume of international trade would have been larger simply because some trade that previously had been "internal" was now "foreign." Foreign trade statistics, therefore, give us merely a sample, and a very inadequate and misleading sample, of the total volume of trade. How often, for instance, is it assumed that the net imports or exports of a certain country have a significance far beyond what the figures carry. When we break down the figures we find that the over-all picture is quite misleading. To take a single example: France normally is regarded as virtually self-sufficient in foodstuffs, having practically no net imports or exports. Yet when the figures are broken down by ports it becomes apparent that France is not one region, but at least two: the northern half of the country is a heavy net *exporter* of foodstuffs to the North sea coastal regions, while the southern half is a heavy *importer* of foodstuffs from across the Mediterranean. Consequently, as in World War II, it is quite possible for the north of France to be feeding moderately well while the south is starving.

The pattern of world trade

The natural trading areas of the world do not correspond in the least degree to national boundaries. It would be an interesting experiment to draw a map of the world in which the distances on the map were proportional not to the number of miles but to the cost of transport. On such a map the oceans would shrink to rivers, for water transport is far and away the cheapest of all forms of transport. We should see the great industrial areas facing both sides of the North Atlantic almost as one huge city: New York, Boston, Philadelphia, Baltimore, London, Liverpool, Glasgow, Southhampton, Rotterdam, Amsterdam, Bremen, and Hamburg would appear as suburbs of the great World-City, separated only by the narrow creek of the Atlantic, with all the other seaboard cities of the world not far away. Stretching away in great expanses from this hub would be the world's hinterlands—the near hinterlands connected by railroad, the far hinterlands beyond. It is hardly an exaggeration to say that international trade is a matter of what happens fifty miles from navigation; it is because Britain has no point more than 90 miles from navigation that her volume of international trade is so great. German international trade is largely a product of the Rhine; the international trade of North America, and much of its internal trade as well, is a product of the Great Lakes. It is well to remember occasionally that the Sault Ste Marie canal between Lake Superior and Lake Michigan carries a greater volume of trade than either Panama or Suez.

The need for interregional investment

In spite of the fact that the significance of international trade in the narrow sense is exaggerated by most writers on the subject, it remains true that the revival of international trade, and especially of international investment, is a problem of great importance for the postwar era. It would be more accurate to say that it is "interregional" rather than "international" trade and investment that is important, for in the event of the creation of a true world government, of course, "international" trade as such would be abolished altogether, and the business of interregional relations could be carried on without constant interruptions and perpetual hindrances. There is, however, a long-range task of great magnitude facing the world in the extension of the best technology to the backward areas. If "freedom from want" is to be a reality on a world scale, the technical standards of the highly developed tenth—the "core of civilization"—must be expanded into the more backward hinterlands. One essential element in this expansion, assuming as we must that the political disunity of the world (that is, its fragmentation into independent nations) will continue for many years to come, is the development of "foreign" investment, by the "rich" nations of the world in the "poor" nations.

—to equalize wealth and to prevent unemployment

Such investment is desirable for two reasons. Not only will it equalize standards of life throughout the world, a process which must go on before real world unity can be achieved, but also it will make it easier to maintain full employment in the rich capital-exporting countries. We have seen that unemployment is the result of a failure to increase consumption in the face of a declining rate of accumulation. Faced with bursting storerooms and stockpiles, an entirely self-contained economy can do only one of two things: increase consumption either by war or by subsidy, or diminish production. For any section of the world economy, however, there is another avenue of escape—the export of capital, or foreign investment. If the country threatened with unemployment can export a greater value of goods than it imports, the threatened glut of the stockpiles can be averted and full employment can be maintained. If therefore, as at present, there are strong prejudices against the sensible solution to the problem (that is, the subsidization of consumption), the only method of attaining full employment apart from war is to develop foreign investment. There is this much truth, perhaps, in the Marxian theory of imperialism, though it is not at all true, of course, that investment abroad necessitates political control of the recipient areas. Assuming, therefore, that it will take at least a generation for the internal solution to the unemployment problem to penetrate the minds of people in authority, there is everything to be said for the encouragement of foreign investment. It will be twice blessed: it will bless him that receives with roads, airfields, machinery, and other modern equipment, and will bless him that gives with more employment and a breathing spell in which to perform the vital task of economic education.

—and to help the transfer of resources

There is still another reason why foreign investment is so highly desirable in the coming decades. It may help to solve a difficult problem of readjustment of the *form* of production and the kinds of commodities produced. One source of the difficulties of the Western World is that our productive machine is designed for a rapidly increasing population. Thus, our construction industry is capable of taking care of the buildings and heavy equipment necessary for several million new people a year. With the declining rate of population growth and the shutting off of immigration, a severe readjustment will be necessary, involving a marked contraction of heavy industry and an expansion of light industry and the service trades. This adjustment can be made more slowly if outlets for the heavy industry products can be found in the export trade. This, however, is only likely if there is a substantial volume of foreign investment.

How can foreign investment be stimulated?

The question now arises, how can a sufficiently large volume of foreign investment be obtained. The solution seems to lie along two lines: the creation of conditions favorable to private investment on the one hand, and the development of public investment on the other. We have already seen that the prime conditions for private investment are political stability and exchange stability. Nothing perhaps illustrates the interrelatedness of the world's problems better than this: that in the absence of a reasonably stable political situation, foreign investment cannot expand, and in the absence of foreign investment or an adequate internal consumption policy, the economic situation will be so disastrous that it will bring down the political order with it—such, indeed, was the history of the interwar period. It is, alas, too much to expect a genuine international order to emerge from this war. There will undoubtedly, however, be some kind of loose international concert and some functional international institutions. It is clear already that the problem of exchange stability is in the forefront of the agenda for international postwar collaboration, as witness the plans prepared by Lord Keynes for the British Treasury, by Mr. White of the United States Treasury, by the joint committee of financial experts in April, 1944, and by the Bretton Woods, New Hampshire, conference. It may be well, therefore, to glance at some of the possible solutions.

The death of the gold standard

The most conservative solution would be, no doubt, a return to the free gold standard, or even to a modified gold standard as long as it included a fixed price for gold in terms of the national currencies and the unobstructed shipment of gold between financial centers. This would, as in the past, insure stability of exchange rates between those countries which adhered to it, though not of course between countries which adhered to it and those which did not. It is fairly evident today, however, that the gold standard, as an automatic, self-regulating international mechanism, is as dead as Marley, even though its ghost occasionally haunts the financial pages and editorial columns. Nations are not now, apparently, willing to accept the uncontrollable limitation on their monetary sovereignty which the gold standard involved. The failure of the British return to the gold standard from 1925 to 1931, and the discrediting of the gold standard in the British mind which followed the revival of 1931, make it virtually unthinkable that Britain will ever return to the gold standard except in a form so highly modified as to be unrecognizable. The United States, of course, because of its enormous gold stock, has a certain interest in preventing the total demonetization of gold. An effective restoration of the gold standard on a world-wide scale would seem to offer a method of disposing of America's "gold brick." Otherwise, the United States faces a dilemma: whether to continue to subsidize the gold-producing industry (mainly located in South Africa) by purchasing all gold offered at the high price of $35 per ounce, or whether to stop the gold purchases, in which case the gold would be effectively demonetized and its price would probably fall as spectacularly as did the price of silver in the 19th century, with consequent bookkeeping loss on the great gold stock now held. Indeed, it may fairly be said that America's only chance of ever *getting* $35 an ounce for her gold is the restoration of actual gold coinage in most other parts of the world—an event that we are not likely to see. But the United States cannot force other countries to adopt the gold standard in any form, and in view of the unwillingness of Britain to return to gold, it is probable that the gold standard will remain a closed episode of economic history. The most the United States will probably be able to do will be to see that gold will constitute part of the assets of any international clearing organization or stabilization fund set up in the postwar period.

Direct exchange stabilization

It seems probable, then, that some form of international monetary authority will be set up with the duty, among others, of stabilizing foreign exchange rates. This will be done mainly by direct "pegging"—that is, the purchase and sale of the currencies of the various countries at fixed prices. This is the technique of the "exchange equalization fund." Whereas the gold standard establishes stability of the exchanges indirectly by enabling currencies to be exchanged for gold at a fixed price, the exchange equalization fund enters the market directly and offers to purchase, say, pounds with dollars or dollars with pounds at a fixed price. It should be noticed that, for a time at least, a single country could fix the exchange rates of the whole world, subject to small differences due to costs of arbitrage, if it offered to buy and sell all other currencies for its own in unlimited quantities at fixed prices. Thus, if the equalization fund of the United States offered to buy and sell pounds for dollars at a rate of $4 to £1 and francs for dollars at a rate of $4 to 100 francs, all in unlimited quantities, then as long as the offer was good not only would it be impossible for the dollar price of pounds and francs in the market to differ much from the above rates, but also the pound-franc ratio would be fixed at about £1 = 100 francs.

Dangers of international rivalry in exchange stabilization

The necessity for international co-operation between national exchange equalization funds, or for an over-all international fund, can be clearly seen, however, if we envisage what would happen if two rival funds tried to peg the exchange rates at different levels. Suppose, for instance, that the British exchange equalization fund was offering to buy and sell dollars for pounds at a rate of $4.50 = £1, and the American fund was offering to buy and sell at a rate of $5=£1. Then people would rush to buy pounds, with dollars, from the British fund and sell them to the American fund, thereby making a gross profit of 50 cents on each $4.50. The British fund would soon find that all its resources were in the form of dollars, the American fund would find its resources in the form of pounds. Long before this point was reached, however, the managers of the respective funds would have to change their buying and selling prices and the stability of the exchange rates would have been lost.

Problems of an international exchange control

Even an international fund would have serious problems, however, especially in deciding the ratios at which it buys and sells foreign exchange. The political question alone is difficult enough—that of reaching agreement as to the operating exchange ratios. Any country which can fix the price of its currency at a level which is low relative to its internal price and income level will have a marked advantage in foreign markets that may last for some years even though it is essentially temporary in nature. Thus, if the British pound were fixed at $4, it would be much easier for British manufacturers to sell in the United States than if it were $5, assuming the level of British prices, wages, and money costs to be the same, for in the former case a British manufacturer could sell an article for $4 in the United States and still receive £1 for it, whereas in the latter case he would have to charge $5 in order to get £1 for it, and would not be able to sell as many. Similarly, American manufacturers would be better able to sell in Britain if £1 were worth $5 than if it were only worth $4. These advantages are essentially temporary, because the very encouragement of exports and discouragement of imports which a low currency valuation gives to a country tends of itself to bring about a situation in the foreign exchange market which will raise the value of the currency. If the equalization fund tries to peg a currency at too low a level, the result will be that the country's excessive exports will create a demand for its currency that will eventually drain the fund's stock, and if the fund is to defend its holdings, it will eventually have to raise the value of the currency to beat off the purchasers. It may stave off this day by borrowing the currency in question, but cannot eventually avoid such revaluation unless it can in some manner affect the *internal* level of prices in the countries concerned.

Internal versus external stability

This raises the fundamental difficulty which is all too likely to destroy any half-hearted attempt at international collaboration in this field. In the long run, the foreign exchange ratios depend broadly on the internal level of prices, money incomes, and wages in the countries concerned. If the United States experienced a twofold rise in prices and money incomes, we should expect the dollar price of pounds to be approximately doubled along with the dollar price of everything else, if prices and incomes in Britain were stable. Stability in exchange rates, therefore, can only be obtained over long periods if the internal monetary levels of all countries change in about the same proportions. If, for instance, there is a deflation in the United States, there would have to be a deflation in Britain of like magnitude if the dollar-pound ratio were to be maintained. If exchange rates are to be kept stable, it means that the monetary systems of the various nations are linked, just as the monetary systems of the various regions within a country are linked. If there is a world deflationary movement, however, it may be very much to the interests of a particular country to break the link that binds it to the world monetary system, and by a devaluation of its currency to insulate its domestic economy from the world movement. Just as deflation broke the gold standard, then, so is any future deflation likely to break any substitute for the gold standard, however carefully devised. If the choice is squarely put between stability of the internal monetary system and stability of foreign exchange rates, most countries will vote for internal stability. It is failure to realize this all important fact and failure to provide for any effective measures against world deflation that make the plans of the monetary experts seem so unrealistic.

How deflation leads to protection

The world deflation of the thirties is the key to the understanding of the growth of protectionist policies during those years. Protection, like its sister, monopoly, is a desperate attempt on the part of a national economy to isolate itself from a world deflation. When prices are falling it seems natural to attribute the fall to a flood of cheap imports from abroad. The raising of the tariff barrier, or the imposition of import quotas, undoubtedly has the effect of raising internal prices; it may have the effect of increasing internal incomes and reducing unemployment. Currency devaluation has much the same effect. It is little wonder. therefore, that when faced with the appalling unemployment problem of the Great Deflation, one government after another sought to solve its own problem by protectionist measures. The restriction of imports means that money which had previously been spent for imports and had gone to swell money incomes abroad, now tends to be spent for home products and raises money income at home. But protection, of course, while it protects the internal system to some extent against deflation, actually aggravates the world problem. The dyke that prevents one country from being flooded raises the height of the flood waters everywhere else. Protection, therefore, is no solution to the world problem; it is a suicidal game of beggar-my-neighbor, but the lack of any respectable alternative made it the only policy open to the individual government. Thus, the shockingly retrogressive commercial policy of the thirties must be interpreted as a desperate attempt, on the part of each individual country, to raise its own level of money incomes by pushing down those of other nations, like the wild scramble of a drowning mob. The result was to drown everybody.

The necessity for sensible short-run policies

The solution, however, is not to utter pious long-run platitudes, nor to deliver sermons on how nice it would be if drowning and desperate men did not try to push themselves up and the others down. The free trade, stable exchanges policy, is impeccable as a long-run argument, with the possible exception of large agricultural countries. But the problems that buzz round the heads of politicians are all short-run problems; a politician, and especially an elected politician, cannot afford to look loftily at the long run, otherwise he will fall promptly into the ditch of the next election. Our dire necessity, therefore, is to discover alternative short-run national and international policies for dealing with world deflation which do not have the disastrous general effect of those hitherto in fashion. The perfect escape from the problem of international relations would, of course, be their total abolition through the formation of a world state. This solution, however, is not for our generation, and while the world waits for it, the question must be asked—and answered—how can we keep the sovereignty of nations and still preserve the essential minimum of international order? It is possible, of course, that there is no answer to this problem and that we will be faced with the plain issue of a world state or world chaos. In view of the present state of emotional development, the latter alternative would probably be chosen. It is all the more necessary, therefore, to develop *national* policies which will not result in international disruption.

The solution of international problems depends on the solution of domestic problems

The first principle of any *international* economic order must be the recognition of the close interrelatedness of "internal" and "external" problems. Any solution of the problem of international exchanges and exchange rates, for instance, which neglects the problem of general and internal stability is doomed to failure from the start. If the last twenty years have taught us anything, it is surely that the whole distinction between "internal" and "external" relations is shadowy and confusing. This is as true in politics as in economics—the rise of an aggressive and imperialistic party within any one country, for instance, cannot be dismissed as a mere "internal" matter, but is something which concerns the whole world. The dismal atmosphere of unreality which pervaded the "Geneva world" of Leagues and Conferences was due more than anything to the failure to realize that there is no clear distinction to be drawn between "foreign" and "domestic" policy. At least, if the division had to be made, its proper place was close to the domestic end of the scale, so that "domestic policy" occupied a small rump of affairs while "foreign policy" included everything of importance. Instead, the line was drawn to make "domestic" policy—which the League and the Conferences could not touch—include every thing of importance, with the result that the discussion of "foreign affairs" had to deal with trivial and peripheral matters. It was a period when even tariff policy was considered to be a purely "domestic" matter, and when if anyone suggested that the discount rate of the central banks or the budget policy of governments were matters of international concern, they would have been met with raised eyebrows and incredulous stares. It is little wonder that it ended in a complete breakdown of the international order.

The international effects of domestic full employment policies

But can we conceive the proud and independent nations of this world submitting to international regulation of such matters as tariff and monetary policy, let alone budgetary and fiscal policy? Clearly not, in the present state of things. Nevertheless, the situation is not hopeless. The trouble with the international order has been that the *domestic* policies of nations have been wrong. If nations can be persuaded to adopt domestic fiscal and monetary programs aimed at the stabilization of money incomes and the attainment of full employment, not only will the internal situations be easier but the international problem will be largely solved as a by-product. It remains, therefore, to consider the effects of *domestic* full employment policies on the international order and particularly to consider the question whether one country could practice such a policy alone, or whether it would have to be applied on a world scale to be effective.

It must be confessed at the outset that a full employment policy on the part of one nation may not be compatible with stability of the foreign exchange rates over long periods, though there is no reason why short-run stability should not be possible. It must also be admitted that the smaller the country, and the more dependent it is upon international trade, the less likelihood is there of a full employment policy succeeding in it. Nevertheless a large country, such as the United States, which is fairly self-sufficient, could in all probability not only make a thorough success of a full employment policy as far as its internal economy was concerned, but could also draw the whole world into its benevolent orbit and contribute materially to the solution of the problem of world stability.

Difficulties of small countries

Consider first the case of a small country, much dependent on foreign trade. Suppose that there was a world-wide deflation, and that the small country tried to counteract this by lowering its tax rate and running a budget deficit. The result would be, of course, to maintain incomes within the country; but if its foreign exchange rate remained the same, the result would be an increase of imports and a decline in exports until it became impossible or undesirable to pay for more imports. If the foreign exchange rate was held constant by the operation of a gold standard, the result of the excess of imports would be a drain of gold that would eventually force the country off the gold standard. If the foreign exchange rate was held constant through direct purchases and sale of foreign exchange by an equalization fund, the same result would follow, for the equalization fund would be forced to buy the domestic currency in order to maintain its value, and the fund would sooner or later become drained of foreign currency and would have to suspend operation. Then the price of the domestic currency would fall in terms of foreign currency. By this means a country could insulate itself from the outside world as far as changes in its own money income went. Nevertheless, this would not insulate it against all the results of depression, for the depression in the rest of the world would mean a real decline in demand for its exports. No amount of domestic maneuvering could prevent a depression in its export industries. Even in this case, however, the depression could be confined to the export industries, and the relatively prosperous home industries could absorb some of the resources displaced from the export industries.

Large countries can contribute greatly to world stability

The larger the country, and the less important the export industries relative to the domestic economy, the easier it would be to insulate the domestic economy from deflationary movements outside. Moreover, in a large country, though its imports may be a small proportion of its own trade, they form a large proportion of the exports of smaller countries. Thus, the imports of the United States are not normally above 5 per cent of its total production; but they form a large percentage of the exports of Malaya and the East Indies. Large countries, and countries with a large import trade, have a grave responsibility, therefore, not only to their own people, but also to the rest of the world. It has been truly observed that no act of the United States—not even the infamous Hawley-Smoot tariff—did so much damage to the rest of the world as the depression of 1929. By allowing itself to have a depression, the United States wrecked not only its domestic economy, but also the economies of a large number of small countries and dependencies, and indeed of the whole world.

Full employment policy in two large countries

The question may now be raised, however—suppose two or three large countries each try to maintain internal stability, independent of each other? Will not the result be an utterly chaotic situation in international trade, so that international trade shrinks to a bare minimum and international investment becomes well-nigh impossible? Will we not be plunged into another period of competitive exchange depreciation? It is true that a situation as above envisaged might lead to a certain instability of exchange rates, particularly if the countries concerned made no efforts at concerted action. Nevertheless, if all countries followed a policy of stabilizing their internal money incomes, the dislocation of the foreign exchange rates would not be very serious, for incomes would tend to rise or fall proportionately in all countries. If in a period of world deflation a single country tried to maintain stable internal incomes, the result would be, of course, a fall in its foreign exchange rate. If two countries tried to maintain stable internal incomes, both the exchange rates would fall relative to the rest of the world but would not change much relative to each other. Suppose, for instance, that we start with a situation in which \$1 = 25 francs, £1 = 125 francs, and \$5 = £1. If there is now a world deflation, but the United States alone maintained her internal money income, she can only do this at the cost of depreciating her currency; we may now have a situation in which \$1 = 20 francs, £1 = 125 francs, and \$6.25 = £1. If, however, Great Britain likewise followed a full employment policy and maintained her money income, the value of the pound on the foreign exchanges would fall, and we might have a situation in which \$1 = 20 francs and £1 = 100 francs; but then we should find that \$5 = £1 again. That is, if both Britain and the United States followed a policy of stabilizing incomes, the exchange rate of their currencies would not fluctuate seriously. In practice, it should not prove impossible to combine an adjustable tax plan with reasonably stable exchange rates among *all those countries that followed the plan.*

It should be noticed that even the victorian gold standard did not give a much better guarantee of exchange stability than this. The gold standard only resulted in stable exchange rates between those countries that practiced it. It did not give stable exchange rates between a country that did practice it and one that did not.

The United States could adopt a full employment policy

In conclusion we may ask "would it be worth the while of the United States to adopt a full employment policy even if other nations did not follow suit? To this question one can answer an unqualified "yes." The foreign trade of the United States yields only a small proportion of her total income, so that she could keep her own income stable without being at the mercy of external circumstances. But even more than this, the imports of the United States, for all that they make but a small part of her total production, are a dominant factor in the trade of many other countries. It is hardly an exaggeration today to say that United States prices are world prices and that a depression in the United States is a world depression. The last great depression unquestionably originated in the United States, and many future depressions are likely to do so. If the United States can keep herself free from depressions, that in itself would be a contribution to the world economic order greater than all the leagues and covenants and conferences that peace may bring into being. If the United States and Great Britain between them could enter into a joint scheme for income and exchange stability, they would without question be able to keep the whole world economy on an even keel. As in the case of the spread of the gold standard, the advantages of the new system would be so apparent that there is little doubt that one country after another would follow suit. Here lies a real possibility of creating something like world order without a formal world government. And once world order has been established, world government may follow.

Duties of an international monetary authority: "Counterspeculation"

It must not be thought, of course, that because an international monetary organization cannot of itself solve the problems of world trade apart from domestic policies, that such an organization would not be desirable or useful. There are at least two functions which are open to an international monetary organization in the present state of the world: one is the prevention of purely speculative movements in foreign exchange rates; the other is the encouragement of long-term foreign investment. It might be preferable to have these functions performed by separate institutions, but there seems to be no weighty reason why they should not be combined. The first function is part of the general duty of monetary authorities which Mr. Lerner has called "counterspeculation." [1] The foreign exchange market is so "perfect" that large fluctuations in exchange rates which are purely speculative in origin may occur in the absence of regulation—that is, the price of a currency may rise simply because dealers expect it to rise and rush to buy it for the sake of the profits which ensue from holding any form of property that is rising in value; similarly, the price may fall simply because people expect it to fall. It is wholly desirable to eliminate these speculative movements which have nothing to do with the underlying forces of international payments and serve no useful economic function. This elimination could be accomplished by the authority undertaking to buy and sell the currency in unlimited quantities at fixed rates. The authority, however, must be given the right to change these rates by small jumps at certain intervals. It would seem vital to the success of any international authority that the right to fix the rates should be vested in the authority itself and not in the participating nations; otherwise, a chaotic situation might develop, akin to competitive currency depreciation.

The irrelevance of gold

The problem of whether gold should be used in the international monetary system is political rather than economic. If

[1] Lerner, A. P., *The Economics of Control*, p. 55. New York: Macmillan, 1944.

gold is not demonetized, any international exchange equalization fund would probably find it convenient to hold a certain proportion of its assets in gold. It may be that current financial superstitions about gold are so strong that purely as a psychological matter it would be advisable for the authority to hold a substantial amount of gold. Apart from these superstitions, however, there is much to be said for the demonetization of gold. It is, after all, a moderately useful metal commercially, and the world's gold stock would probably be more useful in the form of tooth-fillings, rings, and plate than in the form of buried bars. If the demonetization of gold brought down its price to, say $10 an ounce, important industrial uses might also open up. Such a demonetization program would probably have to be accompanied by a program of assistance to the gold-producing areas, but even at that it might be worth the price. The question, however, is not one of great importance, provided that the limitation of the quantity of gold does not become an important limiting factor in the expansion of the quantity of money.

The encouragement of foreign investment

The problem of governmental or international encouragement of foreign investment is also beset with so many political thorns that it is difficult to specify a purely economic policy. There is much to be said, as we have seen, for the encouragement of foreign investment. There is a certain theoretical danger that a full employment policy of encouraging home consumption, say in the United States, would have the effect of discouraging that investment abroad which is so desirable from a world point of view. In view of the political situation and the state of opinion, however, this is extremely unlikely; the danger is entirely the other way, that an internal consumption policy will not be pursued courageously enough, and that foreign investment will therefore be necessary to fill the breach if full employment is to be maintained. An international authority could perform several useful functions in this field. It could act as a clearing house for information on investment opportunities by maintaining field representatives in various parts of the world. It might even act as an underwriting agent for international securities, though this would be risky. The main responsibility, however, rests with the international political order, whatever it may be, and with national governments. If national governments are not prepared to subsidize consumption, it may be easier to persuade them to subsidize foreign investment. If such a subsidy increased employment, it might be well worth its cost.

The problem of access to raw materials

Two other problems may be mentioned which are usually regarded as essentially problems of international relations: one is that of access to raw materials; the other is that of international migration. The raw materials problem was thought worthy of mention in the Atlantic Charter. It has been raised mainly by the so-called "have-not" nations, and is conceived mainly in terms of freedom of all nations to purchase the raw materials of the world, no matter where they are located. Stated merely in these terms, however, the problem hardly exists. There have been very few examples in which a single nation has had a monopoly of any material—the Canadian monopoly of nickel probably comes closest. There are even fewer examples of monopolistic discrimination on a truly international scale, and no examples of which I am aware where such discrimination has been successful or carried on for any length of time. Monopolies are more difficult to maintain than many imagine in these days of chemical substitutes, and the whole trend of modern technology is to lessen our dependence on localized sources of supply. The development of synthetic camphor, synthetic textiles, and now synthetic rubber and perhaps even synthetic gasoline are illustrations of the trend. Indeed, the real raw materials problem is the reverse of what is frequently imagined: it is the poverty and instability of the raw material producing areas, and the difficulty of disposing of their products that presents the greatest problem. Particularly is this true in time of deflation, when the stocks of raw materials pile up, the prices drop precipitously, and the incomes of the producers fall catastrophically. Indeed, no groups in the world have a greater interest in preventing deflation than the raw materials producers, whether it be the farmers of the corn belt, the coffee growers of Brazil, the rubber growers of the Indies or the tin miners of Malaya.

International migration

The problem of international migration is much more real and very thorny. In a unified world, without hindrances to the movement of peoples, we should expect migration to take place from places that are overpopulated and poor to places that are underpopulated and rich. This would have the effect of making the poor sections relatively richer and the rich sections relatively poorer. It might be expected in our fragmented world of independent countries that rich countries would set up barriers to oppose this process, and so perpetuate the inequalities. This in fact happens, as shown by the immigration restrictions of the United States. It might be thought, therefore, that one of the requirements of a true world order would be the removal of all barriers to migration in order to allow the world's population to move where it can earn the best living. Unfortunately, even from the economic point of view, the problem is not so simple. Even apart from political, racial, and cultural considerations such as the desire for a homogeneous nation, there are economic considerations which make it doubtful whether large-scale migration is much of a solution to the world's problem. As we have seen on page 101, where poverty is the result of a real pressure of population on the means of subsistence, emigration is no remedy. The overpopulated area is a perpetual spring of emigrants, for the more emigrants leave, the more food is left, the fewer children die and the more children grow up to replace the emigrants who have left. Unless emigration can take place fast enough, or unless it can be accompanied by a rapid rate of economic progress in the poorer country, it will add to rather than subtract from the world's problems. The migration problem, therefore, is more likely to be political than economic. It would be highly desirable to set up an international migration authority to deal with the displaced, the dispersed, the homeless, the stateless, and the unwanted minorities. But it should not be supposed that migration can contribute a great deal to the world's economic future, unless it can be accomplished on a scale and at a rate hitherto undreamed of.

CHAPTER 11

Right-Wing Illusions

It is the common experience of teachers that the main difficulty with students is not what they don't know but what they do know that isn't so. Particularly is this the case with economics; the student invariably comes to the subject with a mind full of mysterious ideas that he accepts on faith and hearsay, most of which are entirely erroneous. And as truth is frequently seen most clearly against the background of revealed error, it may be worth while spending some time in exposing current fallacies which are preventing us from developing a rational economic system. For purposes of rough classification, I have divided these illusions into "Right Wing" and "Left Wing." The distinction, however, is not as clear as some would like it made. Indeed, the more one studies the interplay of current opinion, the more it becomes apparent that two dimensions are hopelessly inadequate to express its multitudinous shades. Perhaps we should identify opinion as "up" or "down," "back" and "front" as well as "right" and "left." However, the conventional distinction will serve to divide the chapters.

Among the illusions that may tentatively be classified as "Right Wing" may be mentioned: 1. the illusion of national sovereignty; 2. the illusion of sound finance; 3. the illusion of laissez-faire; 4. the illusion of deserving poverty. These illusions have been attacked so strongly in recent years that they are not perhaps such a menace as the corresponding (and intellectually more respectable) illusions of the Left Wing. In spite of the fact that with the exception of the first-mentioned illusion, few can be found to defend them competently, they nevertheless have great importance, for they represent the half-expressed opinions of many people of influence and authority—bankers, industrialists, editors, politicians, and the like.

The illusion of national sovereignty

The illusion of national sovereignty is the illusion that in the modern world nations can be independent and irresponsible. It is the irresponsibility of nations that leads to war, and it is their attempt to be independent that leads to international chaos. It has become a platitude to say that the world is interdependent, but like most platitudes, the trouble is not that it is untrue but that people do not really believe it. It should be obvious to the most casual observer that the policy of an official in Washington may profoundly affect the fortunes of a rubber planter in Malaya or an Eskimo in Alaska, and that a dictator in Germany may profoundly affect the lives and fortunes of numbers of people in Nebraska. That other ancient and neglected platitude—that we are all members one of another—has never been more true than in the modern world. We cannot, as Americans, remain indifferent to the policy of Germany, nor as Malayans remain indifferent to the policies of the Federal Reserve Board in Washington. Nevertheless, our writers and politicians, particularly those of a more isolationist tinge, continue to write and talk as if a sharp distinction could be made between "domestic" and "foreign" affairs, and as if each nation has a wide sphere of "domestic" policy in which foreigners had no business to interfere. In some limited spheres this may still be true; no doubt each country could safely be left to determine its divorce laws, though even here competitive depreciation of the moral standard might ensue, as in the United States. But with the growth of world trade and communications, the area of political action that can safely be labeled "domestic" has shrunk to trivial proportions.

The illusion of "sound finance"

The illusion of "sound finance" is perhaps the most dangerous of all the illusions of the Right Wing, for it is not only influential in high places but it also forms part of the thinking of the ordinary man. It arises because of a failure to understand the fundamental difference between private and public finance. The failure is understandable, particularly in view of the fact that professional economists themselves have only recently come to appreciate the distinction. Nevertheless, one of the principal tasks of education in citizenship should be to increase human understanding in this regard. The untrained mind works principally by analogy, and though this method is useful in many cases it is dangerous, and nowhere more dangerous than in thinking about economic and monetary matters. The ordinary man is aware of income and expenditure as two wholly unrelated streams. It is not easy to make him see that from the point of view of society as a whole income and expenditure are exactly the same thing, for every transfer of money is income at one end and expenditure at the other. The ordinary man is likewise aware of assets and liabilities as two very different things in his personal experience; assets he quite properly regards as pleasant, and liabilities as in themselves unpleasant. It is again not always easy to make him realize that from the point of view of society as a whole, most assets and liabilities are exactly the same thing, for what is an asset to one person or institution is at the same time a liability to another, or to itself. Every debt, every financial instrument, represents an asset to the creditor and a liability to the debtor.

The "solid-money" illusion

To the conservatives, "sound money" is not a reasoned belief, but a fetish. It consists in two ideas—or perhaps they should be called idols: the idea that money must be "backed" by gold in some way, and the idea that the budget must be balanced (except, of course, in time of war when a serious attempt to balance the budget is really necessary!). The ideas that most people have about the gold standard are extremely vague; if they are asked what is meant by "backed" their notions will be even more hazy. They have an idea that unless every note is related, by marriage at least, to a little pile of gold sitting in the treasury, then disaster will inevitably follow. They do not distinguish carefully enough between gold (measured in ounces) and money (measured in dollars). In this confusion they are aided and abetted by the economists and the lawyers, who persistently try to *define* a dollar as a certain weight of gold (or silver), which is like saying that a dollar may be defined as two pounds of cheese, since the price of cheese is 50 cents a pound.

They do not realize that the gold standard simply means a law, passed by the national legislature, which fixes a price at which the treasury or the central bank *must* buy and sell gold. They think that in some mysterious way the gold standard ensures "stability": stability of *what* they never bother to inquire! The gold standard does, of course, insure the stability of the price of gold. It does, when operated by two countries, insure the stability of their foreign exchange rates. But it practically insures the instability of everything that really matters—income, prices, and employment! Under the "stability" and "soundness" of the gold standard we enjoyed the halving of our national money income (from 1929 to 1933), the maintenance of 10-12 million unemployed, the virtual collapse of our banking system, and even great fluctuations in our foreign exchange rates after 1931. Amid all this welter of fluctuation one thing remained nobly stable until President Roosevelt forcibly boosted it in 1933: the price of gold. For this trivial and insignificant item of stability we are apparently content to wreck our whole economic system!

The fetish of the balanced budget

The other fetish of the "sound" school is the balanced budget. Drawing an entirely false analogy from personal and business life, the conservatives argue that just as a private individual must balance his budget, so must a government. Oddly enough, this rule is relaxed in time of war—it is apparently quite proper to finance the destruction of life and property with a budget deficit, but not proper to finance slum clearance, good nutrition, and prosperity! The budget-balancing fetish arises from a misunderstanding of the true purpose of taxation, which is to prevent inflation on the one hand and deflation on the other. The common idea that the primary purpose of taxation is to enable the government to pay its bills is one of the most tenacious fallacies that shackle the human mind. Yet it is quite clear in time of war that the purpose of taxation is to prevent inflation. The government is making enormous expenditures for war purposes. In so doing, it is diverting a large proportion of productive resources away from civilian industries into war industries. The supply of civilian goods is, therefore, diminishing at the same time that the volume of civilian incomes is increasing. Because of the fall in the output of civilian goods, there must be a fall in civilian consumption. This can be achieved in two ways—either by allowing prices to rise until civilians cannot afford to buy more than is available because of high prices, or by taxation until civilians cannot afford to buy more than is available because of reduced incomes. The restriction of consumption is what we really mean by "paying for the war." It is apparent that taxation and inflation are substitute methods for achieving this end. It should be equally clear that in times of depression "negative taxation" and unemployment are alternate ways of achieving another end—the reduction of saving or investment. As capital goods accumulate, the time comes when the rate of accumulation must fall off. That is to say, the excess of production over consumption must fall. This can be done either by raising consumption or by lowering production. The first— and only sensible alternative—can be achieved, I believe, only through the government's tax and expenditure system. If we do not achieve it, the second alternative will be realized through unemployment.

Confusion between budget deficits and wasteful expenditure

Another confusion of thought—for which, it must be confessed, the economists are partly responsible—is the confusion between a budget deficit and wasteful governmental expenditure. There is no excuse for stupid or wasteful governmental expenditure—that is, for a diversion of real economic resources to unnecessary ends. There is no point in building pyramids—or even dams—merely to provide employment, if full employment on useful goods can be assured in other ways. But whether governmental expenditure is wasteful or not has nothing whatever to do with the size of the budget deficit. Expenditure must be judged on its own merits; the budget deficit (or surplus) should be planned without much reference to expenditure as such, except in regard to movements in particular industries. Thus, the government might well seek to mitigate the twenty-year cycle in the building trades by a program of governmental building: government expenditure being large when private expenditures were small, and *vice versa*. But as far as the general income policy is concerned, there is no necessity for linking budget deficits with large, hasty, and wasteful expenditures, nor for linking budget surpluses with large, hasty, and wasteful "economy campaigns."

The fear of increasing national debt: The "ten-year budget"

The advocates of balanced budgets have one fear which seems at first sight to have some justification. This is the fear of an ever-increasing national debt. It is argued that in our highly developed capitalism it will be impossible to increase consumption to the point where unemployment disappears without a continual budget deficit, and therefore a continually increasing national debt. Some writers have attempted to allay these fears by proposing that we should balance the budget over the period of the business cycle—that is, over a decade or so—but not every year. According to this proposal, the budget deficit that is necessary to maintain incomes during a depression would be counterbalanced by the budget surplus necessary to restrict incomes during a boom, and over the whole period of the cycle there would be no net increase in debt. The government would simply pay off in boom years the debt which it had accumulated in depression. The proposal sounds attractive—indeed, a little too attractive to be quite true. The conservatives, with some reason, argue that in fact the surpluses of boom years would not be likely to cover the deficits of depression years. It is much easier to incur a deficit than to achieve a surplus, and hence if the object of financial policy is to balance the budget, this object is much more likely to be achieved by annual balancings than by ten-year programs. In this, the conservatives are probably right, and in fact there is no real reason why the budget should be balanced every ten years any more than every year. We must make up our minds whether the *object* of tax receipts is to balance the budget, or whether it is to stabilize incomes. If we decide the former, then there is everything to be said for annual balancing. If the latter, then there is nothing particularly to be said for ten-year balancings, or twenty, or a hundred-year balancings. The deficit or surplus will be determined solely with reference to the movements of national income; in periods when deflationary forces are strong, the tendency will be for deficits and a growth of the national debt; when inflationary forces are uppermost, the tendency will be towards surpluses and the decline of the national debt. But there is no reason for these movements to cancel each other over any given period of years.

Can the national debt rise without limit?

But, it is said, if the main forces operating in our time in the long run are deflationary, will this not mean that a budget deficit is perpetually necessary to preserve full employment, and will not there be therefore a continually mounting national debt? Even though those who fainted with horror at the thought of the national debt rising above $45,000,000,000 in order to create dams, roads, and employment now face with equanimity the prospect of a debt of $300,000,000,000 in order to create destruction and victory, the question is an important one. Is there not something to be feared in the rise of the national debt? Is there a limit beyond which the debt cannot go without danger? Mr. Lerner thinks not.[1] He points out, quite rightly, that the interest on the national debt is income to its recipients, and can therefore be taxed away. Even a national debt of $10,000,-000,000,000 does not frighten him! However, there are some considerations which lead us to suppose that an indefinite increase in the national debt is not desirable. It is true that if we look at the debt simply in terms of the interest that has to be paid on it, it appears merely as a redistribution of income which is taken from the taxpayers and given to the debt holders. If the debt holders belong to the rich and middle-class groups (as they do), and if the poor pay taxes, the debt may result in an undesirable redistribution of income. However, as we have seen, a tax system that is adjusted to the debt payment can take care of this, and there is no necessity (though there is a likelihood) for the national debt to result in a transference of income from the poor to the rich. Nevertheless, the national debt is not negligible from the point of view of the capital structure of society. Ordinary commercial debt does not in the first instance

---

[1] Lerner, A. P., "Functional Finance and The Federal Debt," *Social Research*, February, 1943. p. 38.

change the total net worth of the people, though of course insofar as it permits investment to take place it indirectly results in the increase of net worths. The growth of ordinary commercial debt results in an equal increase in assets and in liabilities in the balance sheets of the people.

Peculiarities of government debt

Government debt, however, has this peculiarity; that it apparently results only in an increase of assets, and hence apparently results in an increase in the total net worth of the people. The national debt is an asset to the people who hold it; it is, of course, a liability to the government, but oddly enough the government has no balance sheet! I say "apparently," advisedly, for if our accounting system were accurate enough, an increase in government debt, as of any debt, would immediately be reflected in a decline in the value of private capital. The value of private capital depends on the expected income from it, and as an increase in the national debt presumably means a future increase in taxation, the expected income from private capital should decline and the value of private capital should likewise decline. If the government kept a balance sheet, the liability of the national debt should be balanced by an "asset" representing ultimate tax claims. This "asset" of the government would be, of course, a liability of the taxpayers. It is only because we fail to be logical in our accounting practices, especially as applied to persons on the one hand and Leviathans on the other, that we have the illusion that the national debt increased the net worth of the public. Nevertheless, the illusion is an important one, as long as people believe it and as long, therefore, as people are willing to hold the debt as part of their assets.

The danger of increasing debt

There is, however, a grave danger in an increasing volume of debt, whether it be public or private. When debt increases beyond a certain proportion of "real assets" (that is, stocks of commodities and equipment, or "real" capital) the public may become unwilling to hold so large a proportion of their resources in the form of debt-assets, such as bonds, and hence try to shift their assets from the debt-form to the "real" form. When this happens there is, of course, a fall in the price of bonds (a rise in the rate of interest). The results of this fall may be disastrous for those organizations which hold a large proportion of their assets in this form. Particularly is it liable to be disastrous to banks. The banking crisis that accompanies every depression is a result mainly of a fall in the value of the bonds and other contractual debts which form a large part of a bank's portfolio. There is, therefore, a real danger in an increase of debt, which the extreme Keynesians neglect. This danger applies to all debt, whether governmental, private, or corporation. Nevertheless it applies with peculiar force for government debt, and particularly for government debt that is not incurred for the construction of capital goods or for other investment purposes. Private debt for productive purposes tends to raise the total value of assets as well as the total volume of debt; hence, the expansion of private debt does not lead to so large a ratio of debt to total assets as might be supposed. Government debt on the other hand, for consumptive purposes, not only increases the total of debt but may even decrease the total of real assets. Hence, with the increase in government debt, the ratio of debt to real assets increases all the faster.

The danger to banks from increasing debt

We have already seen that there is a peculiar danger in the present situation, where so large a proportion of the national debt is held by banks. Many banks now have something like 60-70 per cent of their assets in the form of government securities. A relatively slight fall in the price of these securities would bankrupt some of the most respected banks in the country. Unfortunately, the prospects of a fall in the price of government securities is not at all unlikely. Rates of interest in recent years have been phenomenally low. The destruction caused by the war will open up new avenues of investment, and hence it is not unlikely that the postwar period will see a rise in the interest rates. The Federal Reserve Banks will be relatively powerless to stop any inflationary movement after the war, for they will not dare to raise interest rates for fear of causing the price of government bonds to fall and so cause a first-class banking crash. Neither will they be able to sell securities to control an inflation, for if they do, again the price of government bonds will fall and the solvency of the whole banking system will be endangered.

Why a full employment policy need not result in a perpetually rising debt

Are the conservatives right, then in supposing that a large increase in the national debt would be ruinous? Are they right also in supposing that any attempt to create permanent prosperity would in fact result in a dangerous increase in the national debt? There are good reasons, fortunately, for believing that they are wrong—I say "fortunately" advisedly, for if they are right in this contention, we may as well resign ourselves to increasing unemployment, chaos, and war. In the first place, it must be pointed out that the present situation is exceptional. We have a budget deficit far in excess of what is necessary to maintain full employment, because of our unwillingness to pay for the war honestly. Consequently, we are having inflation, despite all price controls, and we shall be fortunate, indeed, if we escape the consequences. The potentially dangerous situation of the banks is likewise a result of our fundamentally dishonest war finance—by borrowing from the banks the government can indulge the people by giving them the illusion that they are not paying for the war. The adjustable tax plan would be as much of a safeguard against inflation as it would be against deflation; if it were in operation now, we would see an enormous increase in taxes; the "inflationary gap" between consumers' incomes and the value of available consumers' goods would be closed, and we would not have to resort to the costly and wasteful experiments with price control except in the case of a very limited number of unusually scarce articles.

The control of the national debt

In the second place, it has been shown in Chapter 9 that the adjustable tax plan does *not* necessarily involve a perpetual increase in the national debt, even in a persistently deflationary situation. It was shown in Chapter 9 that a budget deficit may be financed not only by borrowing either from the public or from the banks, but by the issue of currency. Consequently, the growth of the national debt—the growth in interest-bearing securities held by the public—can be controlled in the interest of financial stability. There is much to be said for a policy that will stabilize the price of fixed-interest securities, and the national debt can be adjusted to this end. When the price of bonds is rising unduly, budget deficits can be met by issuing bonds; the new supply of bonds will force down the price. When the price of bonds is falling unduly, budget deficits can be met by issuing currency; the new supply of money will then force up the price of bonds. In times of threatened inflation, also, the budget surplus can be treated in a like manner. If the price of bonds is rising unduly, the rise can be checked by using the budget surplus to retire currency notes; the scarcity of money will then force down the price of bonds. If the price of bonds is falling unduly, the budget surplus can be used to retire government bonds The scarcity of bonds will then force up the price of bonds again. Whether budget deficits should be financed by government bonds or by government currency therefore depends mainly on the state of the bond market. The fear of continually increasing national debt is thus seen to be unnecessary. It might become a reality if a full employment policy were poorly managed, but it is no fundamental obstacle to the success of the plan.

The fear of inflation

Of course, any proposal to finance prosperity by the issue of currency is always met by the cry of "inflation." Even in the depths of the depression the cry was raised. It is odd how conservatives are much more worried about inflation than they are about deflation. Possibly this is because conservatives tend to be bondholders, who are, of course, more likely to be injured by inflation than by deflation. It is unfortunate that our experiences with "managed money" have generally been in times of war or postwar reconstruction when the whole system has been in chaos, government expenditures have been abnormally large, and inflation has easily gotten out of control. If, however, we can persuade people that inflation is impossible as long as there is serious unemployment, for under those circumstances a rise in money demands leads to a rise in output and employment.

not to a rise in prices; and if we can show also that in peacetime, when government expenditures are small, inflation is the easiest thing in the world to control through the tax system, then we may be able to lose our irrational fear of "managed money" and our equally irrational love of "safe," "solid," and "sound" money, which makes us safe only for poverty and revolution, solid misery and sound and fury.

Nowhere does our cardinal logical fallacy—that of mistaking means for ends—stand out so clearly as in monetary discussions. It is a useful substitute for thought to regard "sound finance," "gold standards," and "balanced budgets"—and also on the other side "social control" "planning," "co-operatives," and "collective bargaining"—as ends in themselves, eternal "principles" for which all else must be sacrificed. The *purpose* of the financial system should be to insure stable prosperity. If it fails to do this, no matter how "sound," the system is not doing its job.

The illusion of *"Laissez-faire"*

Another illusion of conservatives is the *"laissez-faire"* or "rugged individualism" illusion. This, like all illusions, is dangerous because of the elements of truth in it, and as we shall see in the next chapter, the corresponding illusion on the Left-Wing side is much more dangerous. There are probably not many people left today in active life who still believe that the "law of supply and demand" is the answer to all economic problems, and who hold the "Bo-Peep" philosophy of government— leave them alone and they'll come home. Nevertheless, this old half-truth is still trotted out by special interests in opposition to the minimum amount of governmental control that the economic system requires, and so paves the way for the much more dangerous and false illusion of the Left—that Government Can Solve All Problems. It is true, of course, that individual initiative is the mainspring of economic progress. The world is divided into the few who create and the many who copy, and there is no substitute for the creative powers of the artist, whether he operates with paint, with machinery, with businesses, or with people. The protection of the creative individual should be one of the main concerns of society, and as we have seen there must be a certain amount of security of property before this end can

be achieved and before economic progress can go forward. It is
true also that freedom and security are in part substitutes, and
a society that is obsessed with security is likely to lose not only
freedom but security as well. Security itself may be desirable;
but the lust for security is one of the most despicable of all
human vices, just as courage and daring are among the most
splendid of human virtues.

Government has economic responsibilities

Nevertheless, it is a gross logical fallacy to deduce from these
truths that all governmental intervention is essentially bad and
that the rights of property must be absolute. Government has
important responsibilities toward the economic order. It is the
principal task of applied economics to find ·out exactly what
those responsibilities are; to find out what tasks cannot be performed properly by private individuals and what therefore must
be performed by government as the instrument of society. Economists have always recognized this fact; from Adam Smith
down no economist has ever preached a pure *laissez-faire* doctrine, though there have been wide differences of opinion as to
where the province of the state ended and the province of private individuals began. It has always been recognized, even by
the most conservative of economists, that one of the principal
functions of government has been the regulation of the monetary system. The differences of opinion between the conservative view and the view of this book is simply in regard to the
aims of such regulation. The conservative view holds that the
main objective of the regulation of the monetary system should
be to maintain a fixed price for gold. My view is that the main
objective is to maintain approximately stable money incomes
and to prevent *general* unemployment and depression.

Property rights are not absolute

It is an equally gross fallacy to deduce from the principle
that some security of property is necessary, the conclusion that
all interference with property rights is unwarranted. Property
is itself the creation of society; there is no "natural right" to
property, or to anything else. "Rights" are in the literal sense
of the word "artificial"—that is, they are artifacts, things created

by man for specific purposes, and particularly for the regulation
of his social relationships. Again, the problem of social philosophy is to discover the principles that should govern the limitation of property rights—the proper definition of property. The
prime function of law is first to define and then to protect
property. The development of the legal framework of our social
and economic life is very largely a matter of the refinement of
the definition of property to include new cases and new moral
beliefs. Thus, at one time human beings were regarded as the
legitimate property of another (slaves). We do not now generally regard this form of property as legitimate—that is, we
have defined the property right that we have in our bodies as
"inalienable." Similarly, the property in a "job" is something
that we are at present in the process of defining, and to do this
certain "rights" both of employers and of the employed have
to be limited. To argue that the state has no right to limit these
rights is to play into the hands of the radicals who would abolish
all private property apart from personal belongings.

The illusion of deserving poverty

The last "illusion of the Right" I have called the "illusion
of deserving poverty." It is the belief that if the people are poor,
it is because they deserve to be so, and that therefore neither
the state nor private individuals have any particular duties towards the elimination of poverty. Again the illusion contains a
dangerous half-truth. It is true that in large measure the poverty of the poor is a result of their personal character. In every
generation there are the shiftless, the drunkards, the spendthrifts, the idle, the stupid, and the unreasonably prolific. These
are mostly to be found among the poor. The fact that they are
also to be found among the rich proves nothing; where they
are so found, they are usually in the process of losing their
riches. One of the tasks of the legal and social framework is
to insure that virtue is rewarded and that vice is not. It need
hardly be said that the legal framework falls far short of this
ideal; but it is an unhappy society in which on the whole, crime
does pay, or even in which unscrupulousness pays. Security of
property does *not* mean that capitalists must not be permitted
to lose their money nor workmen their jobs or the value of

their skills. It might almost be said that the capitalist's job is to lose money and to do it gracefully, for the usual justification for profit is that it is the reward of risk bearing. If the capitalist bears no risks he deserves no profit, and if he cannot lose money then he bears no risks. Hence, there should be in a well-regulated society a certain two-way traffic of the virtuous towards the top and the wicked towards the bottom. In our society this is far from the case, and, indeed, this seems to be an ancient evil, for even the psalmist complained that the wicked flourished as the green bay tree. We cannot even on this account, therefore, justify the continued existence of poverty. Particularly in the case of poverty brought about by the misbehavior of the monetary system is it sheer hypocrisy to suppose that the unemployed, for instance, are in this pass because they are "lazy" or for other moral defects.

There is, however, an even more fundamental reason for believing that society and the individuals which compose it have a responsibility for the abolition of poverty. It is that however rugged we may be, none of us are complete individuals. We are tied by an umbilical cord to the society that produced us. We are members one of another, and of a common body; it is as absurd to suppose that we can safely let one section of this body fester in poverty as it is to suppose that a man can neglect a festering foot because it is so far away from his head. These considerations, however, impinge on moral considerations and will be taken up more fully.later.

The illusion of necessary poverty

Closely connected with the illusion of deserving poverty is the illusion of *necessary* poverty. In all previous civilizations this was no illusion, but a grim fact. All previous cultures have been built on an economic surplus so small that without extreme inequality in the distribution of income they could not have existed. All ancient civilizations were small islands of culture rising out of a black sea of poverty and slavery. Not until the great technical discoveries of the past two centuries was it possible even to conceive of a civilization that did not depend for its very life on extreme inequality. Now, however, the harnessing of power to production has made technically possible for the first time in history, a society in which poverty can be abolished. Yet our habits of thought have not kept pace with technical progress, and the rich everywhere fear the rise in the standard of life of the poor because they are still thinking in pre-technical terms and believe subconsciously that if the poor become richer the rich must become poorer. We still have a lingering feudal idea of what is the "proper" standard of life for the poor, and while in America at least nobody now thinks it improper for a working man to have some kind of an automobile, we still find it difficult to believe that the normal standard of consumption for the ordinary working man should be on the level of a family receiving from three to five thousand dollars a year. Yet this standard of consumption must be maintained in America if we are to have full employment. In a sense, therefore, one of the principal obstacles to the abolition of poverty is the belief still present in so many minds that most people not only have to be poor but ought to be poor.

CHAPTER 12

Left-Wing Illusions
(Marxist)

Dangers of "Leftism"

We have now reached a peculiar stage in our development as a civilization where "left-wing" views have become relatively respectable, and such errors as they contain may therefore be all the more dangerous. Particularly is this true in intellectual circles; the doctrines of the self-consciously enlightened must breathe a radical flavor, and from the pulpit, the intellectual press, the classroom, and the stage the most fashionable pronouncements are those of a pinkish hue. Standpat conservatism is politically extinct. The most conservative political parties have to talk radical doctrines if they want to be successful. There is much in this ferment that is good; in a society where no questions are asked no answers are found. On the other hand, there is a danger that we may be satisfied with plausible but insufficient answers. There is danger also that we attach too much importance to change in itself, and are not sufficiently critical about the direction of change. There is no virtue in "progressiveness" if our progress is in the wrong direction, and the radical heresy "whatever is is wrong" is just as unfruitful as the conservative heresy—"whatever is is right." It is important, therefore, to sift the varieties of left-wing opinion to see what are the constructive and the destructive elements therein.

Varieties of Leftism

There are two principal varieties of Left-Wingers, the Marxist and the Christian-Humanist. There are, of course, a large number of shades of opinion, and the distinction between these two schools is by no means clear. They both have deep roots in

221

Christian idealism, although the Marxist might be loath to recognize them. They are distinguished, however, both by underlying philosophy and by practical programs. The Marxist tends to be mechanistic in general outlook, and revolutionary in theory, if not always in practice. The Christian-Humanist is more pragmatic, more religious, and more evolutionary. Marxism is represented by the Communist party, by the Soviet Union in a watered-down and opportunistic but successful form, and by the Trotskyists in its purest but least effective form. Christian-Humanism is represented by the "Social Gospel" of the Christian Church, by the more idealistic and political aspects of the trade union movement, by Social-Democratic parties, including the British Labor Party and the Socialist Party of the United States, and by the idealistic phases of the Co-operative movement.

Fallacies of Marxism: Mechanism

There are two principal pitfalls in the Marxist way of thinking. The first is the error of mechanism—that of interpreting the complex processes of history in terms of mechanical causation, on the analogy of a machine. The second may be called "aggregative" thinking—that is, thinking in terms of large groups or classes, and assuming that these groups are homogeneous and behave as a unit when in fact they are extremely heterogenous. Both these errors are to be found in the writings of Marx himself, but they are even more characteristic of the thinking of his followers. In its extreme form mechanism becomes materialism—the theory that matter is the only reality and that mind or spirit are in some way illusions, or may be explained away entirely in terms of events in the world of matter. It would, perhaps, be unfair to accuse Marx of philosophical materialism—his thought owes too much to Hegel for that—but some of the appeal of Marxism has come from its broadly materialistic viewpoint. Marxism makes its strongest appeal to minds that are bewildered by the shadowy complexities of the spiritual world and see in the glittering simplicities of the machine a tangible pattern of reality that they can easily grasp. The apparent simplicity, however, is gained only by closing the mind to a large portion of the world of experience, and most of the theoretical and practical mistakes of Marxism can ultimately be traced to this source.

Aggregative thinking

In another direction also Marxism oversimplifies the relationships of social life, in its assumption regarding the class structure of society. It is to Marx's credit that he attempted a task of synthesis which previous economists had neglected; he tried to build up a picture of economic life and relationships as a whole, not merely as a collection of individual phenomena but as an organic unity. But he attempted this synthesis with a wholly inadequate analytical apparatus. Instead of conceiving economic life as a complex system of relationships of a multitude of individual economic organisms, he tried to describe it in terms of vast heterogeneous aggregates such as the "working class."

In fact, there is no such thing as the "working class"; there is merely a heterogeneous mass of bricklayers, steel workers, stenographers, doctors, bureaucrats, and the like, with hardly a single interest in common. If we divide mankind into groups that have important common elements and common interests, and that to some extent act like individual units, we shall find nations, families, churches, trade unions, farm organizations, service clubs, and the like featuring on our list, but we shall not find the "working class." From the point of view of economic conflict also, the working class is too heterogeneous an aggregation to be a useful category. The real lines of economic conflict lie not so much between workers and employers as between city folk and country folk, railroaders and truckers, producers and consumers, skilled and unskilled. Scarcely any act of government or of any other organization is conceivable which will benefit the working class as a whole at the expense of the employing class as a whole. The real pressure-group conflicts lie between agriculturists and the rest of us, builders and the rest of us, and so on; it is the occupational groups rather than the class groups that are the warring elements in economic life. This is seen clearly within the labor movement itself, where it is relatively easy for unions to get along with the employers— often at the expense of the public—but where there is continuous warfare between rival unions. In international life also the "solidarity of the working class" is a hollow fiction. Men feel themselves to be "Americans" or "Germans" much more than "Workers." Marx, probably because of his materialist bent, grossly underestimated the strength of nationalism, and his interpretation of history is one-sided to the point where it is almost valueless for purposes of prediction.

Marx's value theory

The weaknesses of the Marxian system are also exhibited in his value theory. He took over from Ricardo a theory of value that in Ricardo's hands had been a delicate instrument for analyzing the causes of variations in relative prices and turned it into a sledgehammer to beat out a theory of exploitation. The essence of Marx's theory can be expressed in a single syllogism: Labor made all commodities; Labor does not own most of the commodities that it has made nor receive the total product of social activity. Therefore Labor has been deprived of its rightful share by force or fraud. If the major premise is correct, the syllogism stands. If, indeed, all commodities come into existence through acts of labor, then somewhere along the line labor must be cheated, for it is clear that in a capitalist society labor does not receive nor own the whole product. This is the celebrated theory of surplus value—surplus value being merely the difference between the total product of society and that portion of it which goes to labor.

Does labor create the product?

The validity of the theory depends entirely on the accuracy of the major premise. In a mechanical sense, it is true that all commodities can be traced back to innumerable acts of labor. Thus, if we ask ourselves how this page came into being, the answer must be that it appears before us as a result of a very large number of acts of labor; the labor of the men who delivered the book, who sold it, who advertised it, who printed and stitched and bound it, the labor of the author who wrote it, the editor who edited it, the men who made the paper and the ink, the men who made the tools and implements used in all these processes, the men who made the tools that made the tools, and who made the tools that made the tools that made the

tools, and so ad infinitum. But when we have listed all the acts
of labor that made the book, we still have not really explained
how it came into being, for we have not described how these
multitudinous acts of labor came to be *organized* into so miraculous a sequence. These physical acts—the cutting of the logs,
the rolling of the paper, the setting of the type, and so on, are
far from being the whole story. Of themselves, mere physical
acts of cutting, rolling, typesetting and the like would never
produce a book, any more than a monkey pounding on a type-
writer would write the manuscript. There must be organization
of these physical acts into a process of production that con-
sciously looks forward to the satisfaction of a demand before
much in the way of a physical product can emerge.

It would seem, therefore, that Marx is mistaken in supposing
that labor, or even labor and nature, is solely responsible for the
social product. Labor by itself is an amorphous, unorganized
mass that produces nothing. The mechanical operations of hand
or brain produce nothing unless they are *employed*—that is,
organized into a process of production. The total product is produced as a result of a social process in which beliefs, customs,
desires, morale, spirit, expectations, disappointment, and the
whole complex of social institutions and organization play a
part. Marx himself recognized this fact in a crude way in stating
that value is created by "socially necessary" labor. He did not
fall into the error of supposing that the mere expenditure of
labor inevitably produced value, no matter on what the labor
was spent. But putting in the phrase "socially necessary" merely
serves to recognize the problem, and makes no advance towards
its solution.

What institutions permit the greatest progress?

Thus, Marx's theory of value, which he regarded as the very
foundation of "scientific socialism," has, in fact, merely served
to obscure the real questions that he was raising. Arguments
about whether labor does or does not create the total product
lead us nowhere. The important question is what type of social
institutions are likely to lead to the greatest product—or perhaps we should say—to the greatest growth of product. We
must be careful here not to identify the "product" with the

physical product; it is the "psychological product" with which we are concerned, and it would be perfectly possible for a larger physical product to represent a smaller psychological product if it were produced under bad conditions or if people regarded the institutions under which it was produced as bad in themselves.

It is clearly impossible to give any "scientific" answer to the question posed above, for so much depends on judgment. In the first place, it is not easy to say what system of social institutions contributes most to the growth of the physical product. Thus, there is no doubt that the institution of private property has, in the past, contributed enormously to the growth of the product, and it is a fairly safe historical generalization to say that periods of relative security of private property have been periods of great capital accumulation and technical improvement, even if the fruits of this improvement have frequently been dissipated by the growth of population. This is not to say, however, that other institutions and ways of organizing society might not prove even more satisfactory. Over against the growth of the product under capitalism, the communist might point to the great growth of the product in Soviet Russia. Nevertheless, the burden of proof is on the revolutionary. The choice is not a simple one between a system of pure exploitation on the one hand and the ideal society on the other, but between a very large number of forms of economic and social organization, all of them productive in a greater or lesser degree. Even from the point of view of the "working class" the choice is not at all clear. If the communist form of society were exactly as productive as the capitalist form, the workers would presumably be better off under communism. But if communism tends to be less productive than capitalism, the abolition of private property in the means of production, and the consequent abolition of the income of owners of this property might not mean any benefit to the workers; the decline in the total product might more than compensate for the additional proportion of the total product that goes to labor.

Socialism as an ideal in itself

Even if it could be proved that one form of organization produced a larger rate of growth of the physical product than another, the question would still not be settled. The socialist might say that he would rather be poor under socialism than rich under capitalism, or that he would not object to being poor as long as nobody else was rich, or as long as the profit system was abolished, or the cooperative commonwealth established. "Better is a dinner of herbs where love is, than a stalled ox and hatred therewith." Even though some of the motivation for socialist and communist opinions comes from envy, from a sense of frustration and personal failure, this is not the whole story. There is something in the ideal of a society organized for a single common purpose, in which private interest is wholly subordinated to the public good, which makes a powerful appeal, and in many cases the emotional drive behind socialism springs from the identification of the socialist form of organization with this ideal society. Whether this identification is correct is, of course, another matter, but the strength of socialism springs in no small measure from the fact that it exists.

The employer-function

Even though the economist as such cannot be a final arbiter in the socialist controversy, there are, nevertheless, important contributions that he can make. His main duty is to point out the real questions in dispute, which are frequently obscured in the heat of the argument. It should be pointed out, for instance, that the dispute does not center around the abolition of the wage system, nor the abolition of the employer-employee relationship. The dispute ranges around *who* should be the employer-capitalist, the ultimate bearer of responsibility for the process of production. In any society, whether communist or capitalist, it is the *administrator of capital* who bears the immediate responsibility for the employment of labor—that is, the administrator of the money or goods that pay wages and of the equipment and raw materials with which the laborer works. The act of giving or of taking employment is an act of exchange. The worker gives up a certain amount of his time and energy to the employer, and the employer gives up a certain amount of money or goods to the worker (the wage). In the usual wage contract the employer is really exchanging a sum of money (the wage) for a certain amount of physical commodity (the product of the man's labor). Suppose, for instance, that I hire a man to pick beans for $30 a week. At the beginning of the week I have $30, and no beans. At the end of the week, after I have paid my employee, I do not have the $30, but I do have the beans, which presumably will be worth at least $30, or it will not have been worth my while to employ the man. If my enterprise has been profitable, the beans will be worth more than $30—say $35.[1] Now, it is clear that nobody can be an employer unless he has command over property. Unless I had command over (a) $30 and (b) the beans in the field, it would be impossible for me to hire anyone to pick beans. There must be therefore, in any society individuals who are responsible for the administration of the society's capital, and these individuals must also, by the very nature of production, be responsible for the employment of the society's labor.

The case for private property

The real question at issue in the socialist controversy concerns the nature of the institutions under which this employer-task of capital-administration is performed. Under capitalism, it is performed through the institution of private property. Under Socialism, it is performed by officers of the state. The case for private property rests mainly on the assumption that the material and mental equipment of society will be best ad-

---

[1] This fact also has puzzled many people; how can $30 worth of labor be exchanged for $35 worth of product unless there is some kind of fraud or exploitation? Marx based his theory of exploitation on this apparent paradox. Here again, however, we find his materialistic bent leading him astray. He regarded exchange as an *equation*—that is, he supposed that in an exchange "equal values" were exchanged. Thus, if a pound of copper were exchanged for ten pounds of iron he would express this transaction as an equation, 1 lb. copper $= 10$ lbs of iron. If, then, an exchange is an equation of equal values, how can it come about that $30 of labor $= 35 of beans? By exploitation, says Marx. The fallacy in the above argument lies in Marx's materialistic theory of exchange. Only if we view an act of exchange in a purely mechanistic sense can we regard it as an equation. The moment we take account of the psychological elements involved, it becomes clear that exchange is not a single equation but is actually two inequalities. If A gives B one pound of copper in exchange for ten pounds of iron, it must be because A thinks that ten pounds of iron is worth more than one pound of copper, while B thinks that one pound of copper is worth more than ten pounds of iron. Thus, for A, 10 lbs. iron > 1 lb. copper; for B, 10 lbs. iron < 1 lb. copper. Unless both these inequalities hold, the exchange will not take place.

ministered when it is privately owned. The institution of private property dumps the responsibility for the administration of capital squarely into the lap of its owner. He has no alibis; no chance of shifting the responsibility to some other official. If he mismanages his capital, he loses it. It is quite clear what he is responsible for and what he is not; hence, there is no need for the piling up of authorities, checks and balances, and red tape. It is clear that on this count the score of private property is high. We are all familiar with the difficulties of administering common property. A man will take care of his "own," whether his "own" be his body, his house, or his factory. On the other hand, everybody's property is nobody's business, unless individuals develop a higher sense of group responsibility than they now possess. It may be true that the institution of private property is required because of human weakness and selfishness. It is, however, within limits, a method of minimizing the effects of that selfishness. Furthermore, it does not prevent the expression of social-mindedness or unselfishness. There is nothing to prevent an individual with private property administering it for what he considers to be social ends, and there are innumerable examples of such use.

Weaknesses of private property

The case for private property is, however, subject to certain important limitations. It rests on the assumption that the interest of society and of the individual owner coincide, in that both wish to conserve and to increase capital, and to employ it in the most productive fashion. This identity of interest however is subject to certain conditions. That use which is privately most productive is not necessarily the use which is socially most productive. Particularly is this likely to be the case where the private gain is made through fraud or through monopolistic extortion. If the only method of increasing private gain is by increasing the efficiency of the use of resources, then private and social profit are likely to coincide. If, however, private gain can be increased by the restriction of the use of resources, as is likely to be the case under monopoly, private property cannot be trusted to produce social gain. Yet another development of modern capitalism weakens the case for private property—the growth of great corporations has broken the link between the owner and the controller of property. The case for private property is strongest where capital is directly administered by its owner, as in the family-sized farm. The wider the breach between ownership and control, the more ownership becomes absentee, the more tenuous seem to become the social functions of pure ownership and the less justification there seems to be for any income derived from it. In the great corporation, we find most of the objectionable features of socialized enterprise—the bureaucracy, the routine operation, the buck-passing, the indefiniteness of authority and responsibility—without even a theoretical responsibility to the whole society.

The Russian experiment

It is a gross error, however, to suppose that because capitalism exhibits certain important defects, that the communist system would be any better. The more important problems of human relationships are not solved by the replacement of private corporations by state corporations. The communist, of course, can point to the success of the Soviet Union as evidence of the workability of communism, and indeed at this period it would be impossible to deny that a communist state can not only be stable but also powerful. Nevertheless, the experience of Russia gives little comfort to the more dogmatic communists. Russian policy has exhibited a marked cyclical movement towards and away from the institution of private property. The period of "War Communism" led to so great a decline in production that a limited restoration of property rights was granted under the "New Economic Policy," and resulted immediately in an amazing revival of production. A swing back to collectivism followed in the great program to collectivize agriculture; this resulted in a great slaughter of livestock and a famine, which forced a modification of the program in the direction of greater security of both personal and group property. It would seem that the attempt to destroy private property in each case has resulted in a decline in production that has forced a partial restoration.

Imitative character of Soviet Communism

Twenty-five years is all too short a period to compare the two systems from the point of view of economic progress. The technical achievements of Soviet Russia have been remarkable, though it is perhaps significant that the less publicized but even greater achievements of capitalism are not regarded as "remarkable." Nevertheless, it is worth observation that the technical achievements of Soviet Russia are essentially imitative. The dams, the factories, the tractors, are all imitations of techniques first developed under capitalism. It may be, of course, that communism can develop techniques for allowing economically creative and enterprising spirits to command property which they do not personally own, just as under capitalism financial institutions permit such individuals to command much more than they own. It may be also that communism will move even further in the direction of the security of property, taught by bitter experience, just as capitalism is moving in the direction of the limitation of the rights of property. Nevertheless, it can be fairly said that the dogmas of communism, more even than the dogmas of conservatism, are a hindrance to the realistic discussion of the problem of economic and political organization.

Political objections to communism

Perhaps the most fundamental criticism of communism is the political one—that it leads to the severe restriction of political liberty, and substitutes imprisonment or death for insolvency and bankruptcy. That man is most truly free who has many masters; he is least free who has only one master. Under communism, the state becomes virtually the sole employer, and hence is in a position to wield a power over citizens far beyond what can be exercised by the most ruthless capitalist. This power may, of course, be exercised benevolently and humanely—or it may not. In any case it is politically undesirable. The object of a political organization should be the maximum amount of individual liberty. But what is liberty but the wide *diffusion* of power? Let every man be a king in his own household, provided that his kingship makes no other man subject. The supreme virtue of a regulated capitalism is that it permits a wider distribution of power than any alternative system. This is true not only of economic power, but also of political power, for it is probably true that representative democracy can only survive where the economic functions of the state are confined to a relatively small section of the economy.

The communist state as "big business"

It is an odd paradox that perhaps the most important criticism that can be made of communism is that it is too capitalistic! The communist or socialist state is the final outcome of the development of "big business." It is, indeed, a corporation which covers the whole of the economic activity instead of a single sector. Both the attitudes and the problems of "big business" are reflected in communism, even in Soviet Communism. We find, for example, the "business vices" elevated into precepts of national conduct. The materialism which is supposed to be characteristic of business, the obsession with economic activity to the exclusion of all other phases of life, and especially the worship of size as such (megalomania) all these are characteristic vices of Soviet Communism. We find also the organizational difficulties of big business cropping up. Thus, it has been frequently remarked that with the development of large-scale enterprise, there has been a separation of ownership and control. That is to say, the ordinary shareholders of a large corporation, or even the members of a large consumers' co-operative, have little effective voice in the management of the business. The actual direction becomes increasingly concentrated into the hands of a small group of executives who are the real administrators of the property of the corporation, and who may take little account in their decisions of the shareholders' interests in spite of the fact that they ostensibly are elected by the shareholders and are supposed to represent them. This problem is repeated on a much larger scale in the communist state. Ostensibly, the property of the communist state is owned collectively by its citizens, much as a corporation is owned by its shareholders or a college by its trustees. In fact, however, the separation of ownership and control is practically complete. The management of the economic system is in the hands of a clique of bureaucrats, which, like the management of a corporation, is apt to be self-perpetuating. The executive functions of government in such a case are bound to dominate all others, and anything like an effective parliamentary democracy is out of the question. From the organizational point of view also, the administrative problem becomes greater the larger the organization that has to be administered. Under capitalism it is clear that efficiency of operation does not increase indefinitely as the size of the firm grows. This is particularly true in agriculture, where the large firm has always proved less efficient than the small or medium-sized firm, but even in industry it is true after a certain point. There is every reason to suppose that this tendency continues as the size of the economic unit grows, and that the problem of efficient management of a "firm" which included even the economy of a single country would be almost insoluble.

The synthesis of capitalism and communism

In spite of the weaknesses in the Marxian analysis, it has had an enormous and not wholly undeserved influence. The Marxian analysis represented the first attempt to deal with the problems of the whole economic system—with output as a whole. Classical economics, for all that it set out to be an "inquiry into the nature and causes of the wealth of nations" actually turned out to be mainly an analysis of how *individual* prices came into being. It is only within the last generation that the main line of economic thought has succeeded in producing a reasonably accurate account of the forces that determine output as a whole, and only very recently, therefore, that economists have been able to prescribe for the most serious disease of capitalism—its periodic failure to provide full employment. If capitalism can be modified so as to provide full employment, then most of the Marxian criticism falls to the ground. If capitalism can be modified in the direction of greater equality of incomes, then the rest of the Marxian criticism likewise falls. Similarly, if communism can be modified in the direction of greater independence of individual units, greater security of property, and greater personal liberty, many of the objections to communism would fall to the ground. But oddly enough, the modified communism would look very much like the modified capitalism! It is hardly an exaggeration to say that the future of the world depends on our ability to work out a synthesis between the two systems. Communism is undoubtedly here to stay; capitalism likewise is here to stay. If we are to regard them as absolute dogmas, absolutely contradictory, of necessity enemies, then we are undoubtedly in for a period of world warfare on a scale which would make the present effort seem relatively insignificant. If, however, we can regard both American-European capitalism and Russian Communism as steps towards a new synthesis, to be approached perhaps from different directions but with a common end in view, the solution of the economic problem may be in sight even in our generation.

CHAPTER 13

Left-Wing Illusions
(Humanist)

The dominance of Christian-Humanist idealism

At the present, the conflict between communism and western capitalism is somewhat in abeyance, due to the accident of military alliances. Indeed, in the interests of the war effort the "humorless, tight-lipped young men" whose eyes strain from following the party line have been all out for class-collaboration, absolutely no class war or strikes, full co-operation in management-labor councils, co-operation with conservative political parties, and so on. In the United States and in Britain these antics, and their evident connection with the winds that blow from Moscow, have completely discredited the Communists politically—a fact which may have been recognized in the dissolution of the American Communist Party. In these countries, then, the most powerful Left-Wing influence is that of Christian-Humanist Idealism. Though not organized into formal political parties, with the possible exception of the new "Commonwealth" party in Great Britain, it exercises an influence on all parties and on all "liberal" thought. It stems mainly from the Christian doctrines of the brotherhood of man, the unity of the human family, and the Christian ideal of the life of love and service. Its historical origins are to be found perhaps in the "Christian Socialists" of the nineteenth century, and the "Social Gospel" that grew up out of liberal protestantism. It is not particularly a product of orthodox Christianity, whether Catholic or Protestant, which tends to be conservative in economic and social matters, concentrating its attention on the relation of the soul to God and of God to the world.[1] It is, however, highly charac-

---

[1] Note however the development of Catholic Action groups and Catholic interest in the labor movement, following the "social" Encyclicals.

teristic of the humanist quasi-religion which is dominant in intellectual and formally educated circles; it is, indeed, more humanist than Christian, in spite of its Christian origins. It lays more emphasis on happiness than on goodness, on welfare than on salvation, on human brotherhood than on divine fatherhood. In its most developed forms it is completely humanist, and strips itself of all theological clothing. Even in its least ostensibly religious form, however, as in the writings of Stuart Chase in America or Professor Carr in Britain, it preserves a certain note of Hebrew prophecy; a call to economic repentance and a promise of dire things to come if we do not repent, plus the vision of the Kingdom of Comfortable Righteousness.

Fallacies of the "Social Gospel"

This social gospel has made a profound contribution not only to our economic ideals but to our economic practices. Social security legislation, progressive taxation, labor legislation, are all expressions in legislation of the Christian-Humanist philosophy. Nevertheless, its exponents are apt to fall into certain intellectual fallacies which deprive their moral criticism of much of its force.

Identification of the profit system with the profit motive

Perhaps the most common error of the Social Gospel is to identify the profit system with the profit motive. The social gospel has been guilty also of some misunderstanding and misrepresentation of the nature of the profit motive. The general criticism of the profit motive in a narrow sense has on the whole been justified. No economist, of course, has ever suggested that mankind is motivated solely by monetary motives. Even Adam Smith, who is much maligned and misunderstood by the social gospelers, emphasized the importance of nonmonetary motives in economic life. Indeed, without bringing in nonmonetary motives, he could not have explained differences in remuneration in different occupations. The "economic man" is not an invention of the economists, but of those who have failed to understand the economists. Adam Smith also was careful to point out that the celebrated principle of economic harmony—that each acting according to his own self-interest served to promote the common good—was only true under certain circumstances which were not fulfilled in practice. Under conditions of monopoly, or ignorance, or immobility of resources, for instance, self-interest does not promote the common good. Moreover, Adam Smith recognized that there might be social objectives which were more than the sum of individual objectives when, for instance, he said "defense is of more importance than opulence." Neither have the economists, and least of all Adam Smith, held an extreme *laissez-faire* position. Indeed, almost half of Adam Smith's great work (Book 5) consists of a discussion of the proper forms of state intervention, and it comes much nearer the mark to say that Adam Smith's main purpose in writing his book was to discover the correct forms of state intervention. Far from supposing that there was any "natural" tendency for private interest and social welfare to coincide, he regarded the main task of government, and of human organization generally, as that of creating an "artificial" framework of laws, customs, and institutions *in which* private and social interests would most closely coincide.

The critique of selfishness

Now, as a matter of moral principles, the attack on the profit motive is excellent. It is a fundamental principal of ethics that the object which we desire to benefit by our actions should be as broad and inclusive as possible. The completely selfish individual, the man who refers every item of his conduct solely to his own welfare, is regarded as immoral if not criminal. It is better to act in the interests of one's family than of one's narrow self; it is better to act in the interest of one's community or country than solely in the interest of one's family; and we hope the day is not far distant when it will be thought better to act in the interest of the world community than in the narrow interest of one's country. This moral principle is embedded deep in social realities; the immorality of selfishness lies in its untruthfulness. We are not, and cannot be, isolated individuals; our hearts beat with the world's heart; our blood is the world's blood, and we cannot cut ourselves off from the larger body of which we are a member without suffering spiritual death.

"Profit motive" not peculiar to capitalists

It is mere confusion of thought, however, to identify the profit motive with the capitalist pure and simple or with the desire for "profits" in the narrow technical sense of the term. The desire for profits is simply a special case of the general desire for economic advantage to which we are all subject. Every time a union presses for a rise in wages, every time a worker moves to a better job, the "profit motive" comes into play. Indeed, a case can be made out that the workers are more dominated by the "profit motive" than the capitalist—if only because money means more to the poor than the rich.

The selfishness of saints

The criticism of the profit motive applies as much to the wage or salary earner as to the capitalist. It is clearly desirable that men should ask themselves when any decision has to be made, not only "how does this change affect me," but "how does this change affect everybody." It is desirable also even from the point of view of self-interest that non-monetary advantages and disadvantages of each decision should be weighed as carefully as the monetary advantages. It is astonishing how many people think that the "economic man" would always choose a larger monetary reward to a smaller. It may be completely economic, and completely selfish, to choose a smaller monetary reward to a larger, if along with the smaller monetary reward there go certain advantages not measurable in money, such as prestige, or reputation, or pleasant surroundings, or even the sense of doing an important service to the community. Indeed, there is something sublimely selfish about the saint who spurns all monetary rewards—in order to do exactly what he most wants to do. If we were to search for the most completely "economic" behavior, we might well find it in St. Francis or in John Woolman, who, whatever the world thought, did what most completely satisfied their souls. At the other end of the scale, there is a peculiarly maniacal selflessness about the miser, or the "captain of industry" who wears out his life and health not in the enjoyment but in the mere accumulation of wealth.

The profit motive in all systems

The profit motive should not be confused with the profit system. By the profit system, of course, we mean the institution of private property in capital goods and the free private enterprise that goes along with it. There is no reason why the "profit motive" should be necessarily connected with the profit system. In a profit system there is nothing to prevent anyone acting on altruistic lines; there is no law that says a businessman must maximize his profits. If a businessman chose to operate with outputs, prices, and wages that yielded him a smaller profit than the maximum, but which he felt were socially more desirable, there is nothing in the profit system that would prevent him from doing this. Nothing in the profit system would prevent the most ardent liberal from refusing an increase in wages, or from accepting an unpleasant and poorly paid job. At the other extreme, there is nothing in a communist system that would do away with the profit *motive*, or the "advantage motive." Men might still wish to get better jobs, to find more profitable uses for their bodies, to obtain positions of power and influence, to become commissars and dictators, not for the good of society but for their own satisfaction. It is utterly naïve to suppose that the replacement of private by public enterprise would result in the sudden conversion of everyone to selflessness. Indeed, the record of politics even in the most enlightened countries is not such as to convince us that political power makes men angels, or even that it is intrinsically better than the power of private property.

Confusion about "production for use": Critique of restrictionism

Ah, but the liberals will say, should we not have production for use instead of production for profit? This superficially convincing phrase covers a wealth of confusion. The opposition of production for use and production for profit completely covers up the real problem, which is how to make "profit" the test and measure of "use." There are occasions and circumstances, of course, in which "production for profit" is not "production for use." It is possible for a monopolist or a monopolistic organization to increase profit by restricting output, and the liberals point with triumph to the restrictionist policies of the last few years as a horrible example of the evils of the profit system. These restrictionist policies are, however, a result of monopoly or of deflation; and economists have always recognized that monopoly must be regulated in the public interest, for under conditions of monopoly, private and social interests do not necessarily coincide, and they are coming to recognize also that deflation is a preventable evil. It may also be pointed out that the profit system has resulted in widespread unemployment, and the alternative of "production for use" to "production for profit" never seems so clear as during a time of depression when the paradox of "poverty in plenty" seems only to be soluble by the insane procedure of destroying the plenty. Indeed, the main trouble with the profit system is not so much that people do make profits as that they do not! When profits disappear due to deflation, then the system cannot perform the function of providing full employment. I have given reasons in an earlier chapter, however, for supposing that a relatively simple modification of the fiscal and financial system would result in the maintenance of approximately full employment, or at least in the prevention of *general* depressions. If this can be done, the social forces behind restrictionist policies are weakened to the point where they become relatively harmless and easily controlled. Restrictionist policies almost always spring up as an attempted answer to deflation. When prices are falling, two courses seem to be open to us—to make goods scarcer, or to make money more plentiful. Both these alternatives will have the effect of raising prices, and if financial "prudence" or conservatism forbids us doing the latter, we are all too likely to turn to the former. If, however, a sensible monetary and fiscal policy can prevent deflation, the only rational ground for restrictionist policies will be completely cut away.

"Need" versus "Demand"

The trouble with the advocates of "production for use" is that they usually fail to realize adequately the nature of the productive process. It is easy to fall into the old fallacy of mechanism and to think of production as a more or less mechanical process. In fact, production is more of a psychological process; all commodities, even those we usually consider to be consumers' goods, are really means to the end of satisfying wants. Consequently, the problem "what use"—to what end or ends shall the productive process be directed—is much more difficult, and much more important than the socializers think. The productive process is not a machine for filling *needs:* it is a sensitive process for filling individual *demands*. It is frequently regarded as a vice of capitalism that effective demand rather than need is the criterion of what is to be produced. It is true that ignorance, deception, and the unequal distribution of incomes operate to distort the structure of effective demands away from that which seems to be socially desirable. Nevertheless, the principle of "consumer sovereignty"—that consumers shall have the right to choose what they shall buy within broad limits—is a vital contribution of capitalism which must be kept in sight. Basically, demand is a superior motive power than need. A system based on satisfying needs is essentially mechanistic. It is only the mechanical part of the human personality that has "needs"; the personal, individual part has demands. Distribution according to need is all right for robots and slaves, but unless the social mechanism permits the expression of demands, and the adjustment of the productive process to satisfy demands, it has no place for free individuals.

Liberal emotions towards labor

The confusion in regard to the nature of the price-profit system can be seen very clearly in the liberal attitude towards two important institutions—labor unions and co-operatives. The reaction to these names, on the part of both conservatives and liberals, is apt to be emotional rather than intellectual, and a stiff dose of the semantic formula (labor union A is not labor union B, co-operative A is not co-operative B) would have a clarifying effect on the thought of many. The liberal is apt to react to the word "labor" in an emotive-defensive manner, compounded about equally of a maternal affection for the underdog and a Galahad-reaction toward the exploited. The emotion, as emotion, is commendable, and is much to be preferred to the conservative emotion of fear and suspicion. Nevertheless, it is likely to lead to some serious confusions of thought. It leads in the first place to a frame of mind that is not sufficiently discriminating in regard to the abuses that exist within the labor movement. Labor unions range all the way from undisguised rackets to enterprises of industrial statesmanship of a high order, and labor leaders range from criminals to philosopher-statesmen. Liberals are often more interested in apologetics for the labor movement rather than in strengthening it and purifying it.

The complexity of economic conflict

In the second place, the liberal emotions encourage a common misconception—that there are only two conflicting parties to industrial strife, the worker on the one hand and the employer on the other. It is true that there are certain divergent interests between the worker and the employer, insofar as there is a measure of "economic surplus" which may go to one or the other depending on their respective bargaining power. The divergence of interest however is apt to be overestimated, and the community of interest of employer and worker, as common "enemies" of the consumer (that is, of the rest of society) is all too frequently overlooked. The wage gains of organized labor are frequently made not at the expense of employers as a class, but at the expense of unorganized labor on the one hand and the purchasers of the industry's product on the other. There are instances—as occasionally in the building trades—where apparently harmonious relationships between employers and unions conceal a united conspiracy against the public. There are cases in which employers have benefited substantially from the unionization of their industry, because it has enabled them to create a monopoly for themselves. Collective bargaining in such a case may degenerate into a "division of spoils" gained from the monopolistic exploitation of the public.

Virtues of unionism

This is not to say, of course, that labor unions are of necessity an evil and should be abolished. They are an essential part of the framework of industrial government and are capable of playing a vital part in rescuing human relations in industry from the curse of arbitrary power. There are many examples of union-management co-operation in the orderly development of technical change, once the unions are accepted and have passed the "fighting stage." Their economic gains do not always come from the use of monopoly power; they may come from the stimulation which a high money-wage level gives to technical progress, or they may come from the unearned economic surplus of other factors of production. More than all these, unions have an important psychological significance for the individual worker, giving him both a sense of independence and a sense of belonging to a great organization and a great movement. Paternalism and the company union are inadequate substitutes for the sense of dignity and responsibility that are the product of unionism at its best. Then transcending its imperfect manifestation in the unions stands the labor movement—a Church Invisible with its own martyrs and saints, its Joe Hills and Mother Joneses, that is capable of capturing the imagination of men and calling forth from them amazing devotion and loyalty.

Industrial democracy versus the labor cartel

A real dilemma of policy faces us in regard to unions. From the point of view of "industrial relations" in the narrow sense of employer-worker relations they may be entirely admirable. In the adjustment of grievances, the checking of arbitrary power, and in the encouragement of technical efficiency, unions may accomplish much. As the embodiment of the labor movement, they represent a mighty instrument of human progress. On the other hand, from the point of view of society as a whole, a union may be a "labor cartel," and have the dangerous qualities of all cartels—that it may degenerate into a monopoly. Just as a cartel is an organization of firms for the purpose of the joint sale of their product, so a union is an organization of workers for the joint sale of their "products"—the thing which they have to sell being labor.

The dilemma of the closed shop

This dilemma is revealed most clearly in the discussion that centers around the "closed shop." From the point of view of employer-worker relations, there is much to be said for the closed shop. It gives the union leaders a sense of security; it prevents "chiselers" among the workers from participating in the benefits of unionism without bearing their share of the costs; its attainment frequently marks the end of the "fighting union" and the beginning of constructive union-management relations. Without "union security," especially if there is employer opposition, union leaders are bound to be of the belligerent type. Genuine collective bargaining—the delicate day-to-day adjustments of the domestic relationship of employers and employed—is almost impossible, as concessions, even to reason, will be taken as a sign of weakness. On the other hand, the closed shop is the source of most of the abuses of unionism; it is the father of the racket and the breeder of monopoly and discrimination. A union with a closed-shop contract and tightly regulated conditions of membership is in a strong position; it can restrict its membership and gain high wages in consequence. But these high wages are obtained largely at the expense of the consumer and of the non-union worker who is kept out of the union by the membership policy.[2]

Labor is a commodity

There is every reason, therefore, why unions should be brought under a kind of regulation similar to that of the cartel and the trust. The pious declaration of the Clayton Act of 1914 and of the International Labor Organization in 1944 that "labor is not a commodity" is not only economic nonsense, but political nonsense as well. Commodities are things which are bought and sold, and have prices. Labor is bought and sold, and has a price, which is its wage. No logician could avoid completing the syllogism. Labor is, of course, a highly peculiar commodity, very perishable, difficult to measure, and bought and sold under a

---

[2] There are, of course, many varieties and degrees of the closed shop, some of which are less open to abuse than others. The pure closed shop where the union does the hiring is perhaps the most potentially dangerous, though there are examples (in the Maritime and Longshoreman's unions) where union hiring has replaced a much more arbitrary and vicious system. The "Union Shop"—where the employer does the hiring but the employees must join the union after a certain interval—is theoretically less open to abuse, but is by no means proof against unscrupulous leaders. The "maintenance-of-membership" compromise of the War Labor Board is an attempt to combine union security with individual freedom.

great variety of conditions. It is also *more* than a commodity, in that by an employment contract a man accepts a position of subordination in an organized social group; he acquires a "boss" and workmates. But the peculiarities of labor do not absolve it from the general laws which rule the purchase and sale of commodities and the determination of price. Particularly the peculiarities of labor should not exempt the regulation of its sale when conducted under conditions of monopoly.

Consumers' co-operatives

The consumers' co-operative is another institution that perhaps suffers more from the enthusiasm of its friends than from the attacks of its enemies. Essentially, it is another form of business organization, differing, say, from the corporation no more than the corporation differs from the partnership. It differs from the corporation mainly in its financial structure and its constitution of government. Corporations are usually financed partly by fixed-interest securities and partly by shares of stock. The stockholders are regarded as the real owners of the corporation, and they elect the board of directors, voting in proportion to the amount of stock that they own. When a division of profits is made, each stockholder receives an amount proportionate to the amount of stock he owns. A co-operative, on the other hand, is financed in the first place *wholly* by the issue of fixed-interest securities, which are usually called "shares" but which actually are "bonds," as they bear a fixed rate of interest (if any) and do not in themselves entitle the owner to a share in the profits. Profits are divided among the members (stockholders) not in proportion to the amount of stock that they own, but in proportion to the amount of *purchases* made from the business (in the case of a consumers' co-operative) or in proportion to the amount of *sales* made to the business, in the case of a producers' co-operative. Members elect the board of directors or the management on the principle of one vote to one member, so that each stockholder only has one vote no matter how much stock he owns. The co-operative thus represents "personal democracy" in business as the corporation represents "dollar democracy."

Co-operation in Europe and in U. S. A.

The consumers' co-operative has been very successful in the European democracies, such as Britain and Sweden, and has been less successful in the United States. The main reason for its success in Europe is probably to be found in the class structure of European society. The co-operative movement tapped a great unused reservoir of managerial ability in the working class, which it was able to get very cheaply because the class structure prevented an able workman from rising to managerial positions in private or corporate firms. The movement also came along at a propitious time, when the economies of chain store retailing were just opening out, and it was able to take advantage of these developments. In the United States, on the other hand, the more fluid class structure makes it difficult for the co-ops to find and to hold good managers, while the low prices and efficient retailing of the chain stores make it difficult for the co-ops to make profits—and without profits, of course, they cannot grow.

Co-operatives are profit-makers

Hardly anything illustrates the confusion about profits better than the common illusion that co-operatives are "non-profit" concerns. Indeed, this illusion is to some extent responsible for their relative lack of success in this country, because a co-operative cannot succeed unless its members are interested in it as a *business* and not just as a means of saving money by cutting prices. The success of the European co-operatives has been due to the fact that they have made enormous profits (partly by exploiting their management, and in some cases, their workers, but mainly by introducing improved methods of retailing). These profits have been big enough not only to pay large dividends (rebates) to the members, often as much as 15 per cent of purchases, but also to build up huge surpluses. Co-operatives differ from other businesses in the way in which they distribute dividends, but they exactly resemble all other businesses in that they must make profits (that is, increase their net worth) if they are to succeed. The fact that they are owned by their customers does not make them any less a "capitalist" institution. They can only survive in a regime of private property and private profit. They are not particularly revolutionary; they do not represent a new way of life or a new order of civilization, as some of their advocates seem to claim.

The values of the co-operative movement

Nevertheless, when the smoke of evangelical fervor has cleared, the consumers' co-operative can be seen as a very valuable form of business organization, with an important role to play in the world of the future. It is frequently capable of tapping sources of unused managerial ability; even in the United States it has done so, particularly among the middle classes. It can often be an educative force of great power, in acquainting its members with the real problems of business. There are cases where a co-operative in a derelict community has been the means of re-awakening the people to a more business-like and constructive frame of mind. It can also be a powerful "communitizing" force—bringing together on common ground as consumers people of very different social, economic, religious, and political backgrounds. Most of all, perhaps, it is a weapon against monopoly. Indeed, it may be said that the consumers' co-operative is the only form of private business enterprise which can safely be trusted with a monopoly. The reason is that if a consumers' co-operative charges monopoly prices and obtains monopoly profits, these profits tend to come back to the consumer in the form of rebates. Apart from the profits which are added to surplus, then, it is impossible for the members of a consumers' co-operative to be charged *net* prices which are greater than would give normal profits. In retailing commodities where there are great technical advantages in monopoly, therefore, there is much to be hoped from the development of consumers' co-operatives. In milk distribution, for instance, a monopoly has great advantages over the present system of "ten milkmen to every doorstep." Nevertheless, a private corporation could not be trusted with such a monopoly, as it would inevitably be tempted to charge monopoly prices and make monopoly profits. A co-operative, however, would be under less temptation to charge monopoly prices—and if it did, the profits would come rolling back to the consumer. Finally, in Europe at least, the co-operative movement has provided both opportunity and incentive for savings on the part of the working class, and has enabled a large section of the working class not only to save individually, but to become collectively property owners on a large scale. From the point of view of justice in distribution and also the stability of society, this is wholly admirable. It has happened, paradoxically enough, in large part through the operations of compound interest—the high profits of the co-operatives having been ploughed back into the business and not all distributed as dividends.

Dangers of producers' co-operatives

If a consumers' co-operative can be successful, there is, therefore, a great deal to be said in its favor from a social point of view. This is not necessarily the case with producers' co-operatives, and particularly with agricultural marketing co-operatives. There is no social magic in the name "co-operative"—it is just as easy to co-operate for bad ends as for good. Particularly when the end is monopoly, "co-operation" can become a social evil that should be legislated out of existence. Fortunately, most agricultural marketing co-operatives do not cover a wide enough part of the market to be monopolists. There are some examples, however, where under the co-operative form of organization, monopolies have been formed, or at least attempted, for the main purpose not so much of efficient marketing as for monopolistic control of the market. Certain milk co-operatives have attempted such monopolies—not usually with much success. The California lemon growers provide a striking example of monopolistic marketing. Their co-operative during the depression of the 'thirties succeeded in keeping the price of lemons at about double the price of oranges. Before the advent of the co-operative, the prices were about parallel. Orange growers, because of the wider geographical dispersion of the industry, have not succeeded in emulating the lemon growers' monopoly. Here is something that should clearly come under the antimonopoly laws; yet because it is garbed in the co-operative form of organization it escapes censure.

Co-operation vs. the "planners"

The co-operative movement has one great virtue; it is essentially individualistic and practical. It is in reality an enemy of state socialism, and its advocates sometimes even go so far as to deny to the state any significant economic functions. It is "liberal" in the best Manchester sense and looks to private group initiative rather than to state paternalism. Rochdale, after all, is only a few miles from Manchester. This is healthy, even if it sometimes leads to a too narrow view of the duties of the state and too easy an optimism regarding the ability of co-operatives to solve all economic problems.

At the other extreme of the liberal wing lies the "planner," the advocate of the "planned economy." He waxes eloquent about the "unplanned" nature of capitalism and extols the virtues of centralized planning as the cure of all economic ills. He may even have a subconscious picture of himself seated behind a large desk covered with blueprints and charts, while outside a well-ordered and well-oiled machine runs smoothly and brightly to his prearranged order. The very picture reveals the ultimate fallacy of mechanism again. The human world is *not* a machine; it is, in fact, very little like a machine. It is an aggregation of individuals with wills and purposes of their own, and it is absurd to criticize capitalism for its soulless mechanism in making people into cogs, and then to go on to propose an even larger, and more coggy, mechanism. The difficulty with planning is that it is very nice for the planner, but not so nice for the planned. The perfect and completely planned economy is an army; this is the communist state in miniature. The private soldier owns nothing, not even his soul. His needs are taken care of. He is fed, clothed, housed, transported, taught, saved, healed, and buried at the expense of the state. His prime virtue is obedience. He must lose his own individuality into the master plan. He must go where he is sent and do what he is told. He has no economic problems whatever. He has complete economic security. And yet most people, left to themselves, would prefer the life of a free civilian even if the soldier never had to do anything more arduous than march in a parade. Planning is easy, on the assumption that people are willing to sacrifice their liberty. It is difficult, on the assumption that liberty is our most prized possession.

Planning as a necessary evil

This is not to say, of course, that no social planning is necessary. A completely unplanned society—that is, a society without any kind of centralized responsibility for economic life —would soon end in chaos. But it is a far cry from the type of regulation proposed in this volume, whose main object would be to preserve liberty of individual action, to the planning that would seek to impose the planner's will and the planner's objective on all individuals of the system. The analogy of the rule of the road has been used: if people are to travel in safety and liberty, there must be roads and there must be rules. This is the proper function of centralized authority—to provide roads and to enforce rules that will enable individuals to travel where they wish without interfering with the ability of others to travel. Some responsibility must be taken by government in this connection; otherwise, if there were no safe roads and no traffic laws, people would bump into each other, the liberty of one would infringe on the liberties of another, and all our liberty would be diminished. On the other hand, it is *not* the responsibility of government to tell us all exactly where to go and what to do, for that too would destroy our liberty. The excessive zeal of the planners may easily lead to a destruction of liberty, either directly, or by producing a reaction that will deny to government even the right to do the proper amount of regulation.

The fallacy of "social objectives" and the decay of freedom

Part of the general fallacy of mechanism which underlies so much thinking that passes as "liberal" is the "fallacy of social objectives." If we think of society as a machine it must, of course, have a purpose. Society (spelled with a capital S) becomes a kind of deity, with dark purposes of its own quite apart from the purposes of the individuals present in it. The extreme form of this view is perhaps found in fascism, where the national state is exalted as a god with purposes of its own existing over and above the purposes of its individual citizens. But fascism is merely the extreme form of a disease whose symptoms we can, alas, observe everywhere. Nationalism, racism, the growth of hierarchy and bureaucratic control, dictatorship, militarism, aggression: the vices of Nazi Germany can be found in a greater or less degree either in the government or in the social organizations, the parties, associations, businesses, unions, clubs, colleges, and churches even of the United States. Everywhere we see a flight from freedom, and the so-called "liberal" groups are in no way exempt. One cannot study the internal politics of great corporations, of the National Association of Manufacturers, of the C.I.O., or of the churches without noticing the movement towards authoritarianism. Our conventions, whether of manufacturers, unions, parties, or churches become increasingly like the Nazi Reichstag—bodies whose representatives gather not to formulate the broad policies of the executive, but to receive instruction in the policies which executives have previously determined, instructions which they are then supposed to carry home and retail to their subordinates! Our congresses and parliaments all over the world seem to be degenerating into instruments rather than controllers of executive power.

The underlying causes of the decay of freedom are everywhere the same: the atrophy of our ideals and the failure of free enterprise to provide full employment. Unless an individual believes that what he wants to do is important for some larger end than his own personal pleasure, he will not struggle for the freedom to do what he wants. It is the lack of a great ideal that makes men willing to be slaves—for why should one bother to be free to do nothing much in particular? It is the lack of security, brought about largely by unemployment and deflation, that makes men barter their freedom for the apparent security of a regimented society, whether communist, fascist, or "liberal." Previous chapters have indicated the lines along which the problem of full employment may be solved. It remains to add a concluding word on political and moral ideals, without which freedom becomes not a privilege but a burden.

CHAPTER 14

An Appendix on Politics and Morals

Economics and politics

The main purpose of this book has been to outline the principles of economic reconstruction. It is impossible to leave the subject, however, without some reference to the broader fields of politics and morals. Economic problems have no sharp edges; they shade off imperceptibly into politics, sociology, and ethics. Indeed, it is hardly an exaggeration to say that the ultimate answer to every economic problem lies in some other field. Economics is the skeleton of social science; the backbone and framework without which it degenerates into an amorphous jellyfish of casual observation and speculation. But skeletons need flesh and blood; and the flesh and blood of economic problems can only be found in the broader fields. Particularly, the economic problems of the postwar world cannot be solved in a vacuum. It is useless to frame elegant schemes for world reconstruction if there is no political or psychological possibility of carrying them out. Economics of itself is too rational a science to be realistic, for reality in the human sphere is very far from rational. It is not enough, therefore, to give an intellectual solution for the world's economic problems; we must indicate how, from the existing state of war and confusion, men may pass to a better world by steps which are possible under the present framework of beliefs, ideas, and organizations. It is not the intention of this concluding appendix to give any final answer to the social problem; more experienced and more skilled minds than mine are required for that task. I write mainly as an economist, and hence perhaps with a bias against politics, for politics mainly appears as an obstacle in the way of the achievement of the economist's ideals. The economist is by very nature a world citizen, for the economic system is world-wide in its scope. It is difficult for him, therefore, to narrow his interests to the national scale, or to have much sympathy with the objectives of political power. It may be, however, that because of these very facts the economist is equipped to render a criticism of the political system and of the prevailing system of moral ideas that the specialist in these fields is less able to perform. Accordingly, the problem of this chapter is to survey, with an economist's eye, some of the political and moral obstacles to the achievement of the ideals of economic reconstruction.

War as the main obstacle to reconstruction

The most obvious obstacle to economic reconstruction is of course the institution of war itself. It is no exaggeration to say that unless war is brought under control, there can be no possibility of establishing stable prosperity or of abolishing poverty. The memories of the last and the expectations of another war poison the reconstruction after each peace. The expectation of war also is a serious handicap in the way of long-run reconstruction, for it leads to a permanent overexpansion, from the point of view of peacetime needs, of industries that supply the raw materials of war—for example, the steel industry. During war, the armament industry, and the industries that feed the armament industry, are enormously expanded. When peace comes these industries are too large for peacetime demands and the depression which results in them is not only serious in itself, but constantly threatens to become general. As long as over-capacity in these industries remains, therefore, governments will always be tempted to increase armaments as a cure for unemployment. On the other hand, governments are afraid to force a reduction in the capacity of these industries for fear of being caught short in the next war. It is a tempting, though not altogether accurate analogy, to regard the business cycle as a "peak load" phenomenon, with war at the peak. Just as an electric light company must have enough capacity to take care of the "peak load," let us say at 6 o'clock at night, and therefore must have a certain amount of unused capacity at other hours of the day, so a national economy must have enough capacity in the "war industries" to meet the peak load of war, and hence is bound to have its system running at less than full capacity in time of peace.

War as a political problem

In spite of the fact that economic forces are of great importance in interpreting the phenomenon of war, I have called it a "political" problem advisedly. It is true, of course, that certain economic interests are involved in wars. But to suppose that economic conflicts, or even economic difficulties, are the primary cause of war is to shoot very wide of the mark. It is a popular illusion, especially in peacetime, that wars are engineered by big capitalists seeking markets or fields for foreign investments. There have been wars of this nature—for example, the wars of the East India Company. But on the whole, war exists not because of the existence of conflicts but because of the existence of independent nations. It is no exaggeration to say that war is the price we pay for independence, or at least for irresponsible independence. The machinations of armament manufacturers, the greed of capitalists seeking markets, are all unavailing in bringing about war between New York and Pennsylvania, or between England and Scotland. This is not because there are no conflicts between the people of New York and Pennsylvania, or of England and Scotland. It is because New York and Pennsylvania on the one hand, and England and Scotland, on the other, are not independent nations but are parts of a larger political unit. As long as England and Scotland were separate nations there was constant war between them. The union of crowns in 1603 and the union of parliaments in 1707 completely abolished "international" war between them, though civil wars flared up from time to time until the union became one of sentiment and will as well as of political organization.

War as the price of independence

Mere political union by itself, however, is not sufficient to prevent wars. The long struggle between England and Ireland is a good case in point; so is the American Civil War. If one section of a political unit contains enough people who want independence and want it sufficiently to be prepared to fight for it, then the country will be rent by civil war. Civil wars, however, are much rarer than international wars, and if any-thing, have become still rarer with the development of modern armaments. A rebellious district or region has to begin a war almost from scratch, unless the army itself happens to be fairly equally divided in the struggle. Independent nations, on the other hand, constantly direct their thoughts and energies to-wards war. It is only a slight exaggeration to describe an inde-pendent nation as a body of people organized for the principal purpose of carrying on war. Defense has always been regarded as the primary responsibility of an independent national gov-ernment and in the interests of defense all other considerations will be sacrificed. Indeed, the distinction between independent governments and other authorities (such as local or colonial gov-ernments) rests precisely on this ground. The government of the United States is independent, and the United States is a sovereign state, precisely because the federal government has the primary responsibility for the armed defense of the United States. The government of Iowa or of New York State is not truly "sovereign," is not independent, because it is not responsi-ble for the defense of the territories which it governs. Similarly, Great Britain is a completely sovereign state, for no one but herself has any responsibility for her defense. The British Do-minions might be described as semisovereign states, as they accept a large part of the responsibility for their defense; India and the other crown colonies are not sovereign, as Great Britain assumes sole ultimate responsibility for their defense. There are even some countries and empires, such as Portugal, Belgium, and Holland, which though nominally independent actually depend for their defense and existence on the armed forces of another power—in their case, Great Britain. It might even be argued today that Britain and the British Empire are *de facto*, though not *de jure* dependencies of the United States, in that they probably cannot ultimately be defended without the aid of the United States.

War is not the only form of conflict

It is important to realize that war is only *one form* of conflict —is in fact, the form that conflict takes when it runs across the boundaries of independent nations. The abolition of war would not mean the abolition of conflict. Indeed, if we had to abolish conflicts before we could abolish war we might as well give up the task immediately. It is not even desirable to abolish conflicts; conflict conducted in a decent and responsible manner is essential to any form of progress, whether in knowledge, in ideas, or in material things. Competition, as we have seen, is the child of progress; no new idea can come into the world without knocking out an outworn notion, no new methods can come into use without destroying the old. The case against war is not that it is a conflict, but that it is an indecent and irresponsible form of conflict which does not seem to result in progress, but rather in an orgiastic waste in lives and resources. Success in war comes not to the virtuous or the right but to the strong, and unfortunately virtue and strength are by no means always complementary goods.

The extension of peaceful conflict

The abolition of war, then, means not the abolition of conflicts, but the diversion of conflicts into more fruitful channels. In domestic politics we have in great part accomplished this end. We no longer attempt to settle our private quarrels by duelling or feuding, except in remote and lawless regions. The law court, the ballot box, the election campaign, the pamphlet, the magazine article—these are the most fruitful arenas of battle. The great task of the present is to extend the areas of peaceful conflict and to diminish the area where peaceful conflict breaks down. This can only be done by the widespread development of a sense of responsibility, not only among governments but among private citizens, and not only for a limited group, but for all people. It is when the sense of mutual responsibility breaks down that war ensues. As long as the word "we" means the two parties to a problem, a solution is possible and war will not follow. As soon, however, as "we" comes to mean *one* party to a quarrel, and the other party is altogether excluded from the circle of responsibility, then the political structure is split and war of some kind will inevitably follow. We have wars primarily because Americans do not think of the Japanese or the Germans as part of "us," nor do the Japanese or Germans think of Americans as part of "us."

War is not a necessary result of conflict

The truth of this proposition can be seen very clearly if we contrast the conflict between whites and Negroes in this country with the conflict between Americans and Japanese. In terms of the real issues involved there can be no doubt that the Negro-white conflict is by far the most acute. It reaches down into the everyday life of every Negro, and of most white people. A Negro can hardly pass a day of his life without being insulted, particularly in certain localities. He is forced to ride at the back of busses, on Jim Crow cars on trains; he must call at the back door, must kowtow and say "sir," must suffer name-calling and insult. In economic life, he is discriminated against at every turn. Unions keep him out of good jobs; if he is upgraded, riots and strikes ensue. The dirtiest and most unpleasant jobs fall to his lot. He is the first to be laid off in depression, the last to be taken on in boom. On the other hand, millions of white people fear and hate the Negro, partly in an attempt to justify their treatment of him, partly out of fear of his economic competition. He has been used as a strikebreaker. He threatens the comfortable monopolies of many trades. He is a standing reproach to their manners, their customs, their prejudices, their religion, their policies. He is the thorn in the flesh, the prick under the saddle, the nail in the boot, the unassimilated and unassimilable intruder in the body politic. Here is a conflict of an intensity and magnitude that makes one wonder what the war with Japan is all about. Few Americans come into contact with Japanese, or Japanese with Americans. Not one out of a hundred Americans or Japanese could give a coherent account of what *conflict* was behind the war. All that they are conscious of is the war itself. To the vast mass of American people, the attack on Pearl Harbor was a complete bolt from the blue, utterly unexpected, without antecedents, without explanation except that the "Japs" were "dirty rats." To the mass of Japanese also, there is probably no more than a dim sense of fighting for national existence against an immensely rich and powerful enemy, bent on throttling the economic life and imperial ambitions of a competitor. It is significant that a large amount of writing has been deemed necessary since the war began in order to find out what it is all

about. We have the war first, and then find why it is being
fought afterwards.

The American race conflict does not result in war because both parties are "Americans"

Yet the Negro-white conflict, intense and bitter as it is, real
as it is, personal as it is, running as it does deep into the daily
life of almost every American, results only in occasional and
sporadic violence, and does not result in anything approaching
organized warfare. The riots, the lynchings, the discrimination,
the insults, serious as they are, are insignificant beside the whole-
sale destruction of cities, the slaughter of millions of the inno-
cent, the carnage of battle that constitute the incidents of war.
On the other hand, there are few individual quarrels between
citizens of the Axis powers on the one hand, and of the United
Nations on the other. There are no conflicts of economic interest
between, say, Americans and Germans any greater than the economic conflict between Americans and Britishers, or even between New Yorkers and Georgians. Yet in the apparent pursuit
of a conflict that almost eludes definition, the warring nations
lay waste each other's cities, and try to starve and slay each
other into submission.

The reason for this paradox is clear. In spite of the acute
conflict between the races in America, the situation is still regarded as a "problem" rather than as a "fight." In interracial
discussions one still hears the expression "what can *we* do about
it" from both white and Negro lips. The Negro is still an American; America is his country. He recognizes the progress that has
been made, and he is not wholly despairing—yet—of further
progress towards his complete integration into American life. On
the other side, the white man frequently feels a certain responsibility for the Negro. This may take the form of according him
equal rights and courtesies, or it may take the form of a patron-
izing paternalism, based on the theory of the "child race." However unsatisfactory the form of this sense of responsibility, it
exists even in the most racially prejudiced communities. Even
the lyncher cannot deny that in some sense his victim is an
"American." Neither the Negro nor the white communities are
independent of each other. They are neither of them organized

for war on each other. They do not have separate governments, or separate armies. Consequently, in spite of the intensity of conflict between them, war, in the proper sense of the word, is impossible. It may be merely the complete geographical interpenetration of the two groups that brings about this happy result. It may be the common cultural background, for the distinctions between Negro and white culture are trivial. But whatever the cause, it is the sense of community, weak as it is, the sense that we are all "Americans" in spite of our differences, that prevents the conflict breaking out into war.

Lack of "community," not conflicts, cause war

In the case of international war, on the other hand, it is not the intensity of the conflict that matters, but the fact that no sense of community or joint responsibility unites the contending parties. The economic causes of World War II were trivial and in any case were not within the dimensions of the cost of the war. It is not a "race war": yellow Chinese and white Americans fight on one side, yellow Japanese and white Germans fight on the other. It is, no doubt, in part a war of ideologies, though there too we find some strange bedfellows, with the capitalistic democracies and communist Russia on one side, and fascist Germany and semifeudal Japan on the other. There is little, alas, in the German treatment of the Jewish people that finds no parallel in the American treatment of the Indian and the Negro, and little in Japanese imperialism that finds no parallel in the history of the western powers. For purposes of war it is, of course, necessary to emphasize the differences between the opposing parties. While these differences are great indeed, the impartial student finds it difficult to avoid being impressed by the continuity of human affairs. Revolutions are never as revolutionary, nor opposites as opposite as they seem. The complex crystal of social life sometimes turns over and exposes a new facet to public view, but it is the same old crystal; its real changes are slow and continuous, and only its visible appearance changes in revolution. A surprising number of the New Deal inventions were anticipated by Mr. Hoover; an even more surprising continuity appears in matters of detailed policy between the Weimar Republic and the Third Reich.

Nations fight primarily for their independence

The truth seems to be that each nation is fighting the war not primarily for ideas or ideologies, but for its own independence. The cat is let out of the bag admirably by the "Jackson Sun," [1] which observes that the answer to the question "what are we fighting for" is simple: "We are fighting each for the integrity of his own nation—Americans for the United States, English for England, Free French for France, Russians for Russia, and Chinese for China. All the rest is frosting on the cake." The editor might have gone on to add "Germans for Germany, Italians for Italy, Japanese for Japan."

The dilemma of nationalism

Here we seem to be faced with an almost intolerable dilemma. We recognize on the one hand the abominable nature of war, yet on the other hand we must recognize that war springs from the desire for national independence—a desire which is almost universally recognized to be good. The day may come when it will be thought unbelievable folly to kill one another for such abstractions as "Germany" or "England" or "America," but that day is far distant. The love of country and the desire for national independence are perhaps the two strongest motivations in the world today. That they are ultimately stronger than the narrow "economic" motives is proved by the fact that not only nations, but most individuals, are prepared to sacrifice wealth, health, happiness, and life itself for the attainment or the attempted attainment of these national ends. Nor do we feel that there is anything ignoble in this. The love of country is so much better than the love of self that we are apt to praise it as the prince of virtues. We admire the hot-blooded and bitter resistance of the Norwegians, economically foolish though it may be, more than the cool-headed and rather successful acquiescence of the Danes. Nevertheless, it is this very love of country and of independence which is bringing our world down in ruins and which frustrates every attempt to build a better world order.

---

[1] Quoted in the *Nashville Banner*, Monday, April 5, 1943.

Can we separate the love of country from the desire for independence?

There is only one way out of this impasse. It is the separation of the love of country from the desire for independence. It is the love of country that is admirable; it is the desire for independence that leads to destruction. Few people want to have a wholly homogeneous world. There is a positive good in variety, and we could go even further than we have done in developing local pride, local color, local differences. A multitude of interdependent churches, various enough to suit the innumerable varieties of religious experience and yet interdependent enough to permit of united fellowship and common action, is an ideal in the religious sphere more acceptable than that of a centralized uniformity imposed by arbitrary, and therefore necessarily cruel authority. So also in the political life we yet have to solve the problem of order in diversity: how to permit many varieties of political organization within a framework of interdependence and order.

The federal solution

The obvious constitutional framework for the establishment of order in diversity is the federal system, and many voices are raised today advocating federation of one sort or another, whether on a world scale or on the basis of regional or ideological groups. There can be little doubt that ultimately world federation in some form must come; our very technological progress demands it. It has frequently been pointed out that the effective size of a nation depends on its means of transport. In an age of foot travel no political unit much larger than the tribe can persist for long. Most European nations are designed for roads and horse traffic. The railroads permitted the development of the United States. Brazil is a creature of the Amazon, and the British Empire of the seven seas. Now the air age has burst upon us to undo much of the geography we learned in school—an age in which no place on earth is more than sixty hours from home and in which the Arctic Ocean seems destined to become one of the principal highways of commerce. World federation has been made ultimately inevitable by the conquest of the air. Nevertheless, it .may be a long time coming. Our bodies may travel by air, but our minds are still largely conditioned to a horse-and-buggy era. We cannot expect that the nations which have fought so bitterly for survival in World War II, and which, perhaps, will fight in subsequent wars, will voluntarily lay down their independent lives in the interests of peace and progress. Neither the United Nations nor their enemies have been fighting World War II for the abolition of their independence, and it would be foolish optimism to expect a federated world to come out of a war for national survival.

Could a world.federation create world loyalty?

To be realistic, therefore, we must accept the continued existence of independent nations for a long time to come. A nation is essentially a psychological rather than a physical fact; it is a belief in the minds of people. If people stopped believing in the existence of the United States it would cease to exist. Similarly, a world federation must be founded on a belief, on a way of thinking and acting on the part of the people. That belief does not exist at the moment, and without it no world federation can survive. It is possible, of course, that if a world political organization could once be established, the belief and sentiment necessary to support it would grow up under its shadow. It is easier to educate people to be loyal to something that exists than to something which is only potential. The advocates of "federation now" point to the analogy of the United States and show how under the Constitution sectional loyalties have gradually been subordinated to national loyalty, so that even if in 1787 the nation was established on a shaky psychological foundation, the very existence of the nation created and attracted the loyalties that were necessary to sustain it. So, it is argued, if a federation of nations could be formed now, the faith and loyalty necessary to its existence would grow up under its shadow.

Difficulties of world federation

This contention is, of course, a matter of judgment, and for the sake of the future it is to be hoped that the advocates of

"Federation Now" are right. Nevertheless, in view of the wide diversities among existing nations, the tensions and hatreds caused by the war, and the present strength and probable future growth of nationalistic sentiment, one may be pardoned for doubting the optimism of the federationists' viewpoint. The thirteen colonies had a common language, a common tradition, and a common enemy; even these advantages did not prevent the Union from being torn by civil war. The nations of the world today—even the so-called "United Nations"—have no common language, and little in the way of common culture. Their only bond of union is a common enemy—the weakest and most ephemeral of all bonds—which the very success of their common warfare will tend to destroy. It may be doubted, therefore, especially in view of the nationalistic reaction which war always seems to produce, whether any federation could at present survive long enough to make people love it.

Functional international co-operation

This is not to say, of course, that we must despair entirely of international action or of world order. At present, however, it would seem as if the most hopeful avenue of international co-operation is along functional lines. Many such functional organizations have been operating for many years: the International Postal Union, the International Ice Patrol, the International Institute of Agriculture in Rome, the Bank of International Settlements, and the many departments of the League of Nations and the International Labor Office. Already an international monetary organization is on the agenda of the United Nations. The United Nations Relief and Reconstruction Administration could well become a permanent addition to the world's political resources. Many other functional international bodies are needed—for example, an international body to deal with legal problems, such as citizenship and property laws, an international body for the unification of national statistics, a body for the study of population problems, a body to deal with educational problems, a body to deal with communications—especially air transport and radio, both of which are essentially world-wide in their scope. Many others might be added to the list.

Dangers of a world state

None of these developments in themselves, however, will prevent war, for none of them involve any real relinquishment of ultimate national sovereignty. War will always exist as long as national governments exist which are independent and irresponsible. One method of eliminating war, of course, would be the development of a world-state. This method, however, is utterly impracticable at the present time, and also has grave dangers of its own. A world-state, particularly if it is based on military force, might easily degenerate into a world tyranny. Indeed, it might almost be said that a world-state has been tried, and failed: the Roman Empire included almost the whole communicable world, and fell apart mainly because of a failure to inspire internal solidarity. A world in which there are refugees is bad enough, but a world in which there is no place of refuge would be worse. A uniform and authoritarian world-state might easily become a horrible and inescapable tyranny, destructive of liberty, of variety, of creativity and of progress.

World integration through responsible nationalism

There is, however, another avenue of progress towards world integration which offers more hope of success, and which up to the present has been little recognized. This is the development of policies of world *responsibility* on the part of national governments. We have seen that the crux of our international disorder is the lack of any responsible world government. We have war mainly because the government of each country regards itself, in the international field, as responsible only for the welfare of its own citizens, and does not even in theory accept any responsibility for the welfare of foreigners. The government of the United States, in making judgments of policy, considers only the welfare of the people living within the boundaries of the United States. It is sufficient justification for any policy to show that on balance the people of the United States are benefited by it. It is not considered any argument against a particular policy to point out that mankind as a whole is the loser by it. Take, for example, the debate that centers around tariff policy. Both the opponents and the advocates of a particular tariff—say on shoes—are united in their standard of judgment. They both agree that the tariff should stand or fall according to its effect on Americans. The advocates will point to the benefits accruing to the American shoe industry, the opponents will point to the losses to consumers or to exporters. The difference is merely about the effects of the tariff, not about the criterion according to which it should be judged. Anyone who suggested that the tariff was bad because it injured Czecho-Slovaks and other "foreigners" more than it benefited Americans would simply be laughed out of court. Yet this "American only" criterion is precisely what is meant by *irresponsible* government in the international field.

Reasons for hope in this direction: Nations are the real repositories of power

It may be thought too optimistic to hope for the growth of international responsibility in the conduct of national governments. The record of national governments in this respect is so uniformly bad that the attempt to reform them may be thought quixotic in the extreme. Nevertheless, there are reasons to suppose that the efforts of men of good will would be more fruitfully exercised in this field than in many others. In the first place, national governments exist; they are the repositories of real political power at the moment and are likely to be for many years to come. Any international organization, however elegant its formal constitution, will ultimately be the instrument of the "powers," singly or in groups. Hence, an attack on the principles of conduct of national governments goes right to the root of our political disorder. Concentration on world organization merely as organization is likely to be futile.

World government must wait on the growth of world loyalty

Secondly, national feeling is too strong at the moment to permit the establishment of a truly responsible world government. There must be a further growth in the sentiment of world citizenship among large masses of people before a world government could survive long enough to be a reality. Unless this sentiment exists in sufficient degree, mere organization is bound to go down on the rocks of national sentiment and self-interest. As a preliminary stage in the development of world order, therefore, it is necessary to increase the sense of world responsibility among individual citizens and individual nations.

There are precedents for responsible nationalism

In the third place, a policy of international responsibility is not altogether unprecedented, though on a limited scale. The "good neighbor" policy of the United States is a tacit admission that the government of the United States cannot be indifferent to the welfare of citizens of Central and South America. The British Commonwealth of Nations is based ultimately on a certain tradition of decent conduct towards each other on the part of the governments of Great Britain and the Dominions. It might almost be defined as a group of independent nations bound together by a sense of common responsibility. When the British Government wishes to do anything—for example, restrict imports—which might affect adversely the interests of the Dominions, the Dominion governments are consulted, and special arrangements are made with them. On the other hand, to take a single example, where the interests of Denmark are affected, the British government has no hesitation in attempting to ruin the Danish pig industry in the interests of a pressure-group of British farmers, without consultation or even a by-your-leave. It is evident that there is no reason whatever, given the will to do it, why Denmark should not be treated exactly like New Zealand. Nevertheless, the sphere of responsible action extends only to the countries of the commonwealth; to countries outside this sphere no considerations of responsibility limit the self-centeredness of national policy.

The program is capable of unilateral application

A fourth consideration is that a program of world responsibility is capable of immediate and continuous development and need not wait upon the snail-like processes of international agreement and organization. It is capable of *unilateral* application; any nation can immediately begin to apply it without waiting for others. Perhaps the principal reason why the forces of nationalistic reaction were so strong, and the forces of international co-operation so weak in the interwar period was that nationalism—for example, that of the Nazis—was capable of immediate, one-sided expression whereas the international order —as in the Disarmament Conference—waited hopelessly upon unanimous agreement. What nobody will do unless everybody does is never done, and there is a real sense in which all action is unilateral. There is more hope for any policy that can be implemented immediately by existing organizations than for policies that require wide agreement and new organizations.

Institutional implementation of responsible nationalism

It would be quite possible to introduce a responsible foreign policy gradually, and almost imperceptibly, without any change in existing institutions. Nevertheless, there are certain institutional changes that might be valuable in crystallizing the change and making it more apparent. A formal "declaration of interdependence" on the part especially of a large and powerful nation like the United States would have an enormous effect. It would set a formal standard for the internal criticism of irresponsible policies and would act as a constant challenge to those nations which maintained irresponsible policies. At a later stage of formalization, when the policy itself was generally accepted by the people, a nation might establish a "Third House"—a branch of the legislature consisting of representatives of foreign governments with power to legislate on matters affecting foreigners. Such would be the final implementation of a world-responsible national policy.

Democracy is valuable mainly as a means to responsible government

It is no exaggeration to say that responsible government is the key to the whole political problem, in internal as well as in external affairs. We have seen how the development of a responsible foreign policy is the way to the creation of a world order. It is equally true that in domestic politics the achievement of *responsible* government is the basic problem and is still far from full attainment. Democracy, significant as it is for human welfare, is not an end in itself. It is important mainly as a means to responsible government. It is not the peculiar mode of choosing legislators that makes democracy significant; it is the fact that once chosen, the legislators are responsible, in theory at least, to the people who have chosen them. The significant distinction is not between democracy, in the sense of representive institutions, and other political constitutions. Rather is it between responsible government and absolute government—that is, between government which regards itself as a trustee of the welfare of all people and government which is personal, arbitrary, and discriminating. Parliamentary democracy is a mechanism for achieving the end of responsible government. An elected legislator, subject to recall or to the necessity of re-election, is more likely to be responsible than a dictator or a hereditary monarch.

Representative institutions are not ends in themselves

Unfortunately, there is a strong tendency nowadays to regard representative institutions—and even particular representative institutions—as ends in themselves. Such a view leads to great confusion of thought, and is indeed a menace to the very survival of democracy, for it prevents that self-criticism and adaptation which is necessary to the survival of any institution. The greatest danger to democracy comes from within, when it fails to fulfill the end for which it is devised—that is, when it fails to provide a truly responsible government. Unfortunately, in late years, and in many countries, democracy has been failing to do its job, and its weakness, especially on the European continent, may largely be ascribed to this fact. Representative institutions by themselves are no guarantee of responsible government. There must be in addition a tradition of social cohesion and a high standard of responsible behavior, not only on the part of the representatives but also on the part of the electors. Without this subtle psychological cement, democracy degenerates into logrolling, and the representative assembly becomes a squalling cat-fight of pressure-groups and heterogeneous interests. We have seen that the root of war is the fact that national governments regard themselves as responsible only for their own citizens. But many elected representatives fall short even of this ideal. They do not regard themselves as responsible for the welfare of their nation as a whole, but only responsible for their electoral district or for their economic or political bosses. We do not even come up to the relatively noble, if destructive, ideal of "America First"; all too often it is only "Podunk First."

The rise of executive power caused by lack of responsible government

The failure of legislative assemblies to be generally responsible as well as locally representative is at the root of the almost universal decay of representative institutions and the rise of executive power. We see this most clearly, of course, in the fascist countries, where the legislature is completely suppressed and the whole functions of government are centered in the executive dictator. But even in the democratic countries this movement has been going on in a smaller degree. In the United States the powers of the President and of the bureaucracy have been growing until at times it seems as if Congress is either a tool in the hands of the President or a monkey wrench to throw in the machinery of government. In Britain, Parliament, except in times of great crisis, has become increasingly a claque to approve the doings of the Cabinet and the Prime Minister. Can we not see in this world-wide movement a reaction against the irresponsibility of elected legislatures as well as a consequence of the increasing responsibilities of government? Where the legislature represents only the clash of sectional and group interests, people naturally turn to the executive as the only element in government representing the common interest. Even the rise of Hitler may be interpreted in part as a tragic reaction against the partisan loyalties of the Weimar republic. It was no accident that one of the slogans of the Nazi party was *gemein-nutz vor eigennutz*. Narrow and wicked as the Nazi concept of "common good" is, it represents in a perverted form a genuine longing for responsible and integrated government that was not satisfied by the democratic forms. Unless European democracy can satisfy this need for responsible government, no amount of military might can establish it.

Faults of geographical representation

We need to be on our guard against identifying, fetish-like, the true goal of responsible, classless government—by the people, for the people—with particular forms of representation. It can be argued with some force that the principle of representation by geographical areas, on which most democratic legislatures are elected, does not in fact produce as great a degree of responsible government as could be desired. Legislators elected from local areas tend to represent the interests of these areas rather than the common good. The scandalous silver policy of the United States is a case in point, a policy that cannot even pretend to be in the common good, and that exists only because the accident of representation gives the Western states so disproportionate a power in the Senate. On the other hand, were all legislators to be elected at large, the personal tie between the voter and his representative would be broken. Possibly the answer lies in a composite method of representation, with some representatives elected on a regional or local basis, and others elected at large.

Responsibility as a moral problem

In the last resort, the problem of responsible government is more than a political problem: it is a moral problem, affecting the thought and conduct of every individual—even the reader of this page. It is true that environments and institutions modify the character of individuals, yet change in institutions only comes about as a result of changes in the individuals whose character the institutions reflect. It is as true today as in Plato's day that the nature of the state is determined by the nature of the individuals that compose it. Responsible government, whether on a world scale or even on a national or local scale, can never develop unless there are responsible citizens. Every man is in some sense an agent of the great government of human relations. The officials and offices that constitute what we usually call "the" government constitute only a small part of government; the government of the home, of the school, of the business, the trade union, the church, the club, form a much greater part of human activity. Unless there is responsible government here, there can never be responsible government in the capital. And up to a point, the more responsible behavior there is in ordinary human relations, the less need is there for centralized authority. Public authority, however well-intentioned, can never displace the need for responsible private authority. We are all public servants, whether employed by government or not. The father and mother have a responsibility not only to themselves but to the whole community in the upbringing of their children. The director of a corporation is just as much responsible for the public welfare as the head of a government bureau. A teacher in a private school is just as much responsible for education as a teacher in a public school. Unfortunately we do not always recognize these responsibilities and usually have no method for making them effective. We are nearly all responsible *for* much more than we are responsible *to*. One of the main tasks of social organization is to unite these two senses of the word "responsibility." It is the prime task of the moral life to see that when our actions *affect* others we act in their interest as well as in our own. It is the prime task of political life to add the sanctions of law to the moral sanction, and to insure, as far as possible, that those whose actions affect the welfare of others are in some way answerable to those whose lives they influence. But political sanctions are only of limited application and nothing can prevent a society falling apart where the members are not imbued with a sense of responsibility one for another. Particularly is this true where society is organized into groups. A society of selfish individuals might be able to get along, for the power of one individual to injure others is small, and Adam Smith's great "hidden hand" comes into play to turn private interest into public good. But a society organized into selfish *groups* desperately needs the cement of responsible behavior. This is partly because groups can injure each other, and injure society, more than individuals can. Partly, also, it is because men as representives of a group are much less moral than as selfish individuals. Men will lie, cheat, steal, and kill for their country, their class, their trade union, their business—even for their church—with a single-mindedness of evil intent that they would never achieve as individuals. In our days more than ever, then, when the individualistic society

of a generation or two ago is being replaced by a highly col-
lectivized society, organized into labor unions, employers' associations, corporations, and the like, is it necessary to develop
on the part of individuals and on the part of these member-
groups a sense of responsibility for the welfare of all. Labor
leaders must not feel themselves *solely* responsible to the men
that they lead, for their actions affect millions of consumers,
unorganized workers, and employers. Directors and executives
must not feel themselves responsible *solely* to their shareholders,
for their actions affect workers, consumers, and other businessmen. Bankers must not feel themselves solely responsible to
their stockholders and depositors; teachers not solely responsible
to their pupils or employers; writers not merely responsible to
themselves. In the internal strife of society as well as its external warfare only the principle of universal responsibility can
insure peace.

Index

A

Accumulation:
  difficult in poor societies, 7
  involves frugality, 92
  limits of, 7, 127, 173
Adam Smith, 271
Adjustable Tax Plan, 161-167
Age distribution, 2, 3
Aggregative thinking, 223
Agricultural countries, weakness of, 15
Agriculture:
  in World War I, 37-8
  in World War II, 55-57
  maintenance in, 11
  price fluctuations, effect on, 43
Alberta, 151
Alice in Wonderland, 139
American Friends Service Committee, 58
American Relief Administration, 58
Army, as planned economy, 249
Assets, effect of national debt on, 212
Austria-Hungary, 17, 40, 187

B

Backward areas, 96-97
Balance of payments, 30
Bank Act of 1844, 149
Bank deposits, tax on, 152
Bank rate, 146
Banks:
  borrowing from, 167
  central, 145-151
  endangered by national debt, 168, 213
Basic minimum, 120
Bathtub Theorem, 127, 131
Big business, Communist state as, 232
Bimetallism, 154
Black Death, 7
Blockade, effects of, 56
Bombing, effects of, 54
Boom, 1919-1920, 42
Booms, stopped by central banks, 148
Bottlenecks, 11

Boulding, K. E., 5, 33
Brazil, coffee valorization, 21
Bretton Woods, 190
Britain, see Great Britain
British Dominions:
  as semi-sovereign states, 255
  responsible nationalism in, 266
Brookings Institution, 141
Brussels Conference, 44
Budget:
  balanced, fallacy of, 206-211
  deficits, 133, 161-171, 215
  ten-year, 210
Business Cycle: (see also Depressions)
  financial causes, 19
  "peak-load" theory, 253
Business expenditure, 133
Butter, used as axle grease, 21

C

Capital:
  inalienable and transferable, 106
  nature of, 4-7
Capitalism:
  property rights under, 81
  synthesis with Communism, 233
Capitalist distribution, 113
Capitalist, function of, 219, 227
Carr, Professor, 236
Central bank policy, 145-151
Cereals, stock of, 66
Chain store taxation, 81, 93
Chase, Stuart, 236
China:
  agriculture, 97
  large family unit, 85
  population problem, 98
Christian-Humanism, 222, 235-251
"City famine," 13
Class structure, 90
Clayton Act, 244
Closed shop, 243
Collective farm, 82, 83
Collective ownership, 84-86

273